IN THE WRITERS' WORDS

Conversations with
Ten Canadian Poets

VOLUME II

ESSENTIAL ESSAYS SERIES 77

Guernica Editions Inc. acknowledges the support of
the Canada Council for the Arts and the Ontario Arts Council.
The Ontario Arts Council is an agency of the Government of Ontario.
We acknowledge the financial support of the Government of Canada

IN THE WRITERS' WORDS

Conversations with
Ten Canadian Poets

VOLUME II

Compiled and Edited by
LAURENCE HUTCHMAN

GUERNICA
EDITIONS

TORONTO • CHICAGO • BUFFALO • LANCASTER (U.K.)
2022

Guernica Founder: Antonio D'Alfonso

Michael Mirolla, editor
Cover and Interior Design: Rafael Chimicatti
Guernica Editions Inc.
287 Templemead Drive, Hamilton (ON), Canada L8W 2W4
2250 Military Road, Tonawanda, N.Y. 14150-6000 U.S.A.
www.guernicaeditions.com

Distributors:
Independent Publishers Group (IPG)
600 North Pulaski Road, Chicago IL 60624
University of Toronto Press Distribution (UTP)
5201 Dufferin Street, Toronto (ON), Canada M3H 5T8
Gazelle Book Services, White Cross Mills
High Town, Lancaster LA1 4XS U.K.

First edition.
Printed in Canada.

Legal Deposit—First Quarter
Library of Congress Catalog Card Number: 2021949861
Library and Archives Canada Cataloguing in Publication
Title: In the writers' words : conversations with ten Canadian poets.
Volume II / Laurence Hutchman.
Names: Hutchman, Laurence, author, editor.
Series: Essential essays series ; 77.
Description: 1st edition. | Series statement: Essential essays series ; 77
Identifiers: Canadiana (print) 20210365382 | Canadiana (ebook) 20210365455
ISBN 9781771836166 (softcover) | ISBN 9781771836173 (EPUB)
Subjects: LCSH: Poets, Canadian—Interviews. | LCSH: Canadian poetry—
20th century—History and criticism. | CSH: Poets, Canadian (English)—
20th century—Interviews. | CSH: Canadian poetry (English)—
20th century—History and criticism. | LCGFT: Interviews.
Classification: LCC PS8155 .H88 2022 | DDC C811/.5409—dc23

CONTENTS

For Eva

INTRODUCTION

In the 1990s I conducted interviews with eight writers for the book *In the Writers' Words*. I travelled to different provinces to meet the writers in their homes to listen to them speak of the challenges they faced, the complex evolution of their aesthetics and the mysterious nature of the writing process. At that time, I also interviewed Roo Borson, John B. Lee, and Colleen Thibaudeau. In 2018 when I undertook a second volume of interviews with notable Canadian contemporary poets, I decided to include those earlier interviews.

The poets presented in *In the Writers' Words Volume II* have works that convey a wide range of writing styles expressing important trends and concerns of the past half a century. When conducting interviews with these poets, I asked them about their lives, significant issues, historical events, influences, aesthetics, and the genesis of their poems.

George Elliott Clarke speaks about the history of Black people in a national and international context and the "Black Lives Matter" movement. D.A. Lockhart writes about the history of his tribe and the deaths of Indigenous children in residential schools. Brian Bartlett, in the tradition of Thoreau and Dillard, engages the reader with his careful, in-depth observations and responses to nature. Both M. Travis Lane and Roo Borson talk about the development of their aesthetics, and the importance of sound, language, and music in the creation of the poem. Bruce Meyer and John B. Lee chronicle the importance of history: familial, local, national, and international. A.F. Moritz brings surrealism, an acute knowledge of literary traditions, and a global perspective in his work. Sue Sinclair tells us how philosophy became an important part of her poetry. Colleen Thibaudeau and speaks about the development of modern Canadian poetry.

Brian Bartlett grew up in Fredericton, New Brunswick, which had been the home of two Confederation poets—Charles G.D. Roberts and Bliss Carman—and later of Alden Nowlan. He is one of the most significant and active poets in the Maritimes. In his early books he experiments with a variety of lyrical poems, synthesizing personal experiences, literary allusions, and unusual facts of everyday life. Of his "Underwater Carpentry," he writes: "I wanted to experiment with the long sweep of a single poem carried over 10 or 12 pages, but not primarily structured as a narrative—instead of using mosaic, collage, stream of consciousness." He continues his interest in long poems with "Hawthornden Improvisations," written in a Scottish castle, where he muses about history, art, poetry, music, nature, and love. Bartlett began writing haiku in his forties, publishing *Potato Blossom Road: Seven Montages*. His first prose work, *Ringing Here & There: A Nature Calendar*, has 366 entries based on journal notes that he posted on Facebook sharing his observations during his walks in nature.

Roo Borson's early books, such as *A Sad Device* and *The Whole Night, Coming Home*, are meticulous observations of nature and meditations on human behaviour. Later in her career she became interested in the literature of China and Japan, working on the book *Introduction to the Introduction to Wang Wei* with her husband, Kim Maltman, as well as Andy Patton. Her interest in China continued with the book of prose *Box Kite*, written in collaboration with Kim describing their experiences where she explores the legacy of her grandmother, who lived there for two years. The book *Short Journey Upriver Toward Ōishida* is based on the journey of the Japanese poet Basho in which she finds an analogy to her own life. The poems are written in a lyrical, meditative style and, through the unusual juxtaposition of metaphors and shifting perspectives, she creates a wide variety of expressions. In her latest books, whether she is mapping out her community in Toronto or visiting the ruins in Rome, she transforms the ordinary into the extraordinary. In her poetry, Borson has a spiritual understanding of the subtle relationship between the human and the natural world.

George Elliott Clarke writes passionately about issues that have recently been addressed by the Black Lives Matter movement, defining the context of the Africadian and African Canadians and—in his *Canticles I* and *II*—expanding this to the global history of Blacks. In the early work, *Whylah Falls*, the main scenes are developed through dramatic situations, imbued with musical phrases and a language that ranges widely from the colloquial to the literary. Clarke speaks vehemently about injustice in specific instances. In *Beatrice Chancy,* which is influenced by Shelley's tragedy *The Cenci,* he dramatizes the tragedy of a Black slave woman. In *Execution Poems*, he writes about the racism toward two Black Canadians, Rue and George (based on his two cousins), executed in Fredericton, New Brunswick. *Illicit Sonnets* and *Extra Illicit Sonnets* bring the reader a different side of the poet, a celebration of sexuality and love.

M. Travis Lane's poems are distinctive in Canadian literature and have the texture and range of Margaret Avison's poems and the fullness and originality of the poetry of Denise Levertov. She is the consummate artist who aptly harmonizes the stylistic elements of the poem by using musical effects, careful syntax, and lively rhythms. The poems "For Brigid" and "Portobello" show an excellent example of her art. In her interview she says, "but every poem needs its own sound, its own development— the words should be arranged as they are because that is the only way they can say what needs to be said." Travis Lane's intelligent and original poems challenge the reader on many levels so that they can emerge with a different perception of the world.

John B. Lee grew up on a farm in Highgate that had been in his family for five generations. His earlier works such as the *Black Barns trilogy* are largely centred on family history. His subjects become as diverse as hockey and The Beatles. Later he moves to universal subjects such as the Irish famine in *Tongues of the Children* and the African slave ships in a series of poems *Kicheraboo, We Are Dying*. Lee, like Al Purdy, wrote in a number of books about his travels to various parts of the world, including Peru, South Africa, China, the Arctic and especially Cuba. Lee's style is ebullient, creating dramatic narratives through energetic and varied lines, rich, dynamic metaphors, and his own vigorous and original diction, completing the poems with surprise endings. Lee says, "When the language doesn't sing, then there is no poetry."

Recently, there has been a renaissance of Indigenous literature in the works of Louise Bernice Halfe, Billy-Ray Belcourt, Jordan Abel, Liz Howard, and D.A. Lockhart. D.A. Lockhart was born in Chatham and grew up in Windsor. His family belonged to the Lenape tribe. In his first book *Big Medicine Comes to Erie*, he traces significant events in the history of this tribe and writes about the great warrior, *Tecumseh*. In his next book *City at the Crossroads*, he juxtaposes geological, colonial, and present-day scenes of Indianapolis, celebrating the achievement of its athletes, musicians, and writers. In *Wĕnchikàneit Visions*, he writes: "Let me sing of visions had in the places I have been blessed enough to walk through," expressing contemporary versions of this ancient Indigenous quest. In *Devil in the Woods* he provocatively represents famous Canadian characters and demonstrates how Aboriginal culture has been marginalized throughout Canadian history. Lockhart speaks sorrowfully about the tragedy resulting from the recent discovery of the graves of Aboriginal sites at former Canadian Residential schools and the need for reconciliation.

Bruce Meyer's family has been living in Toronto for generations. He grew up in Willowdale and graduated from the University of Toronto. In his writing he draws on the resources of English literature, skilfully using traditions such as those of the aubade, sonnet, villanelle, and elegy. He is a prolific poet developing his books on diverse subjects by employing a variety of narrative techniques, appropriate allusions, and original metaphors. In *The Seasons*, he alludes to Pablo Neruda in love poems that celebrate his wife, Kerry. In *The Madness of Planets*, he pays tribute to poets such as Li Po and Tu Fu, John Berryman and Philip Larkin and Canadian poets Al Purdy and John Newlove. *The Arrow of Time* is concerned with the poet trying to find the permanent in the impermanent and dealing with the complex realities of families, and international events such as the bombing of Nanking as well as the final moments of the Tsar and his family. Bruce Meyer in his excellently crafted poetry writes passionately and with deep insight on history, nature, desire, and love.

A. F. Moritz is a distinguished poet who writes out of his American background and his life in Canada, bringing a broader and more universal vision to Canadian poetry. His works are meditations of different aspects of history, juxtaposing ideas of time, and suggesting how our perception is continually changing. His recent book *The Sparrow: Selected Poems* is a showcase of his talent. We are taken by startling surrealism as seen in his poems "The Butterfly" and "Sentinel" or his philosophical approach in the long poem, *Sequence*. He befriended the artist and Chilean poet Ludwig Zeller, and together with his wife, Theresa Moritz, translated a number of his poetry books and novels. John Ashbery wrote: "An ancient voice, mournful like the wind, speaks to itself yet means to be overheard in A.F. Moritz's amazing poems … We seem to hear shattered echoes from the Bible, Dante, Petrarch, or Scève bound up in Maldoror's cruel eloquence."[1]

Sue Sinclair brings a philosophical approach to poems where she employs unusual arguments that defamiliarize the world, creating provocative new insights for the reader. She writes in her interview: "At its best, philosophy can be world-changing; it can change how you see things and hence how you relate to other beings. So can poetry." Sinclair brings unusual analogies to her poem "Lilies": "The callas, stylish / as the waved hair of women / who do lunch." In "Red Pepper" she compares the red pepper to the human heart. Her poems are often based on a wide range of subjects such as mathematics, biology, astronomy, art, and philosophy. She uses personification to animate things, but also chremamorphism, where the human is treated as an object to bring startling shifts in perspective. Jane Hirshfield writes: "*In Heaven's Thieves,* Sue Sinclair offers us a gorgeous, authoritative, boundary-leaping meditation on beauty and incarnation."[2]

Colleen Thibaudeau grew up in St. Thomas, Ontario, and lived in Winnipeg, London and Angers, France. She graduated from the University of Toronto and was one of the first students to write her MA thesis on Canadian poetry. She married the poet and playwright James Reaney. Her lines of poetry, sometimes short and other times long, have various rhythms, and the images that leap from one to another developing the

1 Ashbery, John. Cover endorsement. *The Sparrow*, by A.F. Moritz, Anansi, 2018.

2 Hirshfield, Jane. Cover endorsement. *Heaven's Thieves*, by Sue Sinclair, Brick Books, 2016.

poem in an unpredictable way reminiscent of French Quebec poetry. In her work she can encompass a larger range: "let this elastic moment stretch out in me: till that / point where they are inside and invisible." Colleen Thibaudeau in her poetry has a wonderful originality, a kaleidoscopic presentation of imagery as she writes about her family, the country, and the world at large.

In this book I present the work of ten significant contemporary poets who create through their innovative styles, original metaphors, inventive language, expressing a philosophical *sagesse*, social engagement and a deep knowledge of literature. They are among the most daring poets in Canada and through their cutting-edge poetry have continued the development of their predecessors, P.K. Page, Al Purdy, Irving Layton, Anne Szumigalski and others, pointing the way to a new direction for young Canadian poets.

Photo credit: Laura Bartlett

BRIAN BARTLETT

Laurence Hutchman: *You have said you began writing at about the age of 11. What provoked you to become a writer at such an early age?*
Brian Bartlett: A keen young listener to jigs, reels and strathspeys picks up fiddle and bow; a fascinated 11-year-old browser of art books and haunter of galleries experiments with paints. After years of living with books, I started to dream of creating them. It's hard to know whether one driving force behind the dream was a grateful desire to give the world one sort of thing I was receiving. Let's hope that's accurate, but we're talking about a state of mind going back over half a century, so it's risky to speak too specifically, even if lapses into self-mythologizing (and why say "lapses"?) are normal. Another reason for turning to writing—common in the lives of would-be artists—was acute introversion. Did I grow attached to pen and paper partly because I often chose to be alone, even with five brothers and sisters? Or, vice versa, did I often choose to be alone because I'd grown attached to pen and paper? The cause-and-effect likely went in both directions.

LH: *In childhood what sorts of books inspired you?*
BB: In the beginning, the Old Testament, the New Testament—and the word-intoxicating picture books of Dr. Seuss. One turning point: a fondness for *Batman*, *Superman* and *Flash* comics switched (how slowly I don't recall) to *Classics Illustrated*. In later elementary school I went through a phase of reading both the *Classics* distillations and the root

17

originals—two very different introductions to Verne, Wells, London, Poe and, above all, Dickens. Another branch of literature, the talking-farm-animal adventures by Walter R. Brooks, had become so much a part of my life that in grades 5 and 6 I drafted over 100 pages of an unfinished novel about talking farm-animals, sometimes returning to school early after lunch to write with nobody else in the classroom. Again, it's a familiar pattern: learning to write partly by unabashedly imitating what you've savoured reading. The human family in the Brooks novels were the Beans; my book featured the Pods.

Quite likely I had a time of unselfconscious pleasure in writing, without considerations of readership. But I don't think it was very long before writing as hobby led to fantasies about becoming a writer; unlike playing Little League baseball and School Boy hockey, writing soon influenced my sense of the adult I might become. With two fingers I typed up pages—blending research from a few sources—and compiled a hefty scrapbook of author biographies. That was an ongoing project, but my memory has never let go of one singular memory: watching the 1944 movie *The Adventures of Mark Twain* on our black-and-white TV, I felt overpowered by a scene of Samuel Clemons (played by Fredric March) signing "Mark Twain" to a manuscript's title page for the first time. The power I felt had nothing to do with the pseudonym; it was in the act of signing a completed manuscript to try with a publisher. The drama of having made a world of words, and of signing one's name to it, hit me hard; no other moment in film has done more to give me a sense of destiny and of a desirable future.

LH: *What were some of the challenges that you faced as a young writer in school?*

BB: No serious challenges, if by that you mean discouragements to get through. Encouragement came from several directions, including the early knowledge that Charles G.D. Roberts, whose "realistic" animal stories differed radically from Brooks's humorous fiction, had lived in Fredericton, where I'd been since the age of four. My mother and grandmothers were all keen readers who gave me books; and in junior-high years I published often in the local newspaper's *Spotlight on Youth* weekend supplement, which featured kids' stories, poems and other sorts of writing. Fundamentally friendless (partly by choice) for three years, and more at home in the woods than in any social circles, I often lived as if my classmates existed in another realm. Sometimes I've been tempted to feel pity for that long-ago skinny loner—who suffered from a sort of eating disorder for a dozen years, and from waves of guilt at not being a good enough Christian (including the failure to pray daily)—then I recall that much of the grounding for a life in writing was being formed before high school. Those junior-high years were in some ways frightened and monkish; in other ways, rich and adventurous. One of my oddest—in retrospect, most laughable—pipe-dreams was to found and edit a mimeographed nature-based magazine called *The Hermit*. (By then an absorption in nature rivalled that in books, and thoughts of becoming a forest ranger or wildlife biologist came into play.) For a while I must've dreamed of being not only a writer but a *hermit* writer—yet I also imagined adult years with a beautiful wife and a house including natural wood everywhere and bookcases reaching from floor to ceiling. (I hadn't a clue that decades later compulsive book-collecting could lead to a beautiful wife pointing out, "Space is limited.")

LH: *When you studied English at the University of New Brunswick you took a course with Fred Cogswell. He was one of the most influential publishers of his generation, encouraging young poets and publishing their books. Some of them, such as Al Purdy, Dorothy Livesay, Alden Nowlan and Roo Borson, became well-known. Cogswell published your first chapbook,* Finches for the Wake. *What did you learn from him in his role as a professor and writer?*

BB: In *All Manner of Tackle: Living with Poetry* I've published a memoir about Fred, so I'd like to confine myself mostly to things not mentioned there. Except in our earliest encounters Fred was more friend than "professor and writer." He was a tireless supporter of poets from coast to coast, and beyond. While he was very dedicated to Canadian literature, from the 1950s on his editing of *The Fiddlehead* was also international; he wanted our country's literature considered alongside that of other countries and continents.

In the early 1970s Fred wasn't a regular Creative Writing prof. When I did a poetry workshop with him, he was a substitute for the regular instructor (Robert Gibbs, maybe?). Early on in the term, Fred said something like, "I'm not sure I even believe in workshops." Sorry, I can't recall much about the course, except Fred assigned experiments with sonnets and villanelles, and oversaw the printing of a class anthology. Several years later, one evening at a summer Maritime Writers' Workshop, he gave an exuberant, off-the-cuff lecture, without a single note in front of him, and spoke with such knowledge and precision about the British Romantics that I kicked myself for never having taken one of his literature courses.

To backtrack: Fred's generosity resulted in the chapbook you mentioned—published a year or two *before* he taught that workshop—a selection of my high-school poetry—soon a source of embarrassment. At least in our dynamic, Fred wasn't a giver of critiques and suggestions; I didn't get specific feedback from him as I did from the Icehouse Gang on Tuesday nights (including Nancy and Bill Bauer, Bob Gibbs, Kent Thompson, Mike Pacey and Dave Richards). Other than the affection and respect he showed talking with someone so young, Fred expressed his kindness by giving me copies of Fiddlehead Poetry books. Back then, I could hardly have known that he published several poets I would write about or edit books by decades later. Only your asking now about Fred has opened my eyes fully to how much his press fed a wellspring for my much later editing. Many other writers can testify to doors Fred opened for them—one of those people who often help make good things happen.

LH: *You have written at length about W.B. Yeats and Elizabeth Bishop. Can you speak about the influences of those writers on you?*
BB: In high-school years (not only in school itself) my po-etry-reading concentrated on Canadians (Nowlan, Layton, Cohen, MacEwen, the Confederation Poets), Shakespeare, the Romantics, Eliot and Thomas—along with Frost, partly be-cause of a Caedmon LP of him reading his own poetry, a much-played gift from one of my grandmothers. (More than with any other major poet, Frost's voices on the page have remained for me inextricably connected to his living, recorded voice.)

Somehow Yeats was left out of the picture until my second year at UNB. Then for the first time I was riveted by his mix of clarity, craft and complexity, and in my final undergrad year I wrote an Honours thesis called "Dialogue as Form and Device in the Poetry of W.B. Yeats." The ways his poems after his first three collections combine natural speech, heightened rhetoric and song-like cadences, relaxation and ferocity, sculpted form and openness to asides, were eye-openers, ear-openers. (One of the repeated auto-correct computer directives I've been most tickled by is that "Yeats" should be "Yeast.") My thesis advisor, Allan Donaldson, was the first person who told me that you can feel alienated by a poet's politics while caring deeply for much of their poetry. While Yeats kept a foot in the 19th century more than, say, Eliot or Williams, part of his originality for me was how he combines textures reminiscent of the Metaphysicals' with 20th-century diction and history.

Bishop didn't enter my reading life until after I'd finished an M.A. in Montreal. I first heard of her the week—maybe even the day—of her death in 1979. Concordia University had announced that the Southern fiction-writer Elizabeth Spencer was going to be its next writer-in-residence, and, mixing up the Elizabeths, I thought, "Oh no, Concordia will have to hire someone else for next year." Soon I had copies of *The Complete Poems* and *Geography III*. Some of the poems instantly became among my favourites in the language, but the bond with Bishop developed more slowly than that with Yeats. Over the decades I've grown to feel more drawn to her sensibility and techniques than to Yeats's. It would be easy to take up the rest of this interview talking about the many exhilarating aspects of her work. For now, I'll cite her unfurling, witty, self-reflexive sentences; restless shifts in tone and mood; subtleties shifting into sudden power; metaphors rooted in immediacies rather than foregrounding the poet's ingenuity; adjectival density combined with moving narratives; wisdom that stays away from pronouncements; harmonies appealing to our hearing.

It's curious how our learning to respond to different poets is far from chronologically aligned with their historical order: I read Bishop as closely and broadly as I'd read any poet, for instance, years before getting drawn down into the mind-dazzling seas of Dickinson.

LH: *In your M.A. program in Creative Writing at Concordia in 1975-76 you took a short-fiction workshop with Clark Blaise—in whose class I met you—and your thesis was a collection of short stories. Was it your intention to become a short-story writer along with being a poet?*

BB: Yes, at the time it was, and it had been earlier. As an under-grad, M.A. student and freelancer I wrote and published short stories in several magazines and anthologies. After the M.A. I also spent much of four years working through several drafts of a novel; a few of its dozen chapters appeared in print, but it never seemed sustained or coherent enough to be published. One of its three main characters was a middle-aged man who had abandoned dreams of becoming a mime artist (a connec-tion to my work decades later writing poetry nourished by the silent-screen comedians Chaplin, Keaton and Lloyd). During a full-time teaching career in Halifax, I didn't write much more fiction, though the old novel got put through the fire again, and about a dozen years ago, having loved Kawabata's *Palm-of-the-Hand Stories*, I drafted a few short-short fiction pieces; I still hope to rework and revise them, and experiment with more short-shorts. Part of the call to fiction-writing has likely been answered by storytelling elements in my poetry; and, in the past decade, by writing three books of non-fiction built in part upon elements of prose narrative.

LH: *At the Université de Montréal you chose to write your disser-tation on the American poet A.R. Ammons, who is known for ex-panding the subject matter of poetry, choosing apparently unpoetic subjects and language, and applying new ways to write about them. Why did you choose this modern American poet, and did you adopt some of his techniques in writing your poems?*

BB: For my three M.A. literature classes, I chose single-author ones on Dante, Chaucer and Milton; I vaguely recall thinking that any would-be poet should know and appreciate the canon (not that in 1975-76 the word "canon" was used nearly as much—or as questioningly—as it would be later on). At the same time, I was starting to read the American poetry I'd not studied formally, and branching out to translations from languages such as French, German, Russian, Italian, Spanish, Chinese; there might've been two or three years when half the poetry I read was in translation. After taking about six years off between the M.A. and the Ph.D., I first planned to do a dissertation on Thoreau's humour, but starting to read A.R. Ammons changed all that.

Ammons was a poet I began to read after picking up one of his books without having heard about him from a friend, or having much idea of his life and his contemporary status; little did I know that Harold Bloom had called him and Ashbery the most significant living American poets. When you first encounter a poet without prior recommendations or awareness of reputation, you can feel a rare excitement in starting to read them. (Keats's "On First Looking into Chapman's Homer" is one of the great poems about reading, but its encounter isn't the sort I'm talking about here, because Keats had known about Homer long before finding Chapman's translation: "Oft of one wide expanse had I been told / That deepbrow'd Homer ruled as his demesne.") So many things about A.R.A. quickly became magnets: a body of sometimes weirdly original nature poetry, a mix of lyricism and laugh-aloud humour, the salt and pepper of vernacular language, a willingness to celebrate and praise, the weaving of essayistic elements into poetry (similar to Marianne Moore), and skill with both miniatures and sprawling, monstrous poems. Rarely had I found poetry so much *fun* to read. In one of his long poems, Ammons writes: "perhaps I will say, / the cosmos, as I understand it, wants you to have fun" ("Hibernaculum"). One appealing thing about Bishop too is her staying clear of lugubriousness, despite the tragedies faced in her life and writing. What an amazing phrase to have carved into her tombstone, the final words from one of her poems: "Awful but cheerful."

A very prolific poet, Ammons is no Yeats or Bishop in terms of sustained polish and striving for perfectionism, but it was bracing to find such a lively, many-toned poet things like "you have so many tones I can't tell / which one's prevailing: the dominant from the / predominant: you have so many, they come in chords, // tonic, subdominant, diminished: I can't tell the / significant significances from the insignificant / significances" ("Hibernaculum); or "I'm sick of good poems, all those little rondures / splendidly brought off, painted gourds on the shelf: give me / the dumb, debilitated, nasty, and massive, if that's the / alternative" (from the book-length poem *Sphere: The Form of a Motion*). In the second quotation, the qualifier "if that's the alternative" matters a lot; it doesn't take much to realize that an either/choice is reductive. What's attractive in the moment isn't the false dichotomy Ammons presents but the comic exaggeration of his speech, the sheer performative chutzpah of his phrasing

Ammons exasperates, yes, with his repetitiousness and verbosity. Yet I still find his work very energizing. What scope, what shining heights and crystalline precision in his poetry!

LH: *Between 1975 and 1990, you lived in Montreal, and like many of us there, you witnessed turbulent times with the election of the PQ in 1976, the Quebec Referendum in 1980 and in 1989 the tragic event of the École Polytechnique massacre. As part of an artistic community, you supported yourself by occasional labour jobs, proofreading for a tabloid, writing book reviews for* The Gazette, *and teaching Creative Writing and English Composition part-time at Concordia University. Which experiences were the most useful in the development of your writing?*

BB: For better or worse, Quebec politics had no obvious effect on my writing, in part because I wasn't (and am still not) a poet prone to grappling with issues of nation and national differences—though I admire much politically inflected poetry, such as that by Amichai, Neruda, Livesay, Milosz and Heaney. My collections have included a handful of poems witnessing the lives of disadvantaged, marginalized citizens, and ones touching on matters of environmental decline—but I've sometimes wanted to write more poems confronting global realities, like Nowlan in "Bobby Sands" and "The Beggars of Dublin," Bishop in "Roosters" and "Pink Dog," and Steven Heighton in several poems I'm recently re-read in preparation for reviewing his *Selected*.

To return to your question about the Montreal experiences that were "most useful." Moving furniture, cleaning apartment buildings and proofreading tabloids didn't do much to help the poetry grow. Book-reviewing and teaching did more, in as much as they encouraged close attention to words on the page—but reading extensively and freely was surely the greater teacher and stimulus.

How about a story? During a few weeks of an extra-cold Montreal winter, I took on an Emergency Manpower job, in an abandoned school used for sorting broken classroom furniture from all over the city. Now and then a truck with a crane would arrive, then swing intertangled chairs and tables toward open windows. Our job was to pull the furniture in, release it from clamps and arrange it in various rooms. But we spent at least 75% of the time just waiting; so I'd settle into one of the less broken chairs and read for hours. I got through a big old Bantam paperback of Tolstoy's short fiction. Such an immersion in 19th century Russia, while I sat there, heavily sweatered, being paid (minimum wage). Though I'd helped Clark Blaise and his Bharati Mukjherjee move to Toronto in

July 1978 during what was supposedly the weekend of the largest-ever departure of Montrealers to Ontario—two years after the PQ's rise to power—I was still in my twenties, without responsibilities or investments affected by the changing social scene. During those days in the abandoned school, it's safe to say, scenes and characters of Tolstoy had more reality for me than Quebec politics.

LH: *In the long poem "Underwater Carpentry," you state that you wanted to write a poem that escapes "time and place." You created that poem by including a taxidermist's wolf, quoted graffiti, a landlady's memories of Auschwitz, post-concert sex, Jacques Cartier, Glenn Gould, spiders and waxwings. How were you able to develop these scenes and move freely through different points in time?*
BB: The zigzagging, subject-switching quality in Ammons' long poems was one prompt for "Underwater Carpentry," as were long jazz-tracks such as ones by Mingus and Coltrane. Memory tells me that much of the poem developed from pulling together fragments from a notebook, with thoughts like *Let's see how these bits can hang out together,* or *Juxtapose like crazy, and see if something sparks.* I'd previously done multi-part poems, and tried mixing up things in shorter poems, then soon after moving from Montreal to Halifax I wanted to experiment with the long sweep of a single poem carried over 10 or 12 pages, but not primarily structured as a narrative—instead using mosaic, collage, stream of consciousness.

You've cited the desire for "a poem without time or place," yet not the rather joking continuation: "… but the four elements / hold me hard, one way out / to sneak in many times and places." The poem expresses a hope to transcend the quotidian, to forsake particulars, then it catches itself and recalls its need for grounding or, essentially, its hunger for imagery (can any image exist without "place"?)

LH: *In "Hawthornden Improvisations," written during a month-long stay at a writers' retreat in a castle in Scotland, you wrote, "I came without much of a plan except to come without / much of a plan," and added that you wanted "the old image-bank" closed, to accept what the days brought. How challenging was it to develop the poem's many parts, to give them the qualities of improvisations while keeping within the tight structure of a five-line stanza?*

BB: Unlike "Underwater Carpentry," the Hawthornden poem appears in sections, diary-like, rather than flowing from beginning to end with no pauses longer than stanza breaks. For that reason and others, including the stanza lengths' regularity, it's more leisurely than the earlier poem, more "prosy" in its pacing. (Since I'm fascinated by interactions between lyrical and discursive modes, sometimes I mean "prosy" descriptively, not pejoratively.) You've asked how challenging it was to synthesize the improvised feeling with the predetermined structure. Truthfully I don't recall giving much thought to difficulties in that process—maybe because it felt natural, both through my decades of private, unrevised journal-keeping and from familiarity with long poems in fixed stanza-lengths (Stevens being a major predecessor of Ammons in that regard).

One other thing: despite the plural in its title, "Hawthornden Improvisations" is intended as a single poem, as a novel stands in relation to its chapters. When one reviewer of *Wanting the Day: Selected Poems* wished it had included some of "Hawthornden Poems" [sic] because he thought the long poem the strongest work in *The Afterlife of Trees*, I was both pleased by the praise and a little unnerved by the misrepresentation of *Improvisations* as *Poems*.

LH: *Classical music, jazz, and other kinds of music play an important role in your life and your work. Poems that come to mind include "Hawthornden Improvisations," of course, and "Bluegrass* in Japan," where the sounds and the rhythms in the first stanza imitate the music. Why has music been an integral part of your poems?

BB: A simple answer: because music has been and remains an integral part of my life.

A longer answer: A day without listening to music has often felt to me like a day without reading. One benefit of having retired from teaching a few years ago I'm finding, is more freedom to truly listen, to simply *listen*—and not while reading magazines, washing dishes or driving the car. Though references to music have often surfaced in my poetry (which might give the inaccurate impression I only listen to jazz and classical, whereas I listen to other sorts of music, including plenty of rock), I don't play an instrument or have much formal knowledge. So the poems reflect the perspective of a listener, collector and concert-goer, whose responses are impressionistic and emotional rather than informed by music's technical specifics. In contrast, Jan Zwicky, Robyn Sarah and Barbara Nickel are three Canadian poets whose practice as musicians has clearly influenced their practice as poets. (Critics and scholars have much more to explore in that direction—as they do with Canadian poets who've trained academically as philosophers—Francis Sparshott, Zwicky, Tim Lilburn and, from a younger generation, Sue Sinclair, Warren Heiti and Darren Bifford.)

LH: *Are the musical references a way of intensifying emotion in a poem?*

BB: Thanks for your question, Laurence, because it's given me pause and helped me recognize that appearances of music in my poems often arise during playful moods. While readers might expect musical references to intensify emotions—like music in a film's soundtrack during an extra-dramatic scene— my poems often bring them in partly for humorous ends.

I'm thinking of a reader-tricking report on concert-going ("Brahms Can Wait Tonight"), a catalogue poem ending with the unlikely image of a Zimbabwean thumb-piano's sounds ("Thanksgiving in an Old House"), and the citing of tunes recorded by trumpeter Clifford Brown in the month after my birth ("Trailing Juniper").

LH: *You have travelled to many places including Israel, Italy, Belgium, Holland, Sweden, Britain, Ireland, Brazil and Costa Rica. Can you speak about how you were inspired on any of those trips?*
BB: Several of those trips led to no writing except on-the-spot or retrospective journal entries. In my first full-length poetry collection, *Planet Harbor*, two weeks in Israel one December resulted in several poems written back in Montreal. One of them, "On the Bus from Beer-sheba," is a sort of political poem, dramatizing both calm and tension when a young Israeli soldier nods off to sleep against an Arab traveller's shoulder. The longest of the poems, "All Fall You Wrote Me About the Desert," was the most ambitious I'd written until then, and in its mix of landscape evocation, love poetry, and contrasts between the unfamiliar/overseas and the familiar/home-based, it flexed its muscles for later, still longer poems. Maybe the poems Al Purdy, P. K. Page and Ralph Gustafson based on their travels outside Canada were influences—but if so, that didn't occur to me for years.

Travel poems risk getting superficially touristic, unless the outsider's perspective is admitted and ironized. Some away-from-home experiences have compelled me to write prose rather than poetry—such as two essays *Brick* published, one about time on Iona in Scotland, another about an ecotour in Brazil. In both those cases, prose seemed the more relaxed medium for exploring and examining impressions received in places I'd never set foot in before.

LH: *Your poem "Foot-doctor for the Homeless," which won the 2001 Petra Kenney Prize, has the qualities of a dramatic monologue, written from a woman's point of view. It captures a dual perspective, the suffering and observations not only of her homeless patients, but also of the doctor herself. Could you speak about the genesis of this poem?*

BB: In my reading experience, dramatic monologues include an implied addressee, a listener in the poem's narrative context (often someone sitting in the same room as the speaker), so I think of the foot-doctor poem as simply a monologue. The poem's seed was a newspaper mention of a young Halifax doctor setting up a clinic like that described in the poem. A while later, in the spring of 2000, I had a major breakdown, a nervous collapse including panic attacks, difficulty breathing and irrational feelings of dread and fears of death. Dr. Paul of the local foot-care fame, by then a GP (everyone seemed to call him by his first name, Paul, preceded by Dr.), helped me through some difficult months. Eventually he moved to New Orleans, where he doctored citizens in desperate straits after Hurricane Katrina. The poem is mostly fictional, yet its expression of distress and need—I didn't realize until it was several drafts old—likely had links with my own distress and need in that anxious spring (though I was far more fortunate than the sore-footed man). Soon I wrote a medically oriented follow-up monologue poem, "The Sonographer," but I'm sorry not to have used personae more often—except in a couple of found poems, and an unpublished satirical group whose speakers are technological devices or features such as a TV remote, Call Waiting and selfies.

LH: *In your poems, especially the longer ones, you leap from time to time to create surprising juxtapositions. In others you are sometimes concerned with simultaneity, which you express in "Always." Why have you been fascinated with creating this sense of simultaneity?*

BB: The two sorts of poems you mention differ as memory differs from the moment. With the multiple-juxtaposition poems, switches in both time and place are crucial, but in a poem like "Always" the poet (and readers) imagine a few of the countless things occurring within one breath of time. In the prose book *Branches Over Ripples: A Waterside Journal*, I overtly champion frequent tense-changing as very much our healthy, daily way of existing in the world and in our lives. Present-tense mindfulness can be a valuable, temporary state of awareness, but I've never thought of it as superior to multi-tense inclusiveness. Alertness takes on many forms. The past and the future are foundational parts of the present. "Living completely in the now" can sound dystopian rather than utopian. Has any science-fiction writer ever tackled such a prospect?

While mindfulness (at least in many meditation practices) rests in the here and now (or in timelessness, which has often seemed to me an inhuman abstraction), simultaneity is a matter of *the now and here and there and there and there* .... Can we bring back the kaleidoscope metaphor?

LH: *You've experimented with "found poems" by taking selections from other writers' works and building poems with them. Why did you choose to explore your family's history through these found poems?*
BB: Annie Dillard's *Mornings Like This* was the major model for the sort of found poems found in "Given Words," the second section of *The Watchmaker's Table*. In contrast to found poems that break other writers' single paragraphs or pages into lines and stanzas, Dillard's often dip into entire books and extract a passage here and a passage there, then combine and order, without adding any words. Writing "Given Words"—arguably editing as much as writing, but still composing—felt like I was helping expand communal, family acts, as well as escaping from the so-called lyric self.

One of my great-uncles, a soldier in World War I, sent letters from a training camp in England to his sister in Canada (later my grandmother). She held onto those letters for more than half a century; one of her daughters inherited them, then they were passed down to me, and eventually I selected and rearranged sentences from them for "Dear Georgie." That poem is a dramatic monologue in the strict sense, in that it has a specific addressee, Georgie. In his book of prose, *Pigheaded Soul: Essays and Reviews on Poetry and Culture*, poet Jason Guriel has an appreciative (and much appreciated) essay about "Dear Georgie." He comments, "Poems' speakers usually sound like poets," and in contrast he says of the great uncle, "He doesn't know he's in a poem." Guriel gets on the poem's wavelength (and recognizes it as a "war poem," though it sees no battles), and finds much of interest in Hermon's language, observing things about it that I'd not consciously noticed.

LH: *While writing those found poems, did you make any surprising discoveries about your ancestors?*
BB: Oh yes. My great-uncle's clear reports and the specifics of his time in England—such as the hardship of cleaning horse harnesses, and his suspicion that plays would spoil him for watching "motion pictures"—were revelations. The longest poem in "Given Words" is "What He Chose to Record," every word of it extracted from my great-grandfather's diaries written between 1889 and 1918. Those diaries are plain-speaking, devoid of introspection, mostly about farm labours, household chores, churchgoing, deaths and weather. A glance at such diaries suggests they're mechanical and boring, but I sensed there might be something else going on under the surface, so I spent a few weeks digging into the diaries and typing out many pages worth of recorded moments and unusual phrasings. C.B. Lawrence (even my father simply recalled him as

"C.B.") only had a grade-four education, so he developed a knack for phonetic spellings. Defamiliarized words like *whife*, *appels, oke, Chrismos, cultervated, hawspittle*, etc. (let's call them spellings, not misspellings) give a Joycean flavour to some moments in his diaries.

You asked about surprises and, yes, C.B.'s spelling was a surprise, as was the discovery of patterns and echoes—even rhymes (separated by dozens of pages), which prompted me to construct the poem's first section in rhyming/off-rhyming couplets: e.g., "repaired fence east of house and brought in last of hay / went to Red Beach to circus   took black cow away." Again, I felt like a contributor to something communal, linking days from years or even decades apart. Reading that poem aloud has always been very moving—though my great-grandfather might've been bewildered by the use made of his hastily jotted-down words.

One last point: relying on an ancestor's letters or diaries is hardly mandatory for a poem to be more than the product of an individual voice. Every poem we've read—every *thing* we've read—is potentially something that feeds into our poems. So I see "Given Words" as escaping from lyric voices but also maintaining the fact of indebtedness that is part of every poem's being.

LH: *In your "Given Words" poems dedicated to your parents (I was fortunate to have known them for a long time), you rely completely on quotations from a newspaper published on the days of their births. Why were you drawn to imagine the larger context of their first 24 hours?*

BB: Those two poems were among the last ones completed for *The Watchmaker's Table*. Now I wish they were a little shorter, more discriminating in what they include. Mining those two 1925 and 1928 issues of *The Telegraph-Journal* was both laborious and gladdening. The greatest surprise were the crossword clues printed on the day of my father's birth—the aptness of words and phrases like *Name*, *Shooting forth*, *Digit of the foot*, *Gazing fixedly*, *To breathe*, *Exist*. Coming across those clues, I have to say, felt absolutely uncanny.

Out of love for my parents, I felt something sacred in learning a few things about the world during the weeks of their births, and in constructing poems built upon those details. If we can stretch simultaneity from the moment to the day, there's an "Always" quality in those two multi-part, rambling poems, at least in bringing together disparate happenings and voices.

LH: *I see in your work a refutation of dualism and Platonism, of worlds other than this one. In "Underwater Carpentry" you give the reader a sense of your change as you moved from a traditional Christian viewpoint to a more of a Thoreauvian belief in nature:*

> When did the tide turn,
>   when did I finally feel
>   the earth was my mother
>   (father) more than any Nameless One
>   was my father (mother)?

Your thoughts remind me of those in Wallace Stevens's "Sunday Morning." Can you speak about why you see Earth as our only reality, without the need for some other spiritual dimension?

BB: Thanks for mentioning "Sunday Morning." Some of its lines are among the ones I've found most sustaining in 20th-century poetry: "We live in an old chaos of the sun, / Or old dependency on day and night, / Or island solitude, unsponsored, free." And those magnificent final lines about the deer, the quail with their "spontaneous cries," and the "casual" pigeon-flocks with their "[a]mbiguous undulations."

Don Domanski once told me Stevens was his favourite poet, and when I asked which poems he'd single out, the first title he gave was "Sunday Morning."

Your question takes me back to a first reading of the famous "Allegory of the Cave" passage in Plato's *Republic*, especially to suggestions that earthly existence only gives us imperfect "shadows" of unearthly, ideal (Ideal) forms. As a second-year undergrad in a "Philosophy and Religion" course, I was still enough of a Christian to write an essay defending one of the classic arguments for the existence of God (the Cosmological or Ontological argument?). But it wasn't very long before I stopped feeling the reality of a monotheistic divinity. That fading of belief went together with questioning the view that bodies are inherently secondary or even, in some Idealist plane, unreal; what seemed to me less substantial, instead, were inventions of the supernatural—as fascinating a topic of study as they can be, and as large a role as they've played in many human cultures. By now some branches of Christianity and other religions are ecologically sensitive, and criticize their own traditions that downplayed or even demonized earthly life; yet beliefs in a soul's heavenly grace-given bliss have helped cause contempt for what we call, for lack of a better phrase, the natural world. To go back to Yeats: even as an undergrad while I responded to the aesthetic splendours of his poems like "Sailing to Byzantium" and "Byzantium," my heart felt much closer to the lived-in qualities of poems like "Vacillation,"The Circus Animal's Desertion" and "A Dialogue of Self and Soul."

LH: *Were questionings of an afterlife part of your questionings of religion?*
BB: That I've written a collection called *The Afterlife of Trees* suggests some sort of faith in afterlives at least in metaphor— but further than that I'm not able to venture. For many years

I took hankerings for an eternal soul as evidence that human beings want to feel extraordinarily special, to be worthy of never truly dying; thoughts of heaven seemed signs of species hubris, of unwillingness to accept one's place in the family of mortal things. But in later years I came to see that it could be another sort of hubris (which aggressively dogmatic atheists fall into) to belittle or caricature beliefs other than your own, and to act as if you understood the convictions and faiths of others. Thoreau was helpful here, as with so many other things. Among the many passages of *Walden* that have helped me live, here's one: "I would not have any one adopt *my* mode of living on any account ... I desire that there may be as many different persons in the world as possible." The second statement is hyperbolic (misused, couldn't it be stretched to defend axe-murderers and brutal dictators?), but Thoreau was an outspoken proponent of hyperbole—"extravagance" was a word he valued—and many of his memorable epigrammatical sentences are qualified by other passages. Still, that statement about "different persons" can guide us while we strive for open-mindedness and love. What a diminished world it would be if everyone had the same religion, politics, sexual nature and aesthetic leanings.

It's hard to assess how much our responsiveness to different attitudes and ideas derives from nature or nurture; and it's a cop-out to say simplistically, "It's all cultural," because we're also creaturely beings. Certainly I've been less attracted to logicians and metaphysicians constructing grand schemes than to more grounded thinkers—Phenomenologists, Existentialists, Pragmatists, anonymous Zen koan-coiners.

Let me pull out my copy of William James's *A Pluralistic Universe* and quote a few sentences I've bracketed: "Philosophy ... lie[s] flat on its belly in the middle of experience, in the very thick of its sand and gravel"; "I asked myself how the opinions of men could ever have so spun themselves away from life so far as to deem the earth only a dry clod, and to seek for angels above it or about it in the emptiness of the sky"; "I am finite once for all, and all categories of my sympathy are knit up with the finite world *as such*, and with things that have a history." In reading philosophy I'm often drawn to Americans, from Emerson and Thoreau to James and Stanley Cavell. Maybe that has something to do with much of my ancestry being from New England, at least three lines going back to Massachusetts/Maine of the early 1600s. Genetics and cultural influences are too interwoven to be separated. Again, nature and nurture: chances are I might feel less at home with eastern North American writers if I were a second- or third-generation Canadian with roots in Germany or Italy or Iceland. Then again, we should be careful not to overdo ancestral affinities. Sympathetic bells also ring in me when reading translations of Polish poetry, Russian fiction and Japanese haiku.

LH: *Alden Nowlan is one of the greatest Canadian poets. You have been reading and teaching his poetry over the years and were friends with him. Why did you undertake the mammoth task of editing his* Collected Poems?

BB: Of the books I've edited since 2006, most were initiated by my making proposals to publishers. Only three, including the Nowlan, were taken on after invitations. On my own I never would've volunteered to bring all of Nowlan's collections and chapbooks between two covers. Though I desired such a book, asking to edit it would've felt presumptuous. Then one day Ross Leckie, head of the Goose Lane/icehouse poetry board, phoned me up with the impossible-to-say-no-to invitation. Whereas with volumes of selected poetry, I'd had to read, re-read and make choices within book-length guidelines, the Nowlan *Collected* was relatively clear-cut. It didn't involve having to choose poems; Goose Lane had already decided that a "complete" Nowlan, including poems that had never gone beyond manuscripts or magazine printings, would be impractically large and expensive. But there were plenty of editorial duties: writing textual notes and bibliography, overseeing blurbs, noting line-breaks when they differed from one printing to another, arranging for art work and, above all, writing a long introductory essay.

LH: *How did your idea of Nowlan's work change while editing the* Collected?

BB: The answer would be brief if I simply said, "It didn't change," but I wonder if anyone editing a poet's collected works would ever say that. At the beginning, part of me was afraid: what if, re-reading the poems in bulk over many months, I'd feel disappointed, dragged down by the amount of sub-par work? Instead, the opposite happened: the poetry grew in my reading to seem even more fulfilling, variously human and artistically crafted than it ever had. None of the poems were completely unfamiliar, yet some of them spoke to me as they never had before. Maybe teaching, aging and decades of reading poetry had made me a more attuned reader. That learning continued during the months when we had celebratory readings from the *Collected* in several Canadian cities: some invited poets highlighted poems that even after the editing I hadn't lit up to; then the poem in another poet's voice did the trick. I could name poems—for starters, "Living in a Mad House," "At a Distance He Observes an Unknown Girl Picking Flowers," "Chopping Onion"—that I felt ashamed never to have responded to strongly. When younger I'd thought certain poems prosy, in the negative sense (and yes, some of the poems still seem that way); but it was a new experience to hear and feel those under-appreciated poems' voices speaking so

exactly, Alden dignifying them with the care of his enjamb-
ments and his careful unfolding of the syntax from line to
line. To harken back to Jason Guriel's comment about the ten-
dency of poems to sound like they're "spoken by poets": one
of Alden's great achievements is that he wrote so many fine
poems that convey the illusion of being direct speech (though
"illusion" is a key word there, and all sorts of indirections and
layers often reside within the seeming transparency).

Earlier I mentioned that Cogswell's Fiddlehead Poetry
Books published several of the poets whose work I've edited
over the past 15 years or so—Alden, along with Robert Gibbs,
Dorothy Roberts and William Bauer; and I've also written
about the Fiddlehead-published poets A.G. Bailey, M. Travis
Lane and Harry Thurston. It's been especially pleasing to edit
volumes of writings by early mentors and friends. Few of us
get so many opportunities to honour good people and poets
who helped us decades earlier; being involved in new editions
of Nowlan, Gibbs and Bauer has truly been a tremendous
privilege.

LH: *In an essay called "Haikuing," concluding your book of haiku
and senryu* Potato Blossom Road: Seven Montages *you say you
were in your forties before you learned to fully appreciate haiku.
Since then you've devoted that full-length collection and three
chapbooks to haiku. Why did you find that Japanese-rooted form
so engaging?*
BB: In "Haikuing" I mention seeing a filmed reading by Robert
Hass sharing his translations of Issa and Basho at a poetry
festival. At last I got bitten and smitten by the form, recog-
nizing the afterthoughts and sensing of depths elicited by so
few words. In later delving into dozens of haiku collections,
anthologies and studies, I've often found that a couple of haiku
out of 50 or 60 approach the illuminating force of the ones

Hass read—but then I remember that similar things can be said about the superlative examples of poems in any form.

Brevity, of course, is essential for haiku and senryu (in "Haikuing" I explain why distinctions between the two don't have much practical interest for me); but brevity is useless without distillation, which means a richness from which the distillation is made. Haiku need a delicate balance between solidity and ellipsis, substance and suggestion, speech and silence. A haiku needs to give enough, but not too much; overwritten haiku stumble, but underwritten haiku are static. Frankly, I find that the maximized minimalism of too many contemporary haiku produces stingy results, as if the poet weren't doing the necessary work for the poem. (On the other hand, I've published some haiku that suffer from having too much packed into them.)

For centuries, haiku have often been given roles in larger pieces of poetry; we tend to think of them as individual three-liners that stand perfectly on their own, yet history tells a more complicated story, one including the presence of haiku within spacious contexts, including mixes with prose, and haiku written in conversation with other haiku-writers. I've mostly written haiku as poems with a secondary role, that of participating in multi-haiku arrangements, forming what I like to call "montages" rather than the temporal-suggestive "sequence." Other metaphors: collage, mosaic and, yes, our old friend the kaleidoscope. Lear's "Speak, and be silent" could be applied to haiku ideals. We could jokingly add that montages seem to follow the guideline "Speak, and be silent ... and speak, and be silent ... and speak, and be silent ...."

A few months ago during a Zoom gathering centered on haiku, one sceptic objected to treating haiku as parts of wholes, which to her was bowing to "Western conceptions of poetry." She claimed that "every haiku must be a gem," and that groupings of haiku are bound to include duds and dull parts that should've been tossed out. Only later did I wish I'd thought to revise her metaphor: let's think of a haiku montage not as a string of gems but as a string of leaves, bark, shells, stones, gems, flowers, feathers. In *Potato Blossom Road*'s essay, somewhat tongue-in-cheek I include "deletes," and suggest why they were deleted. Moreover, in a few friends' copies of the books I've penned in other deletes, like DVD "extras"—or bonus-prizes in a box of cereal? Recipients were amused, yet the penning in of extra haiku expanded on a process of stratification key to the book. Playfulness was intended between the haiku's concentrations and the book's layerings.

LH: *One would not usually think of the comedians of the silent-film era as a natural subject for haiku, but in your latest chapbook,* Safety Last, *you write of the comic genius Harold Lloyd. Earlier you published haiku/senryu montages inspired by Charlie Chaplin and Buster Keaton. What attracted you to writing about these original and unpredictable comedians?*

BB: Most of those haiku were inspired by moments in the actors' silent films rather than their talkies. The silents draw our attention to scene, image, action, gesture, expression, without the distraction of words (though in a few cases I found haiku-seeds in the silents' across-the-screen lines of speech or commentary). Part of the challenge was to give words to wordlessness. Above all, it was Issa's mix of humour and pathos that suggested a Charlie connection. For a long time I'd wanted to write poetry spawned by the films, then one day the Issa parallels became clear: to quote from "Haikuing," Issa is "the haiku master most prone to writing of poverty, hunger, humiliation and childhood—all Chaplinesque themes." I started to imagine Issa haiku as moments in Chaplin films, and moments in Chaplin films as haiku.

Recently I've bought DVDs of early silents by the great Japanese director Yasujiro Ozu. I might enjoy them without feeling any compulsion to write haiku. But after completing the Chaplin and Keaton montages I thought, "That's probably enough"—then, starting to re-watch and watch Lloyd films, I realized there was still more to be done in that haiku-vein.

LH: *Since 2013, you've published three books of prose—a compilation of your prose on poetry* All Manner of Tackle: Living with Poetry *and two books of nature writing:* Ringing Here & There: A Nature Calendar *and* Branches Over a Ripples: A Waterside Journal—*with the third book of nature writing* Daystart Songflight: A Morning Journal *to be soon. Why have you written so much prose in the past decade?*

BB: *All Manner of Tackle* selects from my published writings on poetry going back to nearly 1990, so it doesn't mark a new or relatively recent direction. But the books of nature writing, yes, they've taken much of the attention and energy that earlier would've gone into writing poetry. To me that's more an expansion than a loss. I've always hesitated to think of poetry as the highest form of verbal expression, just as I'd never followed the line that instrumental music is the ultimate form of art (simultaneously, goes the thinking, the most abstract and the most directly emotional). Rating artistic and literary forms, pitting them against each other, can be unnecessary confrontational. Why bother arguing that giraffes are superior to tigers, eagles to herons, butterflies to ants? Poetry, plays, novels, short fiction, essays, journals—kinds of writing, all with potential values and powers; the originality and impact of the work doesn't lie in the choice of genre but in the writer's language and vision.

In retrospect, considering my fondness for the journals of Boswell, Thoreau, Woolf and Merton, it's surprising that I waited so long before constructing books as dated journals.

After a few years developing in that direction, I wondered if such non-fiction prose was better suited to my imagination than fiction, and if I should've taken up the reins of such writing much earlier. *Ringing Here & There*—as a book of days, composed of 366 brief paragraphs running from April 1st to the following March 31st—was transitional: its building blocks are short paragraphs (three fitting onto a page), and some readers consider it prose poetry (but that label seems to me imperfect, a good fit for only some of the 366 bits). But the prose nature of the next two books of nature writing is unmistakable, with long paragraphs and plenty of digressiveness. Partly because of their everything-but-the-kitchen-sink mentality, and their being drafted *en plein air* after walking or hiking, they provided some of my most gratifying writing hours ever. It took a few years before I suspected that the sorts of layering in "Underwater Carpentry" and "Hawthornden Improvisations" had found larger frameworks within the non-fiction manuscripts.

LH: *What has surprised you most about your life as a writer?*
BB: In the years after I turned fifty, my writing activities took a few new turns, into the haiku and senryu, the editing of books of poems by other poets, and experiments in hard-to-classify mixtures of nature writing/travel/journal/autobiography. All of those directions have given me much satisfaction, despite the inevitable regrets and feelings of missed opportunities that are part of creating almost any book. Some writers seem to find their art an ongoing source of unhappiness or angst, both in the day-to-day wrestling with words and in the complications of publishing and other aspects of a writer's public life. Perhaps I'm fortunate, in that writing has always given me more joy than misery.

August, 2021

Photo credit: Steve Schwartz

ROO BORSON

First Interview: 1993

Laurence Hutchman: *You grew up in Berkeley. Were you involved with literature and writing when you were growing up?*

Roo Borson: Involved in a private way, at home. My father always read a lot and he would quote Wordsworth and Shakespeare to me over the toaster at breakfast, just a few lines at a time, with a kind of marvel in his voice. He was a doctor. He practised medicine all day. He was a light sleeper, so he read a lot of the night in bed. He read all kinds of things and had a photographic memory for words. He could call up the pages in his mind, and so could quote whichever passage he wanted, and then give the page number too. He could remember poetry as well as everything else that was written down.

LH: *Do you have this same kind of photographic memory?*

RB: No, not at all. When I was a little kid I had an aural memory for conversations, but when I got older it drove me nuts that I had all of these conversations in my head. Somehow either I dispersed them or they began to disperse because of other pressures.

LH: *Your work is very visual. Are you influenced much by painting and the movies?*

RB: No. I'm influenced by what I see when I walk around.

LH: *Was it difficult adjusting to life in Canada?*

RB: I was twenty-two. I had difficulty adjusting to life at that point, but it was not particularly life in Canada. It was adjusting to life in a completely new place. I had a terrible time getting a job right away and I was newly married. We had very little money and lived in a rowdy, rundown, seedy apartment in Vancouver. I came out of the beautiful countryside of Vermont where I'd been going to school and was in the scuzzy part of a big city and struggling to live.

LH: *That's quite a change, from Vermont to Vancouver.*

RB: Yes. That was a difficult time in my life, but it wasn't adjustments to Canada per se. There were a few linguistic adjustments. The job I finally was able to get was in the Vancouver Public Library and I had the lowest sort of job, a clerk, which meant I was shelving books and filing articles. I had to learn a bit of Canadian. I had to learn what a chesterfield was. I remember saying to myself, I have to change from 'zee' to 'zed.' And how exactly do you say, 'eh'?

LH: *Many of the writers I've interviewed have been influenced by Europe or Canada, but your work seems to come out of the Americas. It seems quite different from the other writers' influence. Are you very aware of this difference?*

RB: Yes, I am. I'm very aware that I come from North America. I've said that before and various people have scowled at me because they think I'm saying North America in some imagined American imperialist sense, as though Canada is a part of the U.S. That's not the way I mean it. I mean I don't come from South America and I don't come from Europe and I don't come from Africa and I don't come from Australia. I come from North America.

LH: *What were some of the key influences in your writing life?*

RB: Starting back when I was a kid, Wordsworth. When I was a young teenager, it was first Dylan Thomas and then e.e. cummings. Before I went off to college I realized that I didn't understand contemporary poetry. What I was thinking of is modernism, I suppose, because I wasn't very up to date. I understood Dylan Thomas. The rhythm is so important and those rhythms are so easy to hear and pick up. I understood e.e. cummings because he's so concrete and his visual imagery plays such a large part. In a certain way he's very simple. I didn't understand some of the ways that a lot of other poetry was put together, and I didn't understand the dark stuff. So, before I went off to college I sat down with Sylvia Plath and said I'm going to learn to read this. It was like learning to listen to more contemporary jazz.

LH: *What about other influences?*

RB: Later, old Chinese poetry in translation, from the Tang dynasty, Wang Wei, Du Fu, Li Bai. And then basically some of the American eastern male poets. I was very attached to Merwin, and to some extent, James Wright. When I first came to Canada, because I happened to end up shelving books in the Language and Literature Department, I started on my short coffee breaks reading through the shelves. I fell in love with the work of Michael Yates. Then I suddenly discovered that he lived in Vancouver. When my marriage split up a year and a half later I went to UBC and he was teaching a course in continuing education and I sat in on that course. For me that was a fantastic opening experience. Here's this guy whose work I love on the page and I can actually talk to him.

LH: *You also mention Robert Bringhurst.*

RB: He was my teacher in the MFA Programme at UBC which I was attending concurrently. He was probably the only one who taught me something about writing. Other poets have taught me something about living as a poet in the world. I took a course from Louise Glück and she was the first poet who gave me a sense of what it could be to be a poet. And I love her work. Robert actually taught me something about the words on the page.

LH: *You studied comparative religion at Santa Barbara for two years. Is there a relation between these studies and your writing?*

RB: When I was a teenager I had probably very natural religious impulses. I am an atheist and never was anything but an atheist, but I was curious about the mystics in various traditions. It seemed to me that mystical experience was very close to what it is that prompts me to write. I was trying to investigate the links between mystical experience and artistic experience.

LH: *When Joyce's Stephen Daedalus was walking on Sandymount Strand he said, "Signatures of all things I am here to read." It seems very much what your work is all about, the constant reading of time and space and place.*

RB: Yes. And actually being sensorially impinged upon by the colour green in that grass. It just blazes, all of a sudden. I've had a lot of that kind of experience from the time I was a child.

LH: *Many of your poems are about the differences of gender and how men and women perceive each other. Your work has a feminist element, but it's not explicit in the way that someone like Erin Mouré or other feminists' work is. How do you express feminist concerns in your writing at this time?*

RB: Right now I'm not concerned with expressing overtly feminist concerns. Always in my writing I'm changing. I'm interested in different things and I'm interested in different content, I suppose. When I first started writing in workshops seriously, I think I had a natural leaning toward using images. I used images from the natural world a lot because that's what impinges on me most. After years of using natural imagery I thought: "Why don't I have any people in my poems?" I'm making it sound much more conscious than it really was, but I thought if I'm going to start to have people in my poems, which I did try to do, then I should pay attention to some of the things I had noticed, growing up female as I did, that are gender related and related to sexism. Much of the first half of *The Whole Night, Coming Home* has to do with adolescent experiences. You're very aware of strange social pressures and strange interpersonal pressures that are not purely biological. You're aware, as a female, of being the underling. At that time I didn't know how to question it or even that I had the right to question that I was the one taking orders, in a way … I think that the sexist experiences that I had were not in the realm of language so much, although they were to the extent that when I was young I was incredibly shy so I didn't speak up, but I never had to lose my language, and in fact I never felt that language was the culprit and I don't feel the sentence is an enemy of mine, in any of its forms. While I admire theories about language, and about power structures—political power, social power—being manifest in language I still don't feel that any sentence is an enemy of mine or any language form or any grammatical structure. I have never seen that women's language is different from men's language. What I see is that men have traditionally held power and that's all.

LH: *Poems like "Jacaranda" and "At Night You Can Almost See the Corona of Bodies" have a cosmic scale for their setting. When some contemporary poets remain close to their experience, why do you choose to express a larger space, as well as a wider sense of time?*

RB: I dislike literature in which I feel claustrophobic. That happens a lot in current American short fiction where the scope really doesn't go outside the psychology of the characters interacting. I have always felt freer when I see us as a species, instead of getting tangled in these endless psychological "Catch 22's." I prefer to see the world in the bigger way and when I'm relaxed, that is in fact how I see the world, so that's how it's portrayed. I am interested in people and how they work, but I wouldn't want to live exclusively inside that world. That's one of the things I dislike about the city. I'm not that interested in architecture and buildings, especially newer ones, like many in North America. What is there in the city? A lot of people and their interactions. I very much miss being able to see the stars and think about other planets and the blackness of space and about trees and other animals.

LH: *In* A Sad Device *the poems are often about the limitations of people's desires, of their inadequacy, of not measuring up. Do you see a darker tone in this book than in the later books?*

RB: I don't know. That's when I was first trying to write about people. Then in *The Whole Night, Coming Home* I found that I *could* write more about people. Looking at it as a technical exercise, which of course for me no poem is solely, I think I was a bit stiffer in *A Sad Device*. I kept relying on trees and space and the figures were smaller. I don't know if it's darker or not. I can't really see that. I think people interpret works as emotionally light or dark depending a lot on their own personalities. My own stance feels almost neutral, but many people interpret my work as sad. I do see sadness, but there's also funniness and lightness and happiness and air and light. I can't answer that question. I don't know which books are darker than other books. They all seem like me in my mind.

LH: *There is a move from a third person narration to a first–person narration in* The Whole Night, Coming Home. *You seem to be more and more comfortable in the first person. Why did you make that shift?*

RB: If you're looking at it as a canvas, first of all I was painting human figures. Once I got more comfortable with writing about people I thought, well I can talk as a person, not just a pair of eyes in the universe. Some of the stuff in *The Whole Night is* third person. Sometimes I speak from the first person when I've identified with somebody else's experience, rather than it having been my own. I think I'm actually more comfortable in the first person, period. When I first started out I had to incorporate figures. They were out there, at some distance from me.

LH: *In* The Whole Night, Coming Home *you have written a number of prose poems. Many of these have a coherence that one finds in fiction. Have you been criticized for using this form, the prose poem, in that some critics question the legitimacy of the form? Are there particular qualities that a prose poem has that allow you to fulfil the possibilities that you couldn't in other forms?*

RB: Yes, on both counts. I certainly have been criticized for using what some people feel is a bastard form or a non-existent form. I think that's silly. For me, those are poems because they have the imagery and density of poetry. They don't tell a narrative, particularly, although there are narrative elements. The way the language moves is rhythmic, melodic. It's something about the combination of melody and leaping from image to image that, for me, makes it poetry.

LH: *Do you think the prose poem allows you to make those leaps, perhaps because there's not the same constraint on line endings and forms?*

RB: I think you can leap all over the place in a poem, but in prose poems it's more subversive. That's how I look at prose poems, as though you're just reading a straight piece of prose, whatever that is, and then, bang, there's something unexpected. It seems more subversive and also less formal.

LH: *Patience Wheatley sees the first section of* The Whole Night, Coming Home *as a chronicle of coming of age in California of the reckless 1960s. Do you think that's an accurate assessment of this section of the book?*

RB: That's certainly part of what's going on. It is a coming of age, although the experiences aren't all mine. It's not just one story exactly, but it does dwell in that adolescent space of not knowing what's ahead of you and not being sure of the rules and not wanting any rules.

LH: *Were you involved in some of the activities in the sixties?*

RB: In high school ... because I was in Berkeley. It was much more politicized than growing up in Fredericton or many other places. I was a high school student during the time of the growing demonstrations against the Vietnam War. I joined in those marches, but I never threw any bombs.

LH: *You don't seem explicitly political.*

RB: No, I'm not.

LH: *You observe from different points of view, such as in the poem "The Night-Blooming Cereus" where at the end of the poem you say, "Imagination on its tether, I was up there with the cats, who prefer to encircle any event from above, defining its borders like gods."*

RB: I don't know if I really do see things from different viewpoints. I'm not aware of coming from different viewpoints. What it is that I'm aware of is that my identity doesn't stop at my own skin. It's not as though I'm shifting around; it's as though I'm bigger than this thing you see here in this chair.

LH: *Your poems are often about the unwritten life, things that somehow don't get into poetry, areas of feeling or consciousness that lie beyond conventional ways of thinking of the world. I'm thinking of the unusual perspectives in "Snowlight on Northwood Path."*
RB: For me it's not unusual.

LH: *At the end of your last book, you talk about "things that didn't get into poems." Do you find areas that you haven't written about, in terms of content and style?*
RB: I guess I'm always moving on. I get really sick of my own stuff. I get sick of my own mind and I want it to change, so I just move along to whatever the next thing seems to be. Often there's a painful transitional period where I'm very uncomfortable, can't really write and hate all my writing. I just went through the longest one like that I'd ever been through. It lasted over a year. I never know what's important to me next until I'm already part way into the next book and then I realize, ah yes, this is what I was after. When I said that in *A Sad Device* I started painting in human figures, I didn't set out to do that. Once I got part way through I realized that was important to me and that was in fact what I was doing, the next project. With each book there's been another project, to expand technically. Technically sounds too dry. It's to interest myself again, to become engaged, to go in a different direction.

LH: *In the epigraph to* Intent, or Weight of the World, *you suggest an approach: "They are not 'truths,' but should be used as phenomenological guides until verified." Rajan Gupta. What did you mean to suggest by this quotation?*

RB: I thought it was fun to use something from a series of highly technical physics lectures as an epigraph and Rajan is a friend. Kim was reading these lectures because Rajan wanted to know if they sounded okay, in terms of is it understandable, well-presented in English, for a group of physicists in China. I was reading over Kim's shoulder and that just struck me. Of course he is talking about something very technical, in lattice gauge theory. That's what the lectures are about, but that one sentence struck me as true for a lot of things. What I meant to suggest was just what it says, except there is a flip side. I'm being flippant, but I also mean it. These are phenomenological guides. The poem contains phenomena that I see. I am a detector: I detect things visually, aurally, sensorially and they end up in the poem. They can't be verified, except by the reader experiencing the same phenomena, either in the poem or outside the poem. I'm being playful with it. I'm suggesting that poems are not truths, or not necessarily factual, or absolute, truths, which, I think, people would now concur with anyway.

LH: *You live with Kim Maltman, the poet. Does he influence you in particular ways?*

RB: In the sense that we edit each other, heavily. We are very influential on each other's writing. In terms of idea, no. In terms of the ways we look at the world, not very much. We talk about technical issues in the writing and some of those stray over into content because you can't really separate them. We do write differently most of the time and admire each other's viewpoints, I think. My mind is much more based on the senses, I'll say it yet again. He has a mind that's capable of taking in great abstractions, although he doesn't feel it's abstract. I'm so close to Kim and so close to his writing. I work in his writing and he works in my writing. Of course there's influence. It's not as easy to talk about as just saying I learned something from Robert about writing. I'm probably always learning things from Kim and I hope he learns a little bit from me, though he's more hard-headed than I am and takes fewer suggestions. He also knows more of what he's after and I'm not as sure of what I'm after, in any given poem.

LH: *It sounds like a very fruitful relationship …*
RB: It's wonderful. The only thing I regret is that he has less time for that kind of editing interaction than he used to because he's doing more physics. He's doing as much writing as he was ever able to, but the amount of time that we can sit down with poetry, working on each other's stuff, has been reduced, although we're actually collaborating right now on a very specific project.

LH: *Do you find yourself drawing on other fields, such as physics?*
RB: Not directly, but I like reading all kinds of books. Things seep into me, but I don't directly base anything on things I've read.

LH: *In* Intent, or the Weight of the World, *there are poems of sadness—"Grief"—and those of celebration—"City Lights"—and some which embody both, as in the title poem. What did you mean when you suggested that the organizing principle was to preserve the dark in the light, and the light in the dark?*
RB: That has to do with the tonal interplay in the book. There's a lot of grief in that book, which is based directly on the deaths of my parents, and at that time, especially my father who died first. There's a lot of that kind of darkness and

there's also some playing with rhetoric that brings in some light and some real happiness. I meant it in emotional terms.

LH: *Your poems seem to be a synthesis of different kinds of consciousness: meditation, imagination, memory, dream. How do you use these various states to try to erase that barrier between the self and the world?*

RB: I don't sit down to try to do anything. When I'm in a poetic state of mind, which is most of the time if I'm relaxed, it's always a mixture of those things. The words are coming to me from a mixed state, I suppose. Dreams are very alive for me after I've just dreamed them. I don't do anything intentional about it. It's just my state of mind that comes out on the page.

LH: *You have a poem about a dream about reading Robert Pinsky.*

RB: That was such an odd little dream. Sometimes I do dream poetry dreams. Once I dreamed that I was reading Phyllis Webb's new work. She was standing up and had it in her hands and I was looking over her shoulder reading it. Another time Margaret Atwood came to me in a dream, though I forget what it was. I take these dreams as good omens. Whenever I dream about poetry I feel good about it.

LH: *Do you think the creative state is close to the dreaming state?*

RB: I feel they're different. They're all shades of something similar. I don't know much about it physiologically and I think that would be the way to approach it.

LH: *In your poems, as well as your statements on poetry, you encourage the reader to become involved with your work. In fact, your poems often create a dialogue or a sense of sharing.*

RB: A sense of sharing with the reader is what I'm certainly trying to do or that's what the poems are trying to do. Again, I don't feel like I'm trying to do anything.

LH: *Even drawing the reader in by saying 'you reader' or comparing your experience with, potentially, the reader's experience, you are conscious, then, of the reader in your poems.*

RB: It's not that I visualize any given reader or even know that there could be an audience, but this is an act of verbal communication, of speech which is meant to be heard. I'm very aware of that. Although I'm writing first for myself, I'm talking to someone, so it's very important that I communicate. That is the prime goal, that I communicate what I see. It feels like I'm in a conversation and someone's listening and I might hear them also. That's the sensation of it.

LH: *So you were anticipating, in some way, the reader's response.*

RB: Yes, although I never fill in the blanks of that response.

LH: *No, that has to remain mysterious, but you are aware then, and the reader is aware, I think, that you are aware of that.*

RB: That's wonderful to know because that's the experience for me.

LH: *The title poem of* Intent, *or* The Weight of the World *is about the difficulty of finding something or fulfilling desire. Expectation, then, will prevent one from seeing the world. One of the major concerns of this book seems to be the conflict between desire and reality.*

RB: I wrote that poem when I was very very depressed and I had no desires. This was precipitated by some bad family stuff that I don't especially want to talk about. I was in a state of unhappiness and desirelessness and, for a relatively long time for me, I wasn't writing much. I thought well, maybe I'll sit down and see if I write anything. Then I started writing from that experience. The writing didn't make the experience go away because the situation was still there, but I was trying to elucidate that state of mind for myself. That's all it is. It's me, thinking through my state of mind. All I know is that I was writing from a state of desirelessness and at the end, that bit about the laughter, that happened. In fact, I think it was Kim who was laughing.

LH: *The form in that poem, the silence, the spacing, the broken forms, the larger stanzas seems to mimic the sense of desire for something.*
RB: Well, I was desiring desire. I was.

LH: *So desire you see as being an essential part of that book.*
RB: Yes, because the kind of dull grief, the endless grief and replaying horrible scenes in your mind, takes away from your desire for the world (*an ambulance is heard in the background*). To be engaged with the world is to be happy and to be disengaged is to be desireless.

LH: *I'm interested in your ideas of landscapes. You've written, "landscape is important to me and sight and smell, sound and touch." Landscape is also connected to memory by part of the poet's life. Do you think landscape has been defined too narrowly in the past by critics and by other poets?*
RB: Some landscape paintings are suffused with emotion and others aren't necessarily. For me, landscape is always suffused with emotion. Landscape is not only land. It's cityscape. It's whatever is around.

LH: *In your poems, landscape has a larger definition than the eighteenth century concept.*

RB: It's the medium we are moving through and we are part of and inextricable from.

LH: *The French talk about the 'passage intérieur' and Rilke talks about the interiorization of landscape. Do you think you interiorize the landscape or is the landscape inside of you?*

RB: Definitely, when I've lived in a particular landscape for a while it seeps into me. I carry different landscapes around inside me, the ones that matter to me. We had a big pepper tree in the yard when I was growing up and it got diseased. It had fungus all over it and finally it had to be cut down, but my mother would still refer to that spot as the pepper tree and so did I. I have that garden in my mind in all of its forms. It changed over time, so I have several layers of memory of that garden and each one is complete and the pepper tree is still there in several of them and it's gone in others. That entire landscape was all burned down in the Oakland-Berkeley fire about a year and a half ago. Now I have that landscape, too. I have the burned landscape which is actually very beautiful.

LH: *It sounds like the different levels of Troy.*

RB: Exactly. Those landscapes are all inside me and that's why I speak from them. I see them still.

LH: *Is it not possible to have many landscapes, dream landscapes, image landscapes?*

RB: Well, all of those merge. A dream landscape, for me, if I remember it clearly, is not different from any other landscape. When I'm dreaming I'm never aware that I'm dreaming. I'm always right in the dream and when I wake up I can be very confused. So those are just as present for me as sitting here in the Icehouse.

LH: *Do you find Don McKay's ideas of poetic attention and the translation of the wilderness relevant for you?*

RB: Don and I have different experiences of wilderness, but it's very important to both of us. Pastoral landscapes are very important to both of us also, not just pure wilderness. I think Don actually does translate the wilderness. He writes bird poems and rock poems, quite intentionally. That is a large part of his material. Wilderness informs my emotions and pastoral landscape informs my emotions, but I'm not trying to directly translate. I am translating my sensory experience into English. I think the focus is different. I am focusing on the interaction between me and that space between, which is really inhabited by both me and the object because I don't end at my skin. Don is actually translating directly from wilderness, whereas I'm translating sensory impressions into English. I think language comes much more naturally to Don than it does to me. I think he's truly much more verbal. I feel that I'm very non-verbal, really, and so the hard work is getting it into language.

LH: *How does a poem come to you? Do you carry it around with you, letting it germinate, or when you feel and think of the poem do you write it down?*

RB: When words really start coming to me, then I write them down. I don't think about poems before the words come to me. I have no forms of the poems before the words start coming to me. Sometimes most of the words will come all at once, but usually not.

LH: *Can you remember a particular poem and how it came to you?*

RB: The most recent poem that came to me isn't finished yet, but if it survives as a poem, most if not all of it came to me all in one lump and it's only a few lines long, less than ten lines, I think. It happened just recently. I was in Italy. We had just been travelling for a couple of weeks, seeing tons of art. I heard some Benedictine monks singing, a Gregorian chant, I have since learned; the main guy had the most beautiful voice I have ever heard. I came upon them all of a sudden, in a cathedral where I wasn't expecting a service to be going on. It was quite an emotional experience. In this context, after a couple of days a few lines came to me. It's not about the monks singing. It's expressive of what happened to me in Italy, I suppose, in a very internal way, but it's not a story poem. It doesn't tell a story. You wouldn't know that's where it came from, if you read it. I think I have some work to do on that poem, but it's too soon to know for sure, because I just wrote it down.

LH: *For the last week you've been teaching creative writing classes here in Fredericton. Do you feel you can teach creative writing?*
RB: Beforehand I never feel that I can possibly teach anything. I feel I have nothing at all to teach and what the hell am I trying to do. Then I go there and start interacting and once I'm interacting it's fine. Then I realize that yes indeed I can answer some questions because I have had more experience now than the students have had because they haven't been writing as long and there are things they don't know, or they want to ask 'how do you title a poem?' Well there all kinds of ways you can title a poem and we can talk about some of the ways. I'm always surprised to discover that I can help.

LH: *Each book seems a different departure, a new direction for you. What are you working on at present?*
RB: I'm working on two things. One is a new book of poems by me as solo writer. It's going to be called *Water Memory*. I've been working on it since the last book, *Intent*. I have about another six months or so of work on it, writing new poems and revising all the poems in it.

LH: *What gave you the idea for* Water Memory?

RB: There are some New Age-y physics experiments that have to do with whether or not water has an electrical or molecular memory. That's where the phrase came from, but in fact I don't deal with that at all and the title poem says water does not remember. In fact, I'm not trying to refute that research, though I hear from sources I consider reliable that that research is itself not reliable.

LH: *You can use Rajan's guide. These are hypotheses until they are proved.*

RB: Somebody told me that homeopathic medicine is based on the idea that water can remember, but as far as I know water can't remember. And anyway my poem says it can't. The other thing I'm working on, which is very exciting for me, is a collaboration with Kim and a painter named Andy Patton, who is a very good friend of ours in Toronto. We're working on a collaborative writing project. It will turn into a book and it will be called *Introduction to the Introduction to Wang Wei*. We're all writing poems for it. It's fully collaborative. We take each other's poems apart and rework them. Each poem has three authors. We are using mostly prose critical texts about poetry and using them as word mines for making poems. They're not found poems because we don't just find a phrase and put line breaks in. We might take one word from page five and then five words from page fourteen and string them together. Basically we're making lyric poetry from what might be thought of as a rather random process, but it's not random. It's just that we're using these words on pages, instead of the images that run through our heads all the time. We're using the texts instead of private experience, although our own experience is certainly what selects from the text. It's a whole lot of fun. I really like it.

The Icehouse, Fredericton, New Brunswick
July 10, 1993

Second Interview (2019)

LH: *It is more than 25 years since I last talked to you at McCord Hall, the Icehouse in Fredericton. I still have recollections of that afternoon. Of course, much has changed in your life. You have now published 16 books and your work has been widely recognized. You received the Governor General's Award and the Griffin Poetry Prize. However, there were difficult times. I have read that you talked about twice giving up poetry. Why did you feel this way?*

RB: I too remember that day in the Icehouse. It must be true for some people that writing poetry gets easier over time, but for me the difficulties seem to increase. The possibilities that present themselves are always new, with no preordained forms or orderly solutions to problems that crop up. Even if we start with certain constraints, as Andy, Kim, and I did in writing *Introduction to the Introduction to Wang Wei*, every single constraint has to be abolished along the way in order to advance or broaden the direction of the poetry, so in the end there's no map or method. There's also the ever-increasing compulsion to get it right, which is to say aligned with whatever a given poem requires as its natural form of speech, its voice. When I began writing, each piece was an unknown; beginnings, endings, bits in the middle, arrived piecemeal; it was like filling in the blanks in a crossword puzzle that hadn't been constructed yet. I couldn't tell whether any attempt would succeed or not. Later, especially with *Short Journey* onward, I still couldn't tell, but if in the end nothing unexpected emerged, I wouldn't be interested in publishing. Somehow I was no longer practicing moves in writing, but just writing. The following two books used variations on forms that had come into being in *Short Journey*, but again they were not predetermined, and their formal complexity seemed to increase in inverse proportion to the simplicity of their nominal content. My friend Andy

Patton has told me again and again that each time I "quit poetry" I nonetheless begin again, often after a long hiatus, and after some years I began to trust his judgement that this cycle could continue. Even so, it seemed I'd finally quit for good after that triptych of books was finished (*Short Journey Upriver Toward Ōishida*, then *Rain; road; an open boat*, and finally *Cardinal in the Eastern White Cedar*). And yet once more I've begun writing again in a new vein, prompted by works I loved early on: some seventeenth century, some twentieth century. Styles that have been dead so long they could conceivably come to life again in a new context.

LH: *In your essay in Tim Lilburn's book* Poetry and Knowing *you say: "Poetry is made of words, yet it is exactly as articulate as music, and as distinct from ordinary speech." This debate has been going on since Wordsworth and Coleridge published A Preface to* Lyrical Ballads. *Could you elaborate on this comment?*

RB: I had no theory, or even older conversations, in mind when I began to focus on Tim's question. What came back to me was the memory of walking past the small music building on the campus of Goddard College in Vermont, and the experience of hearing piano music issuing from that building as if it were speech. It felt as clear and articulate as someone addressing me directly. The piano player was improvising, making it up as he went along, the musical thoughts unfolding as he played, so it felt like the music could move in any direction at any moment. In fact its movement would be limited by the sort of music it was, but not knowing what comes next opens everything up, so the listener can sense the range, the breadth, of a field of possibility. Poetry has two main aspects, music and sense, so this moment seemed a plausible place to begin. A lot of music does seem largely decorative, or descriptive in a limited way, but there are compositions, and playing, that transcend the mood of the moment, and feel open-ended: pieces by de Falla, Segovia, the best of free jazz, J.S. Bach, C.P.E. Bach. Despite the formal and stylistic conventions of their times, these retain a fluidity that, to me at least, remains fresh, freshly uttered. This is one goal of poetry. Think of Wordsworth's "A Slumber Did My Spirit Seal," with its perfect pace and endlessly confounding ending, or Coleridge's "Kubla Khan," jotted down from a dream. We're probably lucky he was interrupted by the person from Porlock, disturbing his recollection and ending the poem before it could accumulate the encrustations of the age.

LH: *In* Personal History *you said that you and André Alexis had a long conversation lasting ten years on whether poetry is fiction or nonfiction. What do you consider poetry?*

RB: In those early years, André and I would talk on the phone several times a day, often for hours at a time. Such an agile, wide-ranging mind. Since the time he was a child he'd looked up to poetry, and I knew I'd never be able to write a novel, so right away we had something to talk about: the seemingly unattainable. This led to trying to work out the differences between these forms of writing, which led naturally to discussions about fiction versus nonfiction. There are fictional poems, as dramatic monologues clearly exemplify, even though poetry is often taken to be the truthful confession or recollection of the poet. And there are autobiographical, more or less nonfictional, novels. But then there's a but: to write a dramatic monologue, doesn't one call on one's own emotions and experience? And in writing an autobiographical novel, doesn't one wittingly or unwittingly display the conventions of one's era? What is it to make up a character that speaks and thinks and has a name? Is a poem just the mouthpiece of a given poet, or is it something entirely different? But to get back to your question: I consider a piece of writing to be poetry if it moves like poetry, and/or if its aftereffect is that of poetry rather than prose. Poetry, to me at least, is a broad category, including prose poetry, even prose poetry of indefinite length. I can think of no single adjective that applies to poetry but not to the novel, and vice versa. If poetry has a ritualistic element, so does the novel. If the novel moves us from one condition to another, so does a poem. The forms blur at their edges, yet their centres remain distinct and palpable. It's like hiking around in Huangshan, trying to discern the contours of multiple mountains in thick, shifting mist: you know they're there, but can't accurately determine their individual outlines.

LH: *In the first interview I asked you about some influences. What writers have been influential for you in the last twenty-five years?*
RB: For me, several of the most astonishing reading experiences in the past twenty-five years have been provided by W.G. Sebald's books as translated by Michael Hulse and others. He was a master of the sublime, with too much highly particular, idiosyncratically curated knowledge of the world for his work to be replicable by others, not to mention his eccentric, wandering, additive style. Earlier, I was fascinated by the books of Peter Handke as translated by Ralph Manheim. Handke's early works are also unrepeatable, with their outsize quantities of sorrow and vengeful pain, more even than the titles of his works acknowledge. Translators rarely get their just rewards, and Hulse and Manheim should be more widely appreciated, though Manheim apparently died sadly aggrieved, without knowing how much he would be missed. These two translators are in my personal pantheon of greats. Hulse, as well, is an excellent poet. Judging by the best of the translations, both Sebald and Handke are poets in prose, and at the same time their novels can satisfy a hankering for either fiction or nonfiction,

or both at the same time. The range of sight in Sebald is vast: from near-microscopic close-focus to grand-focus almost without passing through the ordinary middle distance where most prose, and in fact most poetry, take place. Handke, for the most part, looks at the surround through a magnifying glass, but then introduces paper-thin, almost random characters into certain of his novels, who propel the action forward by the slightest spinning of invisible psychic turbines rather than more overt machinations of plot. Moving away from strictly literary work, many books by Richard Dawkins achieve the poetic, not necessarily in terms of language, his language being pure prose, but in their extreme compression of elegant ideas. All of these writers have exerted their influence over me, making me more demanding as a reader. As a writer, I couldn't begin to touch their work.

LH: *You have written about the importance of reading and what happens to you when you are in the process of reading. Can you speak about how reading a passage of a particularly great book affects you?*

RB: The best works have a discernable music, indisseverable from what we think of as content. A paraphrase won't convey what the original does; a translation has to be really strong, with its own music, to come close, though no doubt some translations surpass the originals. You were also at the Griffin Poetry Prize readings in 2019; you probably noticed Kim Hyesoon delivering the Korean original of the poem translated into English as "Lord No." The structure of that poem, its perfectly arranged sound, rang out in the concert hall, the whole of it seeming to stand there in the air for a moment after she finished reading. I have no Korean, but there is "content" that is conveyed by structure alone. To read a great passage of literature on the page is a similar experience. You hear it aloud as you read, it stands in the mind for a moment, then dissipates, leaving a trace which will propel you toward the book again. Such iconic texts serve as both inspiration and permission. They increase the degrees of freedom available to language and to thought.

LH: *Since I last spoke with you, China has become significant to you. You travelled there and even were motivated to learn Mandarin. Why did you develop such a deep interest in China and its literature?*

RB: I began thinking about your new set of questions while sitting in a hotel room overlooking the Changjiang, or Yangtse River. The long barges carrying piles of multi-coloured materials were passing to and fro on that huge river. Growing up on the west coast of North America as I did, China didn't seem so very far away. I grew up in a house containing pieces of Chinese furniture, Chinese jewellery, Chinese silk and embroidered clothing, translated Chinese books, Chinese paintings. But the opportunity to travel there really came about because of Kim's physics, his conferences. We both learned some Mandarin, and I unfortunately have lost most of what I had, though I can put together a few simple phrases, useful when travelling. I guess what I mean to say is that an interest in China didn't develop; it was already there as a given. At UBC I took an introductory course in Chinese literature, and it was there, thanks to the professor, that the class was introduced to China's first great novel, Cao Xueqin's *Story of the Stone*, also called *The Dream of the Red Chamber* in other translations. We read the first long volume in class, and I subsequently read the rest, though the novel itself was never fully finished by Cao, as he died while still writing it. This novel is a whole world, big enough to convert anyone into a lover of Chinese literature. Not to mention the huge, much older tradition of poetry.

LH: *Your grandmother lived and worked two years in China. Why was she such an influential figure for you? Why was it important to try to find a shikumen residence, one similar to the one in which she had lived?*

RB: It's not that she was influential, but that her absence was influential. I never met either of my mother's parents, as they died before I was born, but both my mother and my aunt would refer now and then to my grandmother and their life with her. I suppose she became a faint but legendary ancestor figure for me. I have one of her coats, which fits me perfectly. Kim and I had already begun working on *Box Kite* when we made the trip to Shanghai during which we tried to find a shikumen, but in fact the idea of telling my grandmother's story, what little we knew of it, preceded the book. I had asked Kim to try to at least begin that story, and it took him a few years to arrive at an entry point for the piece, by which time we were already working on the prose poems that would become *Box Kite*. So the idea of chasing down a shikumen residence came along in the natural course of things. Aside from that, I've found that it's good to have some goal, however small or by-the-way, when one is travelling: it tends to bring unexpected things into focus, even if the goal is never attained. In the end we needn't have tried quite so hard, as we ended up visiting Lu Xun's shikumen residence on a subsequent trip. Nonetheless, that first search engendered memorable experiences we wouldn't have had otherwise, not least drinking tea in the Yuyuan teahouse in Shanghai. Even on our most recent trip, in 2019, I was struck again by the fact that my grandmother would have seen a similar view along the Bund, the street where the old colonial buildings, huge but now understated, still stand along the riverbank, yet she would be shocked, dazzled, by the brilliant night cityscape on the Pudong side of the river. The past and the future can look at each other across that river.

LH: *The book* Short Journey Upriver Toward Ōishida *is based on the life of one of Japan's greatest poets, Basho and his journey to Ōishida. You wrote this book about a particular time in your life, your journey. Can you talk about the genesis of this book?*

RB: I'd been reading Basho in translation for a long time. I'm still reading Basho. He set out on his journey to the north in his mid-forties. I began *Short Journey*, which in retrospect is a book of middle age, in my mid-to-late forties. It seems I was writing through a part of my life that was analogous to Basho's age when he took that particular journey, though Basho lived only a few more years after that. Prior to *Short Journey*, Kim, Andy, and I had been working slowly for ten years on our collaborative book, which was published in 2000. We'd begun that book as a way to shake up our habitual vocabularies and thought processes, and it was approaching completion when I began thinking about how and whether to return to my own solo work, which seemed like a slow lurch backwards, a lonely task compared to the collaborative process I'd by now grown used to. Going back to my own work was necessitated by the fact that the three of us couldn't agree on what project to pursue next. So I stumbled forward into seeing what I could do, or no longer do, in the wake of that intense collaboration. The title, *Short Journey Upriver Toward* Ōishida, inverts Basho's trip: Basho travelled downriver toward Ōishida, but as someone imaginatively arriving in a literary version of Japan from North America, it turns out I had to enter from the sea and navigate upriver.

LH: *I think that there is a change of style in your book* Short Journey Upriver Toward Ōishida. *In "River" there is a lyrical, meditative style in which you capture a wide range of experiences from the "wicked swans," "the haze of after-work traffic," and an astronomical image of the rising of planets to the "Lion sounds* *from the zoo." In these images you create a rapid shift of time and perspective. It reminds me of the shifts in Margaret Avison's poems. How did you develop this idea of the style for this book in which you were able to incorporate so many disparate elements yet still retain a unifying thread of the poem or is it a change at all?*

RB: "River" is a section of the long poem "Summer Grass," which begins the book and was the first piece I finished for it. The poem dictated its own terms: it wouldn't allow me to go further than two or three lines at a time until those lines were pretty well finalized. I suppose this has to do with the fact that this poem is really a piece of music, or music is its continuity, what holds it together no matter which images arrived to fill the aural space. Much of it was written while walking back and forth along a stretch of the River Torrens in Adelaide, as well as in the Botanic Garden nearby, and in the city proper, but related images could arrive from anywhere. Because the speech of the poem is a kind of music, diverse moods and notions could be incorporated, so long as the rhythms and sounds were right. This then allowed more diverse forms to be accommodated in the book as a whole, as long as the sounds were compatible. Compatible, but not the same. No ideas but in music: that could be this poem's motto.

LH: *Art plays an important role in your creative life. You have written extensively on certain paintings of Sheila Ayearst and Andy Patton. I'm intrigued at your observation of painting as you read canvases, almost like texts. Could you talk about a painting that you have not discussed yet which made an impact on you?*

RB: Rather than talking about a particular painting, I'd like to point toward the paintings Andy did after our collaborative book was finished. He wanted a new form, in this case in painting, and worked out a way to display English letterforms as though they were Chinese characters. He used the text of *Introduction to the Introduction to Wang Wei*, combined occasionally with other things he was reading, as a sourcebook for new sets of lines composed of direct and/or recombined excerpts from the poems. These lines were painted in vertical columns, one letter at a time, from top to bottom and then proceeding from left to right. Each small square containing a letter became a miniature painting on its own, side by side with the others, merging through colour and atmospherics, using techniques of Western painting he had perfected in his previous work and at the same time experimenting further with light, shade, disintegration and dissolution. Andy says that for these works he used oils plus Neo Megilp, a combination that is a modern version of the medium Turner used. Our collaborative book thus has an afterlife in his paintings, some of which you can find reproduced online. A few of these beautiful works were exhibited in China as part of a Canadian show curated by Zhou Yan, a fine poet, translator, and curator who lives in Toronto. Wang Wei was known as both a painter and a poet. In their own way, Andy's paintings exemplify the Chinese idea about calligraphic works: they are simultaneously poems and paintings. They are the dual aspects of a single artform. The images are texts. They are, literally, readable, but can only be read slowly, patiently, as paintings and poems are read.

LH: *I notice in* Cardinal in the Eastern White Cedar *that you capture the nuances of the moments, their different possibilities. I'm reminded of Keats' letter to Benjamin Bailey when he writes, "or if a sparrow came before my window I take part in its existence and pick about the gravel." What is behind this need to capture the complexity of natural life around you, your observation of cardinals, squirrels, etc.? I must admit that after reading your commentary on squirrels and cardinals that I'm inclined to observe them more closely now.*

RB: Keats' comment sounds like something Basho might have said. According to Basho, the stance of a poem should be "neither objective nor subjective." It may be something akin to this stance that allows us to communicate with, or participate in, the lives of others, including other human beings. But some of our nearest neighbours are cardinals, squirrels, and others that live in, on, and around the places we inhabit. This would be true for most neighbourhoods in Toronto, much of which is urban woodland. The other evening I looked out the back window and called to Kim to come look: a family of five raccoons, two adults and three kits, were in the cherry tree in the backyard, eating the ripe cherries. The municipal code doesn't allow you to evict a family of skunks nesting under your front porch until the offspring are old enough to fend for themselves. There's an area near Queen Street downtown that's known for its successive generations of white squirrels. What we call the "white squirrel café" is marked by a sign that consists of a picture of a white squirrel, no words. I'm curious about the others we live among: they add both a certain lightness and a certain perplexity to our days. What might sound quaint also has its moments of terror: the summer night drama when you can hear raccoons screaming and the heart-rending bleating of a feral kitten as it's being attacked. Much of this other life might pass unnoticed if you were to move at speeds faster than walking. I walk a lot, and my poetry also proceeds at a walking pace. Read too fast, and there appears to be nothing there. Slow down and there may be more to it. I'm interested in everyday life. One of the impressive things about the classical poems of China is their grounding in a particular voice, the ongoing vitality that arises from a real life, and still feels fresh hundreds of years later.

LH: *For many writers a sense of community is important, but you draw almost a cartography of the community, mapping out the restaurant, "The Bagel Paradise," "the drugstore with the Warhol prints," and Forman's, the old "Men's Shop," but also giving the reader the nature of the urban landscape and history of the characters in your neighbourhood. Why do you feel the need to write about the community around you?*

RB: This half of Baziju (since *Box Kite* is the book you're quoting from, and Kim is the other half of the writer Baziju) would venture that what's important is the matrix we live in, the interactions that ultimately make up a lifetime of experience. Maybe there is a kind of voluntary duty or debt or respect the living owe to their place in time and all that goes on there. The local is simply where we live. All the far-fetched, fascinating disciplines, the grand and withering insights, take place within the matrix of the ordinary days in which they are grounded, and without which they wouldn't exist. The things of daily life are ephemeral, the small outcrops of shops, of street signs, rise up and evanesce, but those who live and work there create the social environment of the city. To pay attention to what is local is to feel in touch with the living.

LH: *Cao Xueqin wrote* The Dream of the Red Chamber, *one of the most famous novels in China. I remember visiting one of his residences in the outskirts of Beijing near the Fragrant Mountain. I was struck by the elegance and simple decor of his quarters. What did you feel when you visited his house? Likewise, the Lu Xun Museum in Fucheng Gate Avenue in Beijing.*

RB: We passed by the residence in the Fragrant Mountains that was said to be the last place Cao Xueqin worked on his novel, but at the time, as I remember it, there was no way to gain access to the interior. Our visit to Lu Xun's residence in Beijing is recounted in "Lu Xun's Desk" in *Box Kite*. One of the interesting things that happened there is that the attendant, an admirer of the Canadian doctor Norman Bethune, who was very famous in China for having helped a lot of people there, asked us where we were from. On hearing that we were from Canada, she was interested but didn't seem particularly impressed by the name Toronto, yet when we added that Toronto is not far from the small town of Gravenhurst (which she recognized immediately as Bethune's home), she was so pleased that she graciously offered to open up the rooms of Lu Xun's house so that we could take a closer look. On another trip we visited Lu Xun's residence in Shanghai, a shikumen. A guide led a small group through the rooms. It was a lovely place, elegantly proportioned though not fancy. I could easily imagine living there. But what really remains of Lu Xun is in his writings, and in his descendants. Cao left most of a huge great novel behind; Lu Xun left outstanding stories, essays, prose poems, and retellings of old tales.

LH: *Travel has long been a source and subject of your poems. You've travelled to many places—Scotland, Spain, Japan, China, Australia and your childhood home in California. What is it about travel that nourishes your writing?*

RB: The Dalai Lama has said that once a year a person should travel somewhere they've never been. It's good advice, as it challenges old habits of mind, stereotypes, worn-out moods. New experiences break up old assumptions. The challenges of travel force one into the present, where the past is always on the point of vanishing and the future never arrives. I like to travel to places that are new to me, but also to places I've been before, finding them transformed over time. The California I grew up in no longer exists, yet there are disarming reminders. I visited the real Japan only after writing about a literary version made up of translations that together had forged what felt like a country. China has seemed a different country each time I've visited, its cities change that quickly: Shanghai, Beijing, Hangzhou, Suzhou, the area around Huangshan. China is still built around the ancient marvels, but the present is ever-changing. Each time a new face is revealed. Returning to poetry is like that too: the goals may remain the same, but everything else has changed in the meantime.

LH: *For many years you have worked collaboratively with your husband Kim Maltman, from* The Transparence of November Snow *to* Introduction to the Introduction to Wang Wei, *which also involved Andy Patton, and your most recent book of prose poems is written by Baziju in* Box Kite. *Why did you give the name of the composite author of this collection, Baziju?*

RB: Kim and I have worked collaboratively since 1975, the year we met. We engage in unusually heavy editing of each other's work even when we're not publishing as joint authors. For that early collaborative book, we used two titles separated by a slash, but the two can be read aloud seamlessly as a single title. Individual poems were written by one or the other of us but edited by both of us, and there are several pairs of echo and response poems. By contrast, *Box Kite* couldn't have been written by either me or Kim; it could only be written by a composite author. The experiences and memories on which the book draws are shared, coalescing out of what is usually thought of as private experience. When two people share an experience, one might remember one aspect more intensely than the other, but then the other compensates by remembering some other feature. Without having planned it, there was a casual slurring of the usual pronouns in this book: "I" becomes "you" becomes "we," and so forth. This slurring could have been edited out, but we chose not to; it seemed a natural outgrowth of the writing process, which was completely collaborative, both in content and in phrasing. We wanted a name for that composite author, just as when Kim, Andy, and I wrote *Introduction to the Introduction* and we needed a name, signifying that the poetry was composed by a threesome. The process of working with others is like working with oneself, except you have more to work with. When the skills and talents of collaborators are complementary to your own, the field of possibility increases. Each choice becomes magnified, as it can be looked at from more angles. Many of the pieces in *Box Kite* were written in tag-team fashion: I would work on them during the day, Kim would take over at night after a full day of physics, and then on weekends we would rewrite, edit, discuss, and revise together. The pieces inched forward, but there was no way to know which direction they would go next. In this way we encountered unexpected ground, and went over that ground again and again, discovering new aspects. What might otherwise fade from memory gained momentum and kept going, fuelled by two imaginations rather than one. It took some time to arrive at the name Baziju, which has several sources, my favourite of which is a grammatical structure in Mandarin referring to a certain type of sentence, the "ba" sentence, in which both the speaker and the listener understand what is being talked about, and the object under discussion is to be disposed of or transformed in some way. This could serve as one definition of writing.

October, 2019

Illustration credit: Lichuanlibuchuan

GEORGE ELLIOTT CLARKE

Laurence Hutchman: *I'm curious about your latest book* Where Beauty Survived: An Africadian Memoir. *Why did you choose this title, which relates beauty to survival?*

George Elliott Clarke: I took my memoir's title from a poem that appears in my narrative lyric sequence, *Whylah Falls* (1990). In "Look Homeward Exile," a poem about the parlous conditions in which many Black Nova Scotian—or Africadian—communities were enmeshed, I write, "But Beauty survived, secreted / In freight trains snorting in their pens ...." Pondering my own childhood and youth in Halifax (NS), but also among various Africadian communities, I could feel that "here," "Beauty survived ...," and its honey palliates bitter pain. In most of my books, you'll find usually at least one epigraph that espouses a definition or aspect of Beauty. In *Where Beauty Survived*, the epigraphs read, "I want to know how I can bring Beauty" (Louise Bernice Halfe) and "But enough. What is all Beauty?" (Wm Faulkner). I think I am drawn to these meditations and interrogatives because I believe that "Beauty" is the "Holy Grail" that all artists seek. "The beautiful seems right ... / By force of Beauty," sayeth Elizabeth Barrett Browning. To me, the revolutionary and the artist want the same thing: Yeatsian Beauty in truth and Keatsian truth in Beauty. For me, Beauty is baroque, rococo, ornate, arabesque, a premonition of the divine. "The poet makes Beauty by pondering the real," says Simone Weil: "How else is born the act of Love?" Aye, and what of Solomon

1:5, "I am black, but beautiful"? And folks survive by insisting on Beauty. "Beauty is … defiance of authority," preacheth Wm Carlos Wms!

LH: *You dedicated this book to your parents, Geraldine Elizabeth Clarke and William Lloyd Clarke, who had a significant presence in your life. Could you speak about their influence on you?*

GEC: My mother Geraldine Elizabeth abandoned this existence on August 6, 2000, and the books I published immediately thereafter—*Execution Poems* (2001), *Blue* (2001), *Québécité* (2003)—are all dedicated to her, who chose my name and initials to designer-match her own, for she was a single parent when I was born, marrying my father a few months later. But once my father passed away on August 30, 2005, I found myself needing to celebrate both. The reason is not filial piety, but a sense of indebtedness that has become a destitution, now that I am bereft of their wisdom and bereaved of their love. I am a twice-divorced child of divorce, who did not agree with or approve of my parents' separation in 1972 and divorce in 1974, when I was 14. Intellectually, I knew that they were not a valid couple: My mother was raised a "have"; my father a "have not." My mother looked white but was profoundly, soulfully black—culturally; my father was definitely black, but was European in orientation. (When we were all together on Sundays, after church, the stereo got a multicultural work-out: James Brown, Beethoven, Beatles; or it was Wilson Pickett, Puccini, Peaches and Herb.) She was a trained teacher; he was an autodidact intellectual working a humble job as a guy who changed the linens on the sleeping cars on the train to/fro Montreal and who trundled luggage back-and-forth the trains at the Halifax station. My mom was doted upon by her parents; my father never knew his father, a Jamaican sailor who may have been paid to marry my paternal grandmother, and then who promptly disappeared. So, these people—both (as I say in my dedications)—"Adepts, Believers, African Baptists"—were classic opposites who were united only by my birth, when he was 24 (going on 25) and she had just turned 21. So, my childhood households were inspiringly artistic—Ian Fleming and Mary Poppins, Bizet's *Carmen* and James Brown's "Bewildered" and "Lost Someone"; Bob Dylan out the radio, "Like a Rolling Stone," and Malcolm X—Malcolm the Tenth to my boy's mind—out the radio news. My father's influence upon me was about being a dedicated artist (he would paint—apply oils to glass—and then back the finished picture with tinfoil, creating a shimmering effect) *and* a *pur-et-dur* intellectual, reading James Baldwin alongside the James Bond adventures, or leafing through Saul Alinsky and *Playboy* mags. My mother's influence upon me was to model the teacher—and a devotion to black culture(s). My father encouraged me to excel in school, and so I did. But he refused to render me any support when I was thinking of attending university. My mother encouraged my poetry, giving me T.S. Eliot to read and Tia Maria to sip, or buying me an acoustic guitar which I never had the discipline to learn to play. But she was financially unable to support my university aspirations. (Help in that regard came from Rocky and Joan Jones, Halifax's "Black Power Couple.") Anyway, despite the impossible tensions between my parents, they created a matrix and a nexus of creativity during my childhood that I savoured—as much as I also loved them devotedly.

LH: *Your growing up in North End Halifax does not seem like a typical Black Canadian experience. Could you elaborate on this statement?*

GEC: As much as I'm Bill Clarke's first-born son, I'm also a Haligonian North Ender. That's most important because Halifax was, like most Canadian cities, organized around class lines that also had an ethnic/racial dimension. The North End was where the factories, docks and wharves were, the city dump (placed right beside Africville), the infectious diseases hospital, the city prison, the slaughterhouse, rusted and half-sunken ships, plus blue-collar and pink-collar workers, the soldiery (mainly sailors), most immigrants, Black, Indigenous, working poor, welfare recipients, pensioners, the addled seniors, and then the whores and the hoods. The North End was the sort of place where, for graduation ceremonies at my grade-school, a humble constable was invited, for at least two years in a row, to tell us brainy, nerdy kids that study was worthless, and that we had better pick up boxing gloves if we were going to survive a nasty, Hobbesian society amid cruel, Darwinian nature. It was a place where teacher "Miss X" would perch deliberately so we teen boys could see up her skirt, and only choose to end that stimulating praxis once she became "Mrs. Y." It was where gals were *bitches* and men were *cocksuckers* and all blacks were *bastoods*. It was the site of the Halifax Explosion of December 6, 1917 (our own backyard Hiroshima—complete with a mushroom cloud); it was where Trotsky was imprisoned on his way back to Russia to trigger the Bolshevik Revolution; it was where the *Titanic* dead wound up, afloat just beneath topsoil. Yet, I loved the smoky aroma of some of my gal classmates (in their hair, their clothes, a kind of woodsmoke, bbq scent); they could also ambidextrously switch between skipping rope and punching my shoulder, or smoking and blowing gum bubbles. I loved the smell of fresh cut wood out the lumber yard—or the smell of chocolate from the chocolate factory. I loved the slow-moving trucks prowling our streets, black men walking behind, yelling, "Maaaackerel! Fresssh maaackerel!" As a paperboy, ages 12-14, I got to peer or step inside some of my North End neighbours' (but strangers') homes. I saw staircases straight out of *Coronation Street*; pictures of Queen Victoria, still mourning long-gone Albert; plus oil stoves and wood stoves, laundry hanging indoors; a prostitute mom who turned tricks in Montreal so she could bring moolah home to her babes in Halifax; boxers—the true heroes of the hood; nominal preachers (a Pentecostal one buggered boys; the United Church one wanted black guys castrated); etc. To sum up, I grew up with class friction because all North Enders—from all backgrounds—were told constantly that "Thou art cannon fodder and cheap labour." We were the impertinent, the insolent, the take-no-guff and talk-no-bullshit Haligonians. All of us ready to die—at a moment's notice—for the far away, saintly Queen. I'm not sure that my North End boyhood was "atypical" for African-Canadians, except that it was "integrated" (i.e. the poor and the working-class and the lower-middle-class were all together and formed families together), and, in my household, there was an unusual emphasis on scholastic success and artistic endeavour.

LH: *In your memoir, you recount some experiences of racism in personal, political, and social ways. How were you able to deal with these situations so effectively?*
GEC: I don't know if I dealt with racist episodes "effectively." I was never a strong boy—never muscled and quick with a punch; so I learned to run—I was a local track star in the longer-metered races; and I also strove to never offend adults, whose authority I never challenged. (I knew that if I did so, my father would be merciless to me once I carried the bad news home.) Besides, because I was a gold-star pupil, I was naturally the teacher's pet! I learned to deal with bullies by

pencilling sketches about them being gobbled by a T-Rex or disintegrated by a laser-beam. These stories—which I was allowed to recite to the classroom—were big hits with junior thugs, and they would beg me to include them in my stories, rather than lurk to punch-me-out after school. So, my good behaviour, politesse, and studiousness allowed me to skate around or surf over most obstacles of race. However, once I was a teen—a mid-teen—the social oppression cranked up because now I was a sexual threat in terms of potentially impregnating a fair maiden from a higher class as well as an economic threat in terms of potentially dislodging a white boy from a coveted post—even if I were smarter, more talented, or better skilled. So, facing racism as an older child, as a youth, and then as a young man, I learned to skirt obstacles rather than confront them directly. So, for instance, when the English Department at Queen's U (Kingston, ON) ranked me so low a doctoral candidate that I never received a cent of Social Sciences and Humanities Research Council or Ontario Graduate Scholarship funds, I wrote film scripts for the CBC and earned dollars *via* other writing gigs. Indeed, I knew my scholarship was worthy, and that fact was cemented when I was hired by Duke University directly out of grad school; and then when I was invited to Harvard to teach. (When the English Department chair heard that I was hired at Duke, he sent me a letter to indicate that it would be a fine place for me from which to find another job once they inevitably let me go. Yeah? Well, when I received the official letter stating that I had passed my mid-tenure review at Duke, I sent him a copy—quite promptly. After all, I had just created the field of African-Canadian literature out of a series of landmark essays!) That has always been my practice: Not so much direct confrontation, but stealthy subversion of the opponent's "traps."

LH: *During the 1960s, there was tremendous social unrest in the United States which included the civil rights marches of Martin Luther King and later his assassination, as well as that of Malcolm X. The Black Lives Matter movement began after the acquittal of George Zimmerman in the shooting of African-American Trayvon Martin and has gained strength recently after the deaths of George Floyd, Breonna Taylor, and Duante Wright, and many others, which were caused by police officers. Unlike the civil protest of the 1960s, which occurred mainly in the United States, the effects of the Black Lives Matter movement are seen worldwide. What kind of change do you see arising from this movement, and do you believe that such change will have long-lasting effects?*

GEC: I should now give shorter answers! To set the (US) Civil Rights Movement (1955-75) in its context, it was a domestic version of decolonization operative worldwide, which had begun in 1947—with India and Pakistan achieving independence; then Mao taking China by strategy in 1949; the French defeated in Vietnam at Dien Bien Phu in 1954; the West fought to a draw in Korea (1953); Ghana achieving independence in 1957; and then the epic showdown in Algeria (1958-62), plus the beginnings of the Vietnam War (1960-75). Indeed, one of the big contrasts between Martin Luther King, Jr. and Malcolm X was that the former steadily disavowed any internationalist leanings (except for borrowing Civil Disobedience techniques from Mahatma Gandhi), while X kept telling everyone that African-Americans would never be free unless they named their cause as a struggle for human rights—along the same lines as the Algerians vs. the French colonists, or the Vietnamese versus the French and Uncle Sam. So, the civil protests of the 1960s were widespread and global—especially by 1968, which saw the Prague Spring, France's May Events, Cultural Revolution in the PRC, bloody repression and assassinations in the US; even Canada was not immune to unrest and disquiet: Juxtapose

"Trudeaumania" that spring with the messianic campaign of RFK: Show me the difference! (Also, in Canada, there was the small-scale, low-level terrorism of the FLQ, directed against Her Majesty's Post Boxes, and incidentally killing Francophone workers.) We must also note that the Ban-the-Bomb, Anti-Vietnam-War, "Civil Rights," and campus "Free Speech" causes also urged on second-wave Feminism and environmentalist movements. So, when I look upon the Black Lives Matter movement now, it is from the vantage point of having lived with and through the tumult and ferment of the 1960s, and my recognition of successes and losses and tangents. My hope for this movement—and for Idle No More—is that they not go astray in chasing down mere symbols—toppling a statue here or a memorial there—but focus on achieving POWER, which means, not "defunding the police" (a Utopian slogan that denies reality), but rather promoting HARSH, public oversight of the police. Achieving POWER also means real self-government. Unless activists target actual, social structures, 'symbolic' protests will be met with 'symbolic' responses—just ephemeral, superficial "change."

LH: *You speak of a significant date of February 21, 1977, as a pivotal point in your life of which you write in your memoir "... where one becomes aware of oneself as Coloured or black, and that one's 'race' is subject to discriminatory abuse." This was a crucial moment because you discovered Malcolm X, yet there were aspects of his actions with which you disagreed. Could you comment on this?*
GEC: Post-1965, almost every Black scholar or public intellectual has read or sampled *The Autobiography of Malcolm X*. Unlike the aristocratic and professorial W.E.B. Du Bois—graduate of Harvard and the University of Berlin—X came from the ghetto gutter as an autodidact, ex-gangsta intellectual. So, it was easier for many first-generation, university students

of the 1960s-1970s to identify with X than with Du Bois or his like—and to aspire to an analysis of socio-political, historical-cultural, and economic concerns based on black folk speech and jive talk. The salient lesson of X was that one could be an organic intellectual, a free-thinker. As a black kid who got called "four eyes" and a "nerd" for reading (MUCH), I had to adore X's unabashed, Buddy Holly spectacles, his concern for punctuation in grammar and punctual appointments in activism. But, I only discovered X when I was 17, in Grade 11 English at Queen Elizabeth High School, and was reading—surreptitiously, Donald Reeves's memoir, *Notes of a Processed Brother* (1971), in the back of my class that day—Monday, February 21, 1977—and I was absorbing Reeves's great passion for Malcolm X's radical thought, and then I realized that it was the 12th anniversary of his assassination, and I began to weep—silently—ashamed that I didn't know—hadn't known—the import of that date. I was a black kid in Advanced (University Prep) high school English, but outdoors, snow was whiting out everything. I suddenly thought I understood my and our oppression. Yet, I didn't read the *Autobiography* until I was 18—in 1978. Then, I saw the limitations of X's 'thought-in-progress': He was anti-Semitic, homophobic, and misogynist. All true. But what I took from Malcolm's example was the need to be able to think and question independently, to seek analyses of political issues that were tied to organic speech and grassroots wisdom. Most importantly, he was—had been—continuously evolving, adjusting his political thought as doctrine gave way to critique.

LH: *One question that I ask poets is, "When did you begin to write?" In your memoir, you say, "It was in Mr. McFee's class, in the spring of 1973, that I wrote my first poetic work, a Hilroy-scribbler of songs and poems." When did you become seriously interested in writing?*

GEC: The key adverb in your question is "seriously," and that elicits sundry answers! When I was in Grade 1 and Grade 2, aged 6-7, in my working-class school, I contributed paragraphs on dinosaurs and/or hurricanes (etc.) to our little Gestetner'd newsletter. And I was also penning screeds about classmates being gobbled up by dinosaurs or sliced-n-diced by laser beams. Then, in 1973, aged 13, out of my shy regard for a Greek-Canadian classmate, I wrote a scribbler of angst-ridden verse and coloured-pencil drawings for her, but only presented it to Mr. McFee—who likely could read the adolescent yearnings that were throbbing there—prima facie—"between the lines," but who kept my secret desires safe between the two of us. Maybe like most teens in those years, I fantasized about being adored as a "rock star," though I had several demerits in that regard: I couldn't sing, couldn't read music, nor play any instruments. Realizing those limitations, I fixated on being a songwriter—to be Bernie Taupin in relation to some unknown, yet-to-be-discovered Elton John. So, on July 1—Dominion Day—1975, I knelt beside my bed—my sudden desk—and began to write—in coloured marker—four 'songs' (because they rhymed) per day. (When I began to write, a year later, "four poems per day," I knew they were poems because they didn't rhyme!) My model was Taupin/John, especially their album, Captain Fantastic and the Brown-Dirt Cowboy, and I took that record whimsically as my model. But, soon, thanks to books on song writing that preached that one had to be a poet to be any kind of decent lyricist, I gravitated toward Bob Dylan, Neil Young, Joni Mitchell, Lennon/McCartney, Leonard Cohen, Cat Stevens, and a host of blues balladeers. Then, at age 16, I read Ezra Pound's version of Li Po's "Song of Chang'Kan," which he titled, "The River-Merchant's Wife: A Letter" (Cathay, 1915), and Tang Dynasty verse seemed reborn effectively, poignantly, as Mississippi blues. Add one more year, and, at age 17, I felt suddenly connected to Rimbaud, Baude-laire, and the Beats. My first publication? A letter to Rolling Stone mag, late December 1978, in defence of Bob Dylan's Street Legal LP, signed, "General Electric, Halifax, NS"!

LH: *I would like to turn to some technical aspects of writing. One of the essential features of poetry is its sound. Poetry was tradition-ally dependent on the element of sound, along with metre, rhythm, and all kinds of rhymes, as in the writing of Blake, Keats, Shelley, and Tennyson. When you write, do you read the poems aloud to get a sense of each poem's sound, rhythm, and overall development?*

GEC: To amend Dylan's "Just Like Tom Thumb's Blues," I started out as a (post-)modernist, but soon hit the harder stuff. What I mean is, as a teen, I deemed poetry to be *vers libre*—unrhymed, ironic, surrealistic, absurdist—while "tra-ditional verse" was either outmoded or only acceptable as (pop) song. I twigged to the mode of T.S. Eliot—ironic, priggish, sacerdotal; bemoaning Christianity overthrown by Commies in the factories and suffragettes in the bedrooms. I didn't aim for "Spoken Word," for it seemed to have been superseded: William Carlos Williams versus Otis Red-ding; Walt Whitman versus The Supremes. My first book, *Saltwater Spirituals and Deeper Blues* (1983), despite its tit-ular references to song, was closer to Eliot's Missouri River than it was to the Memphis of black poets or the Motown of Holland-Dozier-Holland. But I suffered a Paul-*en-route*-to-Damascus moment when, in 1986, at a fundraiser in Hal-ifax for the Black Cultural Centre for Nova Scotia, I took to the stage as a (post-)modernist poet, reciting verse as wood-enly (stoically?) as *La Dame* Atwood, only to be nigh booed offstage by the black-majority audience. Luckily for me, I'd just written a piece (included in *Whylah Falls*), "Love Letter to an African Woman," that the assembled mass adored. When I finished reciting that piece—to rapturous, earth-shaking applause—I knew that I could never eschew the oral or the musical in reciting/performing my verse. However, I didn't begin to regularly rehearse the reading aloud of my poetry until I authored the opera libretto, *Québécité* (2003) for composer D.D. Jackson. Using octosyllabic couplets (modelled on the style of *Les Parapluies de Cherbourg*, 1964), I wanted to sound each word, to test the rhythm and the rhyme.

LH: *More than most poets, the presence of songs in your poems is very important—from blues, spiritual hymns to rock 'n roll and folk. This is especially true in* Whylah Falls, *where you seamlessly incorporate the songs into the drama of your poem. Quite often, your poems are songs. Why is it that music is such an integral and essential part of your work?*

GEC: I grew up in a household where recorded music of all types—except, strangely, church music (not even spirituals)—got played, and where my father whistled along to arias and even instrumentals, and my brother Bryant proved adept at recorder, ukulele, and drums (which he preferred), and wherein I practiced trombone unenthusiastically for two years (although I was told that I had "perfect pitch"), so it had to seep into me. Then, becoming a teenager, affianced to Top 40 radio (CJCH), I discovered that the hit parade—or many 45s in that number—were all about *my* amours, my crushes, would-be love affairs (were I not TOO shy), my yearnings and disappointments. So, it makes sense that my coming to voice as a writer was all about trying to write songs—those mini soap-operas, polemical anthems, bluesy diatribes, saccharin proverbs. Then, at about the same time that I discovered the Bob Dylan of *Another Side of Bob Dylan* (1964) up to *Desire* (1975), I picked out of a school trash bin Louis Dudek's perfect anthology, *Poetry of Our Time* (1966), which groups together "Modernist"

British and American poetry (from Whitman and Dickinson to Ginsberg and LeRoi Jones) backed with Canadian and French-Canadian poets (Archibald Lampman hanging out with Anne Hébert), and there I found Pound's translation of Li Po (Rihaku) and his "Song of Chang'Kan," retitled, "The River-Merchant's Wife: A Letter." I heard the wife's longing as something that Billie Holiday could have wept out her lungs. I knew I wanted to write such singing poetry!

LH: *How do you feel about being one of the most celebrated poets in Canada?*

GEC: I'm always shocked to hear such statements! I don't think I'm acclaimed as much as I'm avoided. So, I delight in the unexpected arrivals of e-mails or letters, especially from foreign climes, where someone announces that they have staged a version of a poem from *Whylah Falls* in New Zealand; or a court-appointed, Death Row, Texas lawyer writes to say that *George & Rue* spoke viscerally to him as a defender of condemned black men; or a Brazilian student does a PhD dissertation comparing my verses with those of a great Afro-Brazilian poet; or a Chinese scholar translates *Whylah Falls* into Chinese and an Italian scholar renders *Beatrice Chancy* into his tongue; or I win a poetry prize from Romania for my poems in Romanian translation; or a student in Florida makes a video of my poem, "Everything Is Free"; or I'm at a poetry reading in Halifax and an African woman approaches me afterward to ask that I sign a copy of *Whylah Falls* that she found in a house that she was renting, and then, having memorized several of the poems, begins to recite them to my amazed ears. Etc., etc. Oh, I love these surprises!

LH: *Speaking of the blues, you mentioned the influence of Langston Hughes: "My soul has grown deep like the rivers." Your* *style reminds me of his work with its musicality, direct simplicity, and rich emotional depth. When did you discover him, and what effect did he have on your writing? What other Black Canadian or American poets did you read?*

GEC: Strangely, the first Black poet I knew of was also the first to publish a collection, in English, in the revolutionary climax of The Enlightenment. I refer to Phillis Wheatley, who may have been literate in Arabic in her girlhood in Sénégal, before being captured and sold and bought as a household slave, aged 9, for the Wheatleys of Boston. Becoming aware of the slave-girl's capacity for instruction, Mrs. Wheatley made it her project to see Phillis educated. Eventually, the young black woman published *Poems on Various Subjects, Moral and Religious* in 1773. I learned about Wheatley as a boy because she was a personage mentioned in the Classics Illustrated comic book, *Negro Americans* (1969). When I decided, at age 15, to write songs and then poetry—to be a better songwriter, I did take up the volumes of African-American poetry available to me at the North Branch Library, and so, of course, I fell under the spell of Langston Hughes. I also loved the idea of The Harlem Renaissance, with ragtime and jazz burgeoning, Josephine Baker becoming a very flexible model for Picasso and co., and Beautiful (Black) People strutting in silk suits or stockings, or kicking up their heels in speakeasies, etc. My reading soon branched out from the key group of the 1920s— Hughes, Claude McKay, Sterling Brown, and Jean Toomer (an unadulterated genius who was saluted by Hemingway, fucked adulterously by Georgia O'Keeffe [Mrs. Alfred Stieglitz], but exploited by the mystical Gurdjieff)—to the poets of the 1940s/50s—Hughes, but joined now by Gwendolyn Brooks, the impossibly intellectual Melvin B. Tolson (who out-Eliots Eliot and out-Pounds Pound), and Conrad Kent Rivers, whose singular poem, "Four Sheets to the Wind and a

One-Way Ticket to France," had me vaunting a clichéd vision of berets, wine bottles, scarves, and French-kissing (*oui*) ma-demoiselles. Next came the poets of the 1960s, starting with LeRoi Jones (later known as Amiri Baraka), Nikki Giovanni, Sonia Sanchez, Ishmael Reed, Henry Dumas (who was the first to draw rural folklore and African motifs *organically* into his verses), and my all-time fave—as a teen and on deep into my 20s—Robert Hayden, who had been a student of W.H. Auden, but was breathtakingly brilliant in his portraiture of a gallery of African Diasporic heroes—and also so viscerally picturesque, so audibly, unabashedly musical. It is now—hap-pily—a strange thing to say: I read no African-Canadian poets as a teen because I did not know of those who had published books (and they were very, very few). I was 19 before I read the chapbook, *To My Someday Child*, which Gloria Wesley Daye (now Gloria Ann Wesley) published in 1975. Still, her little book was electrifying because Gloria was writing about Black Nova Scotia; her poems talked about CN Marine fer-ries as well as seaweed, rats, and broken glass. (For the record, the first book of African-Canadian poetry to be published in English was R. Nathaniel Dett's *Album of a Heart*, which was released in 1911—in Tennessee! The first book of verse in English by an African-Canadian woman was Anna Min-erva Henderson's *Citadel*, which appeared in 1967—when she was 80.) I met Dionne Brand in 1978, and visited with her during trips between Halifax and Waterloo—where I spent my undergraduate years. I remember viewing the galleys for either her first book or her second—on the floor of her To-ronto apartment near Spadina. But I was 19 before I read her few poems selected for *Canada In Us Now* (1976) which billed itself as being the *First* anthology of Black writing in Canada, when it was actually the third (the first two were published in 1972 and 1975 respectively). So, I have to say that, yes, I grew up—as a poet—with African-American scribes, though I also read two Afro-French poets closely: Aimé Césaire and Léopold Senghor. They were Négritude poets, who'd been influenced by The Harlem Renaissance bards. They returned the favour by influencing the "revolutionary" black poets of the 1960s. But, once again, I did not answer your question directly! Hughes was an influence (especially his blues poems; see his unfortunately titled, *Fine Clothes to the Jew*, 1927). But the black poets who were most vital for me were Toomer, Tolson, Brooks, Jones/Baraka, Dumas, Giovanni, and Hayden, with Césaire, and then Rita Dove (her poem, "Pomade," is electrifying—*the* model for *Whylah Falls*) and Derek Walcott joining this group, but not until my mid-20s.

LH: *Your readings are passionate performances evoking the drama of the poems. You engage your audience. Your approach perhaps comes from your experience as a professor. How did you develop this style of reading?*

GEC: I'll try to be shorter now! After being almost booted off the stage during my Black Cultural Centre fundraiser reading in 1986, I resolved to be more emotive in my readings. What I've learned to do—as a professor/critic—is to seek out the emotion in the poem. If I can find the emotion, I can voice the poem with a degree of authenticity and efficacy. Every poem is essentially a soliloquy, expressing ideas encased in emotion.

LH: Whylah Falls *is a narrative poem with a variety of characters and dramatic situations. It is one of your most popular books and has gone into several printings. In it you use "monologues, songs, sermons, sonnets, newspaper snippets, recipes, haiku, and free verse." (Wikipedia). How did this poem come about? Critics have described it as a mythological work, but does it relate to the actual Africadian (a term you invented) community?*

GEC: Another big question! But I'll strive to be succinct! *Whylah Falls* arose from several autobiographical experiences: a) childhood and teenage visits to Three Mile Plains due to my love of its vistas and later my mooning over girls and then very irregularly having passions requited alongside grassy, forest paths; b) organizing, aged 18-19, a Black Youth Organization, and visiting and adoring the rural demesnes and *demoiselles* of the Annapolis Valley—Windsor down to Weymouth Falls; c) working as a social worker, aged 25-26 in bucolic—if oppressed—Africadian villages and hamlets, and falling in love incessantly with incredibly lovely women with copper or beige or sable tints and smoky voices; d) visiting Weymouth Falls over a year of weekends (52), aged 25-26, and recording the folk speech—"Shakespeare with a blackened tongue" (says my companion and *le-mot-juste* poet Giovanna Riccio); e) studying "Tradition and Experimentation in Modern Poetry, 1880-1930" with *the* John Fraser (author of *Violence in the Arts*) at Dalhousie University (1986-87); and f) loving Milton's *Paradise Lost* so much that I did end up "blackening" blank verse, stealing his idea of "The Argument" to open each section; but then also taking as my subject the rural Black locale that Toomer explores in *Cane* (1923), which is also a work employing song forms, free verse, and prose sketches. (Come to think of it, I think I'm pretty much alone—save for Richard Greene—in employing *vers blanc* as a regular poetic form.) So, yes, *Whylah Falls* is rooted utterly in Africadia, being a composite, really, of Windsor Plains and Weymouth Falls. I just loved the idea of black women posed beside apple blossoms, or lounging luxuriously in high grass; and I loved the idea of ornery and lusty preachers and sexy church gals comin up outta baptismal waters, their wet robes suddenly tight-fitting and also translucent; not to mention the trains crying and hollering; the guitars and pianos caterwauling; the tearful outflowing of flowing rum and ale. Yes, yes, yes!

LH: *Opera is not a usual form that poets choose. James Reaney is one of the Canadian poets who used this form. What drew you to opera, and what challenges did you face in writing operas?*

GEC: Opera—i.e., the libretto—is a form that I fell into accidently. The catalyst was a letter from composer James Rolfe who had read a few of my poems in the anthology *Poets 88* (1988), and thought that I had a certain lusty bravado in my diction, a nice mix of the scatological and the scriptural, the visceral and the intellectual. His own tendency in music was to be experimental, atonal, aloof (re: audience), and laconic. He guessed that I would push him towards more lyricism, more chromaticism, more Romanticism. When I received James's letter, I had no idea what a libretto was. For his part, once we knew our subject would be an enslaved woman murdering her father, master, and rapist (a double villain in paternal guise) in rural Nova Scotia in 1801, James set to work studying British military music, reels, Acadian fiddling, African-American spirituals and ring-shouts, as well as the parlour operettas and arias so popular in the "better" homes of the colonial bourgeoisie. And I started buying operas so I could study their libretti ("little books"). It was wonderful to encounter Pound's radio opera on François Villon; Jean Cocteau's text for Stravinsky's *Oedipus Rex*; Wayne Koestenbaum's pop art text for Michael Daugherty's *Jackie O*; Thulani Davis's text for Anthony Davis's *Malcolm X*; Richard Strauss's Salome based on *Oscar Wilde*'s play; and Alice Goodman's unexcelled octosyllabic couplets so befitting John Adams's *Nixon in China*. I soon learned that the challenge in writing libretti (I've also scribed two for D.D. Jackson) is in finding plot, characters, and wording pleasing and inspiring for the composer. In that regard, James was tyrannical in wanting a text as spare as possible, while I wanted to be baroque. In the end, because I didn't like having to sacrifice language that I was wedded to, I gave him the libretto that he needed, and then I wrote a separate, longer work—a verse-tragedy—to suit myself.

LH: *I've observed in your work a plethora of literary allusions to many other writers. In* Beatrice Chancy, *you base your play on the famous story of Beatrice Cenci, who killed her abusive father. There were numerous versions of the story taken from Percy Bysshe Shelley's* The Cenci *to Walter Landor, Antonin Artaud, Alberto Moravia, and many romances, chronicles, films, and operas. Can you speak about how you used and adapted these sources to write about the slave Beatrice Chancy? Why did you choose to tell this story in the form of an opera?*

GEC: When James and I first met in person, in November 1992, in Kingston (ON), where I was half-way through my doctoral work, it was to choose an operatic story we both could relish. It just so happened that, in writing my comprehensive exam in English Lit, I'd decided to focus on the seldom-employed genre of closet drama. Exemplary was Shelley's *The Cenci* (1819) because it is so visceral—a text besotted with blood, wine, gold, dirt, chains, a fat corpse plummeting into an olive tree far below a mountain'd castle's balcony …. It was all out-of-character for that most dreamy and idealistic of Romantic poets. You could expect Byron to be bawdy and Coleridge to dip his bread and butter in opium, but Shelley? To get down and dirty in literary sheets rather than bed sheets? Yet, his zeal in retelling this more-than-twice-told tale was fascinating, and also understandable because the story of the Italian nobleman and villain, Francesco Cenci (who is a murderous, greedy lecher, who purchases forgiveness from the Church), is also a sweet vehicle for the atheistic, communard Shelley to attack all the pillars of Moral Authority: Patriarchy, Religion, and Aristocracy, by dramatizing a historically true story of an allegedly rapist plutocrat, protected by the

Church, getting whacked *via* the plotting of his vengeful, victimized daughter, Beatrice. I think James had seen Tarantino's *Reservoir Dogs* (1992), but he was definitely a fan of David Lynch's oddball films with their occasionally subtle violences (for instance, there's a brooding shot of Guido Reni's portrait of *Beatrice Cenci* in Mulholland Drive [2001]), particularly *Blue Velvet* (1986), so, he loved a story that would involve blood ejaculating from bodies and saliva born outta sweat. So we settled on that story immediately. But I made two adjustments that James okayed: a) To translate a Renaissance, Papal State "Italy" story to slaveholding, colonial Nova Scotia, in the year 1801; and b) to make our Beatrice a mixed-race daughter (and legally a slave) of a rapist and slaveholding father. So Beatrice Cenci became *Beatrice Chancy*. I wanted to write a work centred on slavery because every self-consciously black writer—in the African Diaspora—does: Sooner or later. As for the various sources of the Cenci story that I consulted, I have to say that I became intrigued, enthralled, obsessed with the multiple, *other* Beatrices I encountered: from Dante's spiritual guide through the Inferno to Shakespeare's leading lady, and from the Beatrice (Cenci) of Julia Margaret Cameron (in an Art Gallery of Ontario show of Cameron's photos in 1998, they wrongly thought that one snap was a portrait of Beatrice Portinari) to Béatrice Harnois of *Las mil y una perversiones de Felicia* (a porn flick, 1975). I soon discovered that there is an artistic underground of persons fascinated by the Cenci story and its star heroine: Surrealists, dissidents, dissenters, decadents. Percy Shelley's Beatrice is the perfect, resuscitated bride for Mary Shelley's Creature. I read *all* of the treatments of her story that I could get my hands on in English. I did write my own version of the story, though I accepted Shelley's decision to suggest that incestuous rape was the motivation for his heroine's homicidal plot against her father. My major revision—accomplished with James's ecstatic agreement—was to have our Beatrice commit the murder herself: her lover, Lead (first rhyming with *dead* and later with *speed*), chickens out, so Beatrice does the grisly deed herself. But the other complication that I invented was the white stepmother's jealousy toward her beautiful-but-black daughter—who earns her father's rapacious wrath because her black, fiance is her father's slave.

LH: *In* Execution Poems, *you write of two characters, George and Rue (your cousins), who are convicted of murder and hanged in Fredericton. When describing this city, Fred Cogswell wrote: "O snow-washed city of cold, white Christians, / So white you will not cut a black man's hair." You provide a disturbing background of these two characters who witnessed many crimes and experienced violence in their lives, so it seemed inevitable that they would end up as felons.*

GEC: One of the paucities in Can Lit—and in African-Canadian literature itself—is any description of the lives of Black Canadians—as *lived*—from 1605 up to Austin Clarke's stories and novels that begin to canvass the lives of Caribbean and European immigrants in Toronto, as of the later 1960s. Save for very few diaries, memoirs, autobiographies, biographies, socio-historical (oral) interviews, and trial transcripts (mainly of capital cases), the archive and data of African-Canadian lives—of folks born, bred, and died in Canada—is distressingly disappeared—buried under blizzards of "Canada-is-better-than-the-U.S." snow-jobs. So, when my mom, Gerry, stricken with dementia, blurted out, in the spring of 1994, "You know you have two cousins who were hanged," I knew at once that story would be a novel. Indeed, my mom mentioned this suppressed truth to me on a Friday morning; by the following Sunday eve, I had received a 1949 newspaper clipping, announcing the execution date for the brothers, George Albert Hamilton, 23, and Rufus James Hamilton, 22. I began to write the novel—*immediately*. I knew that their story would be a way for me to understand the world of my parents' childhoods: Gerry was 10 and Bill was 14 when the brothers hanged, back-to-back, in a barn behind the Fredericton City Gaol. Who else had written *anything* about Black Maritimers' lives between 1925 and 1950? To write the novel, I had to spelunk into the pages of the Fredericton *Daily Gleaner* newspaper, January to July of 1949, finding obvious racism in the coverage of the crime—the murder and robbery of a white taxi driver by two Black (Afro-Métis) ne'er-do-wells in early January; the three trials (preliminary hearing and then two separate capital murder cases); and the conviction and executions. But I also found George's prison diary, and read through the trial transcripts for both men. Therein also were the judge's recommendations (No Mercy!), his description of Black citizens as constituting "a Negro camp"; but also letters (including a couple from the Ku Klux Klan—who also paraded outside the prison in the early morning hour—3 a.m.—of the executions); the testimony of others. I even found a clue for George's Africadian speech: When he said *beers*, the court reporter heard *bews*. My research opened up for me a black-and-white, *film-noir* world with a soundtrack of honky tonk country and rum-n-coke blues. A place where two unemployed, barely literate, Black-n-Indigenous ex-cons, outta Three Miles Plains, NS, found themselves hungry, thirsty, and freezing on a frigid January night, Friday the 7th to Saturday the 8th, and figured that the solution was to call a taxi driver, knock him out, and steal his stash. Their weapon? A hammer. But the blow struck had such force that the bones of the victim's skull were shattered, and he either died at once or through exsanguination. Then, the brothers took everything worth taking—cash, watch, wedding ring, cigarette lighter; burnt up what evidence they could; then put the victim's body in the trunk of his car; and then went driving about New Brunswick, partying, gambling, guzzling bootleg…. George even found a "shady lady" in Saint John to keep him company in exchange for $20 and a pair of nylons (or polyhexamethylineneudiapide—a word that turned up in a *Gleaner* ad coaxing ladies to try the *just-invented* hosiery). So, the novel took shape, and I wrote a first draft in the summer of 2000. But it was badly flawed: I'd decided to cast Rufus an intellectual—and a poet. I wrote a couple dozen poems that were intended for the novel. After I had submitted the first draft, Andrew Steeves wrote to ask if I had any poetry he could publish in his *Gaspereau Review*, his now-defunct literary journal. I sent him the poems that "Rufus" had written for the novel, "George & Rue." Two weeks later, Andrew wrote to say that he'd publish the lot as a chapbook. When I heard that, I imagined that the publication would be photocopied pages stapled together. But he flew me down to the press, then headquartered in Wolfville, NS, and there I witnessed coming off the rollers these huge sheets (each page was 2-feet-long by 1-foot-wide), the titles in red ink, the text in black, and then the pages sewn—hand-sewn—in the binding. Wow! Thus was born *Execution Poems* as an "experiment" in collector-edition printing. The print-run—only 66 copies (6 leather bound, 60 cardstock-covered)—was exhausted, with the "ordinary" copies selling for $50 each and the leather-bound for $250 each. But the demand was such that a trade edition was launched in 2001, winning me the Governor-General's Award for Poetry—but also an Alcuin book design award for Andrew. To complete this narrative, I have to say that HarperCollins rejected the first draft for *George & Rue*, but when I went back to it in 2002, I wrote chunks of it in "Blackened English," so

Joygee could say "bews" and Rufus could be "Rupe." But that process was helped along by my attempt to pen a screenplay of the story for Picture Plant. Maybe now—in the wake of the George Floyd Martyrdom—someone will think that it's a story that should be produced for the screen.

LH: *In the libretto* Québecité, *you celebrate Quebec writing in the introduction: "Quebec is a cinema of words, a cathedral of jazz, a catwalk of politics, a theatre of art, a* fête *of nostalgia, a gallery of passion, and a theme park of dreams." You said that the issues raised in this play were gender and race, not language. Yet, you experienced some objections to the points that you made in this work. What were they?*

GEC: My whole life has been defined by my brown complexion, my black consciousness, *and* my 'white' (European) acculturation. Even though it took decades for me to accept myself really for the full complexity of who I am—all my inheritances, I've always been mixed-race (*métis*) in soul and multicultural/cosmopolitan in sentiment. So, my first marriage was to a Chinese woman from Hong Kong, and my second was to a Brahmin-descended woman from Mauritius (an Indian Ocean isle off the east coast of South Africa); however, my non-marital but long-term amours were with a white Québécoise translator (my daughter' Aurélia's mom) and a white Finnish translator. And my most heartbreaking love was for a part-Chinese, Afro-Jamaican, British-accented woman, whom I met at Waterloo, but who did not reciprocate my feelings. (Intriguingly, almost all of my loves have spoken English accented in some way.) So, in writing *Québécité* for D.D. Jackson (commissioned by the Guelph Jazz Festival), I wanted to ponder interracial relationships—based on my own experiences, but also the romance between D.D.'s parents, an African-American professor of Spanish at Carleton

University and a Chinese woman, gifted in languages, who became one of the first builders of Official Languages policy and governance for the PET Guv-mint. And I nodded to a slew of films: Radley Metzger's randy sex-romp, *The Lickerish Quartet* (1970), Sanjay Leela Bhansali's posh, Bollywood-baroque, romantic tragedy, *Devdas* (2002); Alfie Hitchcock's Québec City-set, noirish thriller, *I Confess* (1953); Mira Nair's spicy, Af-Am & South Asian mash-up, *Mississippi Masala* (1991); and above all, Jacques Démy's brilliant, *bossa-nova*-scored, *nouvelle-vague* masterpiece, anti-war "musical," *Les Parapluies de Cherbourg* (1964). My plot was elementary: Two lads meet two gals in Québec City: Everyone is bilingual, and so language politics don't matter. Instead the Africadian jazz saxophonist—Malcolm States—woos Colette Chan, a Chinese-Canadian law student (whose parents object to their match, thus breaking them up). In the other pairing, the problem is sexism, not racism, with Laxmi Bharati, a student architect, rejecting the playboy philosophy of her suitor, the architect Ovide Rimbaud, who is Haitian. White Québécois prejudice is hardly mentioned. So, why was there such a virulent reaction against a light, comic opera, where the problems highlighted were anti-black, Chinese racism and black-male sexism versus a South Asian woman? Well, more than one Québécois critic (Francophone or Anglophone) objected to the staged presentation of a Québec City where white people are *not* front-and-centre. *Quelle horreur*! How dare I focus on BIPOC characters (and Malcolm is Afro-Métis) in a space that is pictured as "*pur laine*," or "as white as the virgin snow." Indeed, I called the opera, *Québécité*—a Québécois word meaning "Quebecness"—to accent (pun intended) my claim—our claim—that BIPOC are also Québécois, and may also possess *Québécité*. Other critics objected to the "puritanical" attitude of Laxmi, even slagging her as "Victorian" because she refused to okay premarital sex. Yes, it had a rough reception, but the music and songs are imperishable.

LH: *Few Canadian poets have written about a Canadian politician. Your dramatic poem* Trudeau: Long March & Shining Path *is about the Canadian Prime Minister, Pierre Elliott Trudeau. You view him as a politician, but also as a man. Yet, you state, "This dramatic poem is purely a theatre of imagination." Why did you write about drama as a fantasy, including scenes with Mao Tse Tung, Fidel Castro, Pablo Neruda, John F. Kennedy, and others? Why did you choose to write this as a play with politicians as characters who would not have met in this way?*

GEC: *Trudeau: Long March / Shining Path* is about that rarity in English-North-American politics: The intellectual. Papa T was that; Baby T is not. Yet, there is a tradition in French politics of leaders who read and fighters who write and thinkers who drink (and drinkers who think). As a crusading journalist attacking the illiberal orthodoxies of pre-Quiet Revolution Québec, PET modelled the combative intellectual; and his writing is superbly acerbic, but also satirical, insightful, and witty. Yet, the wealthy PET was also glamorous—and had a JFK-yen for adventure. I believe that he globetrotted through all of 1948 to make up for not having seen combat during the Anti-Fascist War. (The stories he tells about his bravery are only *his* reportage; there are no witnesses; no one to verify that, for instance, he stole a would-be mugger's knife and brandished it at him while quoting Rimbaud, on a set of ziggurat steps in Baghdad.) I was also fascinated by what I saw as the unexamined basic fact of PET's politics—his understanding that Québec was decolonizing—getting rid of blunt, Anglo control of its economy *via* capital and control of its politics *via* corruption. Unlike every Anglo-Canadian politician of his era, PET was schooled enough in global politics to realize that Québec's decolonization could follow the violent and "socialist" models of China, Algeria, and Cuba (to name but three readily available examples), resulting in loss of life, property, and liberty; or, it could unfurl "democratically," and in a managed way (*Reason Over Passion*—PET's slogan); but there were not many successful examples of such a process; instead, nations split: India into India, Pakistan, and Bangladesh; or fell into spasms of never-ending civil wars; or, following a first, 'free' election, fell into cycles of coups enacted by disaffected generals wanting to have their turn at looting the treasury (see Sierra Leone, for instance). So, PET's singular quality as a PM in that time of tumult was to have read his Fanon and his Mao, his Rousseau and his Marx, and to have been a student of revolution and to have witnessed both the birth of Israel and the triumph of Mao, to have dropped in on Moscow for economics and leafed through assorted, national constitutions at Harvard. So, he was gung-ho to ensure that Québec's decolonization would unfold constitutionally, reasonably, to forestall terrorism, civil war, or brutal suppression. (Of course, the War Measures Act invocation in October 1970 revealed that even civil libertarian Papa T could bare the fangs—or "lightning bolts" [his phrase]—of the state.) For all his success at trying to guide Québec's decolonization through the 1960s, most especially by bringing in the Official Languages policy to suggest that Canada was not an English-only state, PET never understood English-Canada's own decolonization (from Great Britain), even though his own election in 1968 was a result of that inchoate yearning to no longer be either an English vessel or a Yankee vassal. Nor did he understand the decolonizing imperative of Indigenous peoples. Even so, the fact that he was a "*citoyen du monde*," and not a parochial, insular chap, meant that he was a free-thinker, cosmopolitan, and even a libertine (ferrying Liona Boyd under furs in his limo; courting Barbra Streisand by Prince-Rainier-stealth). I wanted to play up those aspects of his personality, and show him in dialogue with leaders that he admired (and I do remember that, as a teen, he admired fascists—strong men, dictators), such as Mao and Castro, both of whom he met, and I could imagine him in dialogue with JFK. On the domestic side, by marrying a 60s Flower-Child, he helped usher into the Canadian public mind a woman who could recite poetry at affairs of state and party with The Rolling Stones in Toronto, become a celebrity photographer and a symbol of scandal-mag feminism (lusting for Lou Rawls and taking to the disco dance-floor minus her panties). Along with the Charter, PET remade Canada by championing multiculturalism—a word he uttered *once* only in the House of Commons, i.e., when he announced the policy in October 1971. I guessed that all of these facets of his personality could be best sounded by positioning PET both outside Ottawa and outside Canada; for, he brought into Canadian public life, regularly so drearily provincial, the excitement of thinking that we could have philosopher-kings paddling canoes and jazz-club playboys quoting Mao's Little Red Book. (Only in Canada, eh? Pity!) And I believe that PET's knowledge of Mao's Long March gave him wanderlust; but his "Shining Path" was constitutional liberalism, producing the Charter of Rights and Freedoms (so indebted to Red Tory Dief the Chief's Canadian Bill of Rights, 1960). Finally, the opera version, composed by D.D., allowed him to relish and import revolutionary Chinese opera, Brazilian *bossa nova* (for the Cuban scene), light Italian pop (for PET's meeting with Margaret Sinclair in Tahiti), and even a Rolling Stone vibe for Margaret's personal liberation anthem. It was a lot of fun to pen, and I still wager my understanding of PET's politics is correct. Neatly, when George Walker produced his woodcut-illustrated book of Papa T's life in 2015, he asked me to pen a Foreword, but he also asked Baby T for permission to reprint his funeral oration for his father. So, when the book was published the week before Baby T's first election victory, George signed the limited edition in black ink, Baby T in Tory blue, and I—in Harvard-crimson (or, um, socialist-red).

LH: *There are not many Canadian poets that are overtly political in their work. I'm thinking of Gary Geddes in his writing or the Quebecois poet Gaston Miron. In a recent interview at the launch of your literary memoir by your publisher, you said, "Art is never political." Is it the role of the writer to be political in their work at certain times?*

GEC: Well, there is a strong tradition of political poetry in English Canada. Think of *Civil Elegies* Dennis Lee or feminist-socialist Dorothy Livesay; or even of the nationalistic Atwood of the 60s and the environmentalist and feminist Atwood of the 70s; think of Milton Acorn—a stogie-chomping Commie; Earle Birney adored Trotsky; F.R. Scott was an intellectual daddy of the Charter because he mentored PET; but he was also an intellectual father of the CCF/NDP (and won two literary GG prizes: one for politic poetry; the other for essays on the Constitution [he was totally devoted to the BNA Act]); even E.J. Pratt was political in terms of making heroes out of French martyrs in Nouvelle-France, a hero out of Sir John A. for thrusting the railway (with Chinese labour) through the mountain ranges betwixt Alberta and the Pacific coast, and a hero out of Christ for being a decent role-model. E. Pauline Johnson was also political—in advocating early on for Indigenous people; as was A.M. Klein for his fierce denunciation of Hitler in *The Hitleriad* and of anti-Semitism and anti-Native prejudice in *The Rocking Chair*; of course, currently, Brand, Lillian Allen, Erin Mouré, Jeff Derksen, Garry

Thomas Morse, Sky Dancer (lb. halfe = £ & ½) and other Indigenous poets also embrace political agitation. *Et cetera.* Maybe the real division in contemporary Anglo-Can-do poets is between the pomo-absurdists (there is no truth or meaning that is—or should be—sensible; the poem is a series of PSYOPS and disjunctive ellipses) and the poco-realists (who fancy that poetry may speak to readers about 'real' personages and discernible events with even a hint of political persuasion). Many poets do straddle the middle, going in one direction for one book or poem, and then reversing course in another. I think that both approaches have their strengths and their devotees. My personal bias is for variety—indulging the many forms of verse that have been incorporated into our 'canon' in the last century, from haiku to ghazal, the sestina to the glosa, not to mention the ballad stanza and the blues. For me, "Form is as form does," and inspiration is possible from every quarter. At times, blood-curdling, spine-chilling, cold-blooded propaganda is justified; on other occasions, surrealist, whimsical confections are operative. Like Emma Goldman (if out of context), I don't want to support any school of poetry that denies that poetry is also about freestyle dancing. When I said that "Art is never political," I think that I was really trying to say that good Art, in the end, is not partisan; that it transcends the immediate political motive of its creation. So, when Pound eulogizes Mussolini and fascism in that incredible opening line of Canto LXXIV, "The enormous tragedy of the dream in the peasant's bent shoulders," I don't need to be in favour of either Il Duce or his politics to recognize the agony and the trauma that move Pound's hand.

LH: *You have mentioned in an interview that you were influenced by the Jewish Canadian poet Irving Layton whom you called a "libertine lyricist." Were there other writers who influenced you in* *the way that they wrote about sex? There is a continual presence of sexuality in your work, from* Whylah Falls *through* Extra Illicit Sonnets Canticles. *Why is it so vital that you express eroticism in your poetry?*

GEC: Wow! Another huge question—and I keep trying to be succinct. Lookit! I'm a son of the 60s—all of it—from Hugh Hefner's topless-pixies-next-door to burn-the-bra lady-libbers; from painters using nude women as *paintbrushes* (Paris, France, 1960) to the sensation of barely-there micro-mini-skirts and nipple-accenting halter-tops (not to mention see-throughs). Yes, there's now an on-line porn bonanza, but just as disturbingly prevalent are puritanical or censorious ideals that equate any sexual desire to sexual assault. Contrasted with the current mood—both smutty and shaming (a satanic coupling indeed), the Sexual Revolution was awesomely radical—despite patriarchal hypocrisy that insists perpetually on dividing the maternal from the carnal, the "virginal" from the "liberated." Keeping in mind the steady efforts of phallocentric, masculinist, and heterosexual regimes to suppress women *and* other sexualities, the Sexual Revolution was liberating—so insurgent, dynamic, and upsetting of bourgeois conventions and expectations. I'm glad that I grew up at a time when liberation was lauded and experimentation was wide-open, when PET said "The state has no place in the bedrooms of the nation" and *Playgirl* could attempt to one-up *Playboy*. Yes, Lizzie Borden's film, *Born in Flames* (1983), was right to question whether anything had really changed; and it is also true that, in tandem with "liberation," there followed a tsunami of "sexploitation." But, exudes Wordsworth, "Bliss was it in that time to be alive!" Though he was born in 1912, Layton was—along with the generation-younger Leonard Cohen—right on-time for the 60s *Zeitgeist*, maybe because they were both luxuriating in sunny Greece, the birthplace—perhaps only in name—of "Lesbos" and Apollonian hedonism, "French" tongue and "Greek" love—along with the Platonist sort (!). But the other connection was both were Jewish artists/intellectuals who came of age in a repressive, fascistic-flirtatious, fervently Catholic, and repressed/repressive Québec. Was not half of the victory of the Quiet Revolution the ending of censorship, the ending of the suppression of exotic dancers and of jazz clubs (both detested by Duplessis)? So, in his 1960s collections, such as *Flowers for Hitler* (1964)—whose outré title winks at Baudelaire's *Les Fleurs du Mal* (1857)—Cohen is sacrilegious, scatological, and calling for "free love" in Cuba, in Greece, even in North Hatley (QC)! Likewise, Layton wants to tease the prudes of Catholic Québec and protestant Anglo-Canada by presenting images of Byronic, Adonis-he-man-*he* penning eulogies for Aviva coming to Paris like an all-conquering Jackie Kennedy (not yet Jackie O), or poking fingers in feminists' eyes (for him they were just newfangled morality cops) by cheering on the sight of "titties" jumping in ladies' tops as they jounced their way along rue Sainte-Catherine Ouest in 'swinging' Montréal. What a spirit of *joie-de-vivre*, of ecstatic life, animates such vigorous paeans! We know from Harriet Bernstein's memoir (2019) that being married to Layton was tricky—because he was egotistical, a womanizer, and controlling. And yet, if you sample the titles of his later output (from the *Collected*—1965—onward), many announce themes of love, sex, romance, presenting a speaker who is all Byronic fun-in-the-sun (as well as all Sadean enmity for anti-Semites and Israel critics). As for me and my house, my own view of authorial liberty—of artistic freedom—is that I can write about sexuality just as I like. I note that the "Negro Revolution" and "Women's Liberation" both worked to affirm the "Sexual Revolution" (with Hefner's *Playboy* backing all—plus anti-war policies, decriminalization of drugs, exposure of U.S. Crimes Against Humanity, and applauding *beaucoup* jazz). So, for me, *freedom* as a black male (heterosexual) poet means that I must claim the right to write about whatever I like, so help me God. In *Canticles I* (both volumes—*MMXVI* & *MMXVII*), I canvass two millennia of vicious imperialisms, and I know that an additional motive for conquest and pillage was rapine; that oppression was colonial, racial, sexual. Imperialism is sadism—exported.

LH: *Ezra Pound has been one of the most significant poets in the 20th and 21st centuries. In Canada, Louis Dudek, his secretary when the American poet was held in St. Elizabeth Hospital, was greatly affected by him in his longer poems. What brought you to Pound, and what kind of influence did he have on you, even when you were critical of aspects of his character?*

GEC: "Pound, Pound, Pound, Pound, Pound, Pound, Pound. / Why wouldn't the man shut up?" That's a line from John Thompson's ghazal, "IX," except that he writes "Yeats," where I say "Pound"! Yep, I came to Pound due to his translation from Li Po/Rihaku, "The River-Merchant's Wife: A Letter." I was thunder-struck by how the projected woman's voice reached my boyish heart all the way from Tang Dynasty China *via* the Mississippi River. I found that poem in Dudek's fine anthology, *Poetry of Our Time* (1966); I liked all the Pound selections, particularly "N.Y." and "Commission." Also present was a fragment of "Canto LXXXI," and so I soon picked up a copy of *The Cantos* from the North End Library and started trying to read it in 1977—when I was 17. Not only that, in the same summer, I first attempted to write a pint-sized version of Pound's deft, difficult (and daffy) poem of poems. Mine? Only the length of a *Hilroy* scribbler! I recall that I wielded biblical allusions plus French phrases that I knew, plus smatterings of phrases copied out of dual-language translations of works by exotic poets. I denounced Pound's politics. But how thrilling to read, at age 20, his denunciations of bankers while I stood in pay-day line-ups at a Royal Bank branch! I made another half-hearted attempt to compose my own 'Cantos' at age 23; but those pieces were hardly much longer than haikus and my effort did not even fill a scribbler. I returned to *The Cantos*, in my mid-30s, while drafting *Beatrice Chancy*. Soon, I fixated on *Italiana*:

> Dante—Morricone—Puccini—Verdi—
> Corso—Portinari—Madonna—Cicciolina—
> Piccioni—Venezia—Ferlinghetti—Fellini—
> Pasolini—Moravia—*Gialli*—*Punt e*
> *Mes*—Limoncello—Martini—Grappa—Pizza—
> Vespa—*et cetera*.

And that attention delivered me back to Pound, to observe that his tripartite structure of *The Cantos* echoes Dante's Inferno, Purgatorio, and Paradiso. So, by 1995, I was reading *The Cantos*, wholly, biennially, a duty that continues. My epic—"Canticles"—gestures to Pound, but also to my Black Baptist roots. The work is unfinished, but is intended to evince a Dantean structure: *Canticles I* (2 vols.) ponders hellish history; *Canticles II* (2 vols., *MMXIX* & *MMXX*) is a purgatorial revisiting of scriptures; the work will conclude with the 'paradise' effected by the construction of the African (United) Baptist Association of Nova Scotia in the 1850s; that narrative will unfold in "Canticles III" (2 vols., likely "MMXXII" & "MMXXIII"). A strange dream is pertinent here. When I was 25, I dreamt that the elder Pound and I were ambling about Toronto. He is peering straight ahead, while I'm looking over at him sheepishly. Finally, I screw up my nerve to ask him for his view of my verse. Then he speaks a single sentence: "Some of it is bad;

some of it is very good." I can only pray that, 36 years later, the "bad" has shrivelled in balance with the "very good"!

LH: *You have taught in several universities in Canada and at Duke University and Harvard. As an Africadian, did you perceive any differences between the African-Americans and African Canadians? How was this experience reflected in your poetry?*

GEC: Before I went to live and teach in the United States, at Duke University, in Durham, North Carolina (1994-99), I had both a demonic view of the U.S.—being a Canadian nationalist—and a romantic view of Black America—being a Black Canadian. Both of those viewpoints got tempered and transformed by my American life. But the acclimatization was subtle and all-encompassing. Some changes were superficial: I went from a Canadian life where there were no black radio stations to a city that boasted five. I went from a "visible minority" status in Canada to an empowered minority status in Durham (a city 30% black). But other changes were psychological. In Canada, I was shy about my unruly, kinky hair. In the U.S., I could forget to 'comb' my Afro and walk about with my hair gone clearly wild. In Canada, I felt constrained in my writing; but in the U.S. I began to feel FREE—truly FREE— *for the first time in my life*. I began to just write whatever the hell I wanted—more like Layton and less like Atwood. The poems in *Blue* (2001, 2008, 2011) resulted from my liberation from Canuck politesse and strictures of conformity: Rambunctious, cranky, in-yo-face, dirty, fresh, frank, spiky, insouciant. I also began to document other African-Canadian writers, writing paeans for some, or complaints bout others, but acknowledging our mutual existence and struggle. The downside to the mood of liberty? The African-American erasure of my Canadian identity: To be black was to be "Black American." So, for instance, when many of my colleagues were sure that O.J. Simpson was framed for the murder of Nicole Brown-Simpson and were exhilarated by his acquittal, I could not join in the chorus of acclaim, even though I did defend the jury against (racist) criticisms of their decision. Too, when colleagues invited me to walk along with Lou Farrakhan's Million Man March, I could not: I watched it on television—and I did feel a connection. But I was also happy that I did not have to pay implicit homage to one of the instigators of Malcolm X's assassination. In my opening essay in *Odysseys Home: Mapping African-Canadian Literature* (2002), I list seven principles of "African-Americanness"; but its main tenet is, the supreme group of black peoples on Earth are not in Africa, but in America; indeed, while African-Americans remain an oppressed people (especially the ghettoized underclass), they are also a constitutive element of American society and culture and history (in *every* way); and so, as America projects its values abroad—militarily *and* culturally, African-American culture and history also go global. So, when the Berlin Wall fell, Berliners sang, "We Shall Overcome." Rap and Hip Hop are universal cultural expressions now. In other words, there is an African-American cultural imperialism that gets projected right alongside Hollywood's blockbusters and Broadway's musicals. The African-Canadian response—as my scholarship has proven—is to take African-American cultural formations and "ring changes pon them." So, Richard Wright wrote a short story collection, *Eight Men* (1961), and Austin Clarke answered with *Nine Men Who Laughed* (1986). Because the vast majority of African-Americans have roots going back to the early 1800s, they are capable of monolithic thought—as well as unity. African-Canadians are far more various and variegated—and the vast majority have 'roots' going back to (take your pick) 1955, 1965, 1975, 1985, 1995, 2005, or 2015; too, the vast most of us are from British West Indies isles, or Haiti, or Africa, or the U.S. So, African-Canadians are multicultural, multi-ethnic, polyglot, if mainly Christian (evangelical or Anglican, but Catholic if Francophone). The upside is, we are open to influences from everywhere, are cosmopolitan in our art, but are seldom unified on socio-political issues—even in anti-racism. While the US black population is centred in major northern cities and southern rural districts; the Canadian black population is centred in Toronto, southwestern Ontario (Mississauga/Brampton/Hamilton/Windsor), Ottawa, Montréal, Calgary, and Vancouver, but seldom in communal numbers large enough to sway even a city council vote let alone decide a provincial or federal riding outcome. (One exception is the provincial riding of Preston, in Nova Scotia [which still boasts the largest, historically rooted Africadian population], which was crafted to give black voters a chance to elect a black MLA. Yet, the successful candidate in the riding is usually white, who amasses most of the white vote and enough of the black—to win.) To sum up, African America is really a sub-civilization of the U.S. (not a mere subculture) with its own *national* media, educational, religious, and entertainment infrastructure. African Canada is, in contrast, a clutch of (mainly) integrated, urban neighbourhoods, where folks are marginalized by class as much as race, but where the poor are allowed to be poor together. The growing professional class of African-Canadians can seldom express a collective sense of identity: Some Black Canadians still see themselves as British or French or American or Nigerian or Haitian; and a few others, like me, carry the values of the black communities of Sweet Home Nova Scotia (Africadia). African-Canadians are lucky to have such dynamic diversity! But it does make it more challenging for us to act as one. You did also ask about how this acknowledgment of Canadian and American differences shows up in my poetry. Well, given

Canada's elitist (hierarchical, monarchical) orientation, we are bound to generate writers who are less about "roots" and being "accessible," and more about relishing cosmopolitan, cultural complexity and unabashed intellectuality. See Brand, Wayde Compton, Kaie Kellough, André Alexis, Chantal Gibson, etc. I do have a foot in that camp (some of my lyrics are abstract, ethereal, opaque, requiring human-flesh-hunt search-engines, i.e., the—Chinese-dubbed *Rénròu Sōusuǒ*). But I started off as a song-wright born in rural Nova Scotia among folks who put a premium on orality and emotive expressiveness (more like Af-Ams). Yessum, I prefer Bob Dylan to Anne Carson, Henry Dumas to Edward Kamau Braithwaite. Tear-jerking melisma over cold-eyed, pomo musing. So, in almost every book, I place a blues song, or homely ballads, and I feel free to drop g's and replace *be* with *is*. Such moments are not affectations! Lookit! They represent just how I speak. So, I'm proud that Spoken Word stars like Andrea Thompson count me as a progenitor; just as I'm glad that Rosella Zorzi writ a comparative essay, juxtaposing Pound *et moi*, in the book, *Roma/Amor: Ezra Pound, Rome, and Love* (2013).

LH: *You have been very supportive of African Canadian writers producing more than four anthologies. You have edited two volumes of* Fire on the Water: An Anthology of Black Nova Scotian Writing. *Why was it so crucial for you to do this?*

GEC: Now, I will be brief! I edit anthologies. Why? To repel an absence with a presence. When my debut book outed in 1983, a few critics pronounced me the first Black Nova Scotian poet "to break into print." Untrue! After all, I knew of Gloria Wesley's publication, eight years before, of her *To My Someday Child*. But I wanted to be sure. So, Lesley Choyce of Pottersfield Press accepted my idea that I ransack libraries and archives to locate materials for an anthology that became

Fire on the Water. Not only did I retrieve—as "Africadians"— slave narrative authors such as John William Robertson (see his apocalyptic pamphlet, *The Book of the Bible Against Slavery*, 1854), I also showcased Floyd Kane, who now produces the CBC TV program, *Diggstown*, and directs other films. Similarly, sick of being told that Black Canadian writing began with Austin Clarke publishing his first novel in 1964, I assembled *Eyeing the North Star: Directions in African-Canadian Literature* (1997), whose historical overview, names the true pioneers, such as Amelia E. Johnson—born in Montréal, raised in Toronto, who published *Clarence and Corinne; or, God's Way*, the first African-Canadian novel, in Baltimore in 1890. I also highlighted our perfect diversity, featuring authors from Canada, migrants from the U.S., the Caribbean, and Africa, plus Francophone authors. At first, some resisted my approach; they felt that non-Caribbean, pre-1964 authors didn't matter (see M. NourbeSe Philip's comments). But the forthcoming *Handbook to Black Canadian Literature*, vaunts historical articles and groups migrant and "native" writers together, which was exactly what I had argued for "all those years ago" (John Lennon). But will there ever be a comprehensive, *Atlantic* Canadian poetry anthology? Eh?

LH: *In his work, Derek Walcott speaks about his attitude to the works of the English canon. He writes about imperialism and slavery in a global context, the way you have done in your Canticles books. In a recent elegy, "In Memory of Derek Walcott," you write "a la manière d'Auden"—"Is this Walcott's mission to reclaim / The Commonwealth due each ex-slaves name?" I was curious why this poem came to you when visiting the tomb of Ezra Pound in Italy.*

GEC: In truth, I went to Pound's grave deliberately to write Walcott's elegy. I sought to join a chain of associations: Auden's elegy for Yeats; Walcott's for Auden (with Yeats' ghost attending); and mine for Walcott—but imitating Auden's syllable-count and rhyme-scheme (line by line), while letting Pound haunt my margins. You know, in *Omeros*, Walcott alludes severally to Pound (as well as Yeats, and the epic is a homage to Homer in plot and to Dante in the loosened and often slant-rhymed tercets). When I interviewed him in Victoria, B.C., in 2010, he said, "Pound is great in the way that poets know he is great." That's a cryptic line, avoiding £'s anti-Semitism and fascism; and yet it is also accurate. £ be the modernist who tried hardest to wed vernacular speech with a democratized classicism. But Walcott pursued a like ideal: To write blank verse infused with patois, or to write rhyme bouncy with the calypsos of Trinidad and Barbados. I love the fact that, in *The Bounty* (1997), Walcott resurrects Jack Clare—the Peasant Poet—to remind us of the Burnsian vigour and Hopkins-like inventiveness of *the* people parleying in pubs or in the lover-liberated parks hind cathedral backsides. So, for me, to pay correct homage to Walcott (with whom I dined on lobster and Champagne in September 2012), it was vital to be at Pound's grave, with Auden's example before me. And he merited that elegy, for he had surmised that the tragedy of slavery was also a gift: That the imposed language—English (or other European tongues)—expanded immensely the registers of expression available for African-heritage poets. To write in English is to lay claim to the entire Commonwealth (including that drop-out state, the U.S.), whose language informs our very names.

LH: *In the introduction of* Canticles I *(MMXVI), you write that the subject "is* History, *principally, of slavery and the resistance to enslavements: of imperialism and the struggle for independence" and also the presentation of the "image or symbolism" of the "Negro." What was the genesis of this book? Did your ideas change as you researched the subject of slavery?*

GEC: As I mentioned above, since encountering *The Cantos* at age 17, I'd always wanted to write my own epic hodgepodge, helter-skeltering bout history. In some ways, *Whylah Falls* was an epic, though I've always felt more comfortable describing it as a verse-novel (or a narrative lyric sequence). *I & I* (2009)—my second verse-novel—was writ in the shadow or Enlightenment of Walcott's *Omeros*, Bernardine Evaristo's *Lara* (1997) and her *The Emperor's Babe* (2001), and that unusual fusion of Tang Dynasty, Chinese poetry and pomo-litcrit that is *An Introduction to the Introduction to Wang Wei* by Pain Not Bread (Roo Borson, Kim Maltman & Andy Patton, 2000). My first two "epics" (or epyllia) were anchored in Nova Scotian or Africadian lived experience, if slightly fictionalized. But I was moved to attempt directly an epic due to the examples of Pound—*and* Walcott, given the latter's fulfillment of the Aristotelian scale of poetic achievement that ranks lyric as the lowest, verse-drama as the middle-level (with tragedy trumping comedy), and epic as the highest. I've tried to follow Aristotle and Walcott by writing verse in all genres, and have always felt that epic would be—had to be—the "crowning" effort of whatever my gifts may be. I also trust Pound's definition that "an epic is a poem containing history." For me, as a black writer, that means looking at the history of the Christian era, and especially the last 500 years, all marked by enslavement and colonization and then liberation struggles. In my view, *all* of the major contretemps in our world were triggered by Columbus's discovery of "Turtle Island"; the (Western) European exploitation of the riches and resources of the Americas which fuelled imperial rivalries and a naval arms-race; which led to (Western) European domination of Earth by the end of Victoria's reign; but which also mandated the sacking of the labour and resources of Africa; plus slavery in the Americas and serfdom in Europe; plus eventual rebellion by America and its rapid growth to become an undeclared empire rivalling and then besting (and dwarfing) Britain's; plus "global wars" of empires vs. would-be empires; plus ancillary civil wars (see China, Korea, Vietnam, etc.); plus revolutionary "liberations" (China, Russia, Cuba, etc.) or coups that exchange one foreign-backed despot for another foreign-backed despot (see Egypt or Syria); plus wars of liberation versus colonialism/imperialism; plus "democratic" political decolonization often followed by either military (aligned) dictatorships or economic control (by the rich, white, west, north nations: NATO & the G7 & the EU). *That* is a fair and just summary of the last 500 years, and *that* is what I elaborate upon in *Canticles I*. Once I was ready to commence, I flew to Africa—to Tanzania—to Zanzibar, in February 2008, to pen my first musings. I had planned to write just one volume—maybe 800-900 pages—like Pound's *Cantos*. Yet, when Michael Mirolla and Guernica signed on to the project in 2011, I had already amassed material for two volumes. Next, I planned to do biblical rewrites in one volume. But, I ended up writing two volumes for *Canticles II*. I've now published over 2,000 pages of verse, and likely have another 1,000 on tap for the final volumes of *Canticles III*, dealing with the formation of the African Baptist Church of Nova Scotia. My logic for this sequence is simple: The history of colonization and enslavement forces upon black peoples Judeo-Christian spirituality, which they then incorporate in their Freedom movements, which can foment new brands of Christianity (or other faiths).

LH: *Like Ezra Pound, you shift through many different periods and different countries, portraying a wide variety of historical characters, and use languages other than English throughout your work. In* Canticles I, *you create portraits of many historical figures such as Christopher Columbus, George Washington, and Thomas Jefferson in which you deconstruct popular representations of them. For example, you write of Columbus, a "royal pirate" responsible for many crimes against Indigenous people. Why is it so important to re-evaluate the interpretations of these characters and their roles in history?*

GEC: I'll keep this answer short! Once I began to ink *Canticles I*, I soon realized that history becomes more dynamic if one sets personages at odds with each other or allows devils to state their diabolical beliefs. If Canticles is a "lyric epic"—an epic composed of individual lyrics, most of these are dramatic monologues, so that, *par exemple*, Phillis Wheatley can attack Thomas Jefferson—and he can ridicule her in turn; or Napoléon can spit upon Toussaint L'Ouverture, but not before L'Ouverture massacres the French soldiery; or Jamaican guerilla-army-slave-liberator Nanny-of-the Maroons wars upon the British slaveholders, while a British officer at Isandlwana, South Africa, in 1879, records their rout at the hands of Zulu warriors. Other episodes treat black participation in imperial oppression, such as the exodus of African Americans to Liberia, 1822-47, who, as the ruling-class, oppressed and enslaved the Indigenous peoples. *Canticles I (MMXVI)* opens with a meditation "by Dante" (writ at his tomb in Ravenna) on how poets haunt graveyards, but I end with Mao celebrating his 1949 victory at Nanjing/Nanking. (Was this the pivotal, decisive moment for *21*st century history?). The shifting kaleidoscope of scenes and the proliferation of voices, along with interjections of translations, indicate that the panorama is international and perpetually historical.

LH: *In* Canticle II, *you create adaptations of The Bible from ancient times. For example, T.S. Eliot in "The Wasteland" juxtaposes his contemporary England and Europe with ancient scenes. Al Moritz, in his book* Sequence, *juxtaposes scenes from different times. Throughout* Canticle II *while speaking of events in the Old*

Testament, you refer to contemporary events PSYOP and "Nixo-nian Minority and State Multiculturalism*." Why did you con-textualize Biblical scenes using modern situations and language?*

GEC: Tis true! I was awe-struck by Eliot's "The Journey of the Magi" with his modern lingo recapitulating a double-mil-lennia-old tale; Pound also reproduces historic personages as "modern" types. His Mussolini is the Second Coming—so to speak—of Sigismundo Malatesta, a military strongman, con-queror, architect, and poet; and Pound turns both Confucius and Thomas Jefferson into precursors of "Musso"—due to the overarching conceit that, for him, history isn't just circular, but a vortex, wherein historic events and characters are repeated—in different contexts—as they are swirled about in nauseating repetition (so long as nations fail to overthrow bankers and arms merchants). But Northrop Frye is also an inevitable influ-ence, for, in *The Great Code* (1982), he argues that events in the Bible are always presented as types—archetypes prophetic of later events, including those that transpire long after the Bible has been closed. So, the Messiah is always still to arrive—OR is still to return; or the Slaughter of the Innocents forecasts the Holocaust; or the contest between Moses and Pharaoh fore-shadows the struggle between Af-Am slave and Euro slave-master; or the Great Whore of Babylon needs to be locked up—basically again and again. Sometimes she's Rome; other times she's Washington (DC). Walcott also fields a Viconian vision: Empires rise, collapse, and the shambles produce new nations, even new empires, and especially lingos; so English is indebted to Roman, German, Norse, French, interlopers. Then again, being a (bad, i.e., independent) Christian, I read all the biblical personages as being vividly human, enriched by divinity in some cases, but enlarged by passions—always. I believe that our Saviour was sinless; could never have felt, for instance, an iota of lust for Mary Magdalen. But I also believe

124

that He would *not* have *not seen* her pulchritude. Moreover, I believe that our Saviour belched, yawned, farted, scratched at an itch, guffawed, performed His toilet with godly cleanliness, but still noticed the stink of our waste. So, for me, the Christ who attacks the moneychangers is the same Dude who should chastise the IMF. In February 2009, I found myself in Bethlehem—ahem—Pennsylvania! How impossible to NOT set the Xmas story in the cradle of Bethlehem Steel, to let "Joseph X" muse, "I look across this precipitation-walloped landscape / (almost a seascape), / and I set our mules slouching toward Bethlehem…. / Mary is the apogee of spice. / About her, the rain blurs down as flurried confetti."

LH: *I'm interested in knowing more about the techniques that you used in the* Canticles II *MMXIX. In the introduction you touched on this point by saying, "My method? Oulipo, elliptical, and seren-dipitous." You speak about how the more your characters changed, the more you meditated on them during the act of writing.*

GEC: All of the poetry in all of the *Canticles* was the result of a magical process wherein I would decide, for instance, that I would write a poem in the voice of Jezebel; next, I'd scan my journal jottings, and I would twig to a word like *homicidal* or a phrase like *Peace, Order, and Good Government*. Instantly, I'd know that Queen Jezebel would say, in her defence:

> And Governance requires kings
> to be homicidal,
>
> for *Peace, Order, and Good Government* demands
> the dismantling of conniptions—
>
> via mass public hangings
> (as in El-Sisi's U.S.-bossed Egypt),

imprisonment under trumped-up charges,
geniuses become palpable dung…,

a lot of loud, gory pigment—
squalls as grave as gravel tumbling, squabbling:

To be dirty,
inside and out.

LH: *Another question I like to ask a poet is, "What are you working on now?"*

GEC: Now, I'll truly be succinct! I explained recently to Shane Neilson that my fecund (not, I pray, fecal) productivity is a result of "projects" (my word for my verse *works*) appearing hand-over-fist, but which have been in separate production—usually over years. So, my memoir—*Where Beauty Survived*—contracted in 2015, begun in 2017—has materialized in 2021. In rapid succession, as we approach year's end, I'll publish my latest "colouring book"—or miscellany of poetry, *White* (#5 in this series since 2001), with Gaspereau Press; and then, only a few days or weeks apart, *J'Accuse…! (Poem* Versus *Silence).* Of this textual trio, "J'Accuse" took shape fastest. Unable to respond—i.e., unable to see a critical essay published as my riposte—to the vitriol hurled at me in the winter and spring of 2020 (and which persists, though the immediate, acidic tidal wave has receded to vinegary sprinkles), I decided to answer—in strong poetry—those who argued insanely that my unwitting assistance to a poet who murdered an Indigenous woman a quarter-century-plus ago, somehow made me an accomplice to the crime or a supporter of anti-Indigenous violence. Though I've penned "J'Accuse" with pure empathy for Indigenous peoples (I am one), I denounce—scathingly—the muck-throwing journalists and piss-the-bed profs who tried to blame an Afro-Métis poet for the evils dealt an Indigenous woman, *rather than* the bigoted, misogynist, Saskatchewan justice system, which explained away rape, downplayed murder, and assigned the killers to a Club Fed prison, from which they exited a mere 3.5 years after sentencing. So what am I working on now? The completion of "Canticles III" (for 2022 and 2023) and the writing of poems for the 6th "colouring book," "Green," due out—on schedule—God willing—in 2026! I've also been contracted by classical violinist Emmanuel Vukovich to pen the libretto for his musical project to correct Wagner's racist erasure of Parsifal's black brother, Feirefiz. On-the-go are commissions to composers to turn selected, Canuck poems into songs. Thus far, I've commissioned 13, and I hope for 2 CDs by 2 different composers (both Canadian) to result. But everything is in God's hands. I close with my fave Pound quotation: "The production IS the beloved" (Canto CIV).

October, 2021

Photo credit: Stephen MacGillivray

M. TRAVIS LANE

Laurence Hutchman: *You published your first poem when you were 11. When did you start writing, and at what time did you decide to become a poet? Were there particular books that inspired you as a child and provoked you to become a poet?*

Travis Lane: I started "composing" poems before I could write—because my family recited poems, sang songs, read poetry to me—*Mother Goose, A Child's Garden of Verses, The Little Small Red Hen, Johnny Crow's Garden,* etc.—the house is still full of children's books—and my sister has half of the books we had when we were kids. My father and his father told Uncle Remus stories, and my mother's father had a large repertoire of comic songs—and my mother recited poetry while we washed the dishes: favourites were Matthew Arnold and W.S. Gilbert.

LH: *Your parents were great storytellers. Can you talk about your mother and father and what influence they had on you when you were growing up? Were they supportive of your writing?*

TL: My parents very much supported my writing and poem making—my father had made a few poems himself, and mother had written some prose—both were fond of good books.

LH: *Your father was Colonel W.L. Travis in the United States Armed Forces. As a military family your parents moved yearly to different locations. How did this affect your childhood? Did you feel lonely not having a permanent place called home?*

TL: My family was widespread but personally close, most of them in Colorado or Georgia. We visited my grandparents, aunts, uncles, etc. frequently—so if I had no geographical "place" I did have a "place" in terms of family. People ask me often where was home, where was I brought up—I was brought up by books, and within a close knit if far sprung family—so I wasn't lonely—but have no "hometown/origin"—and had no long-time friends from early childhood, but instead a constant supply of new friends. Because my father was regular army air force, and because most of my childhood was mid-war, we moved almost annually: Maryland, Florida, Colorado, Texas, Connecticut, New York, Georgia, Hawaii, Alabama, and Okinawa. As an intellectual I was a bit "odd," but was always treated with friendliness, asked to edit the high school yearbook, invited into clubs, had a happy time!

LH: *In the poem "What I Remember, 1935," you talk about some of the scenes of the past. Do you have significant memories from your childhood?*
TL: Lots of memories but not a lot of stories.

LH: *You studied at Vassar College, a prestigious American college in Poughkeepsie, New York. It was the first degree-granting institution of higher education for women in the United States, whose alumnae included Edna St. Vincent Millay and Elizabeth Bishop. What was your experience as a student there working on your B.A.?*
TL: Oh, Vassar was wonderful! It was the first time I lived in a place where many others had read the sort of books I had read! I was active in the Outing Club—(overnights in the Adirondacks, country dancing, hiking)—and with the *Vassar Review*, (editing and contributing poetry). This was the era of folk songs and the whole outing club learned them and sang them, and "stuck to the union". I campaigned for Eisenhower

year one in fall, for Stevenson, after that, and have stayed happily Left ever since. I won Junior Phi Beta Kappa and they let me do as my senior's thesis a short novel (not in my opinion good enough to be published, but fun to write, semi-historical about the gold rush days in Colorado.)

Perhaps the most educational thing during my years at Vassar was the first summer when I signed into the Quaker led "Internes in Industry"—a chance to learn something about American history after 1860 (because that is when high school history shut up). We lived in a Baptist church upstairs rooms for a few weeks in the slums of Philadelphia, blacks and whites together (girls and boys separate). We looked for jobs in industry—learned that if I applied for a job with Willa (black) we neither of us got a job so we separated and she got a job with hat trimming and I got a job at pamphlet binding. We went to lectures about labour history, unions, Quakers, Zen Buddhism, etc. One evening, Philadelphia having said it was ok for people to give political speeches downtown in a square as long as we didn't impede traffic—some of us agreed to go down and help distribute leaflets against extending the Korean war into North Korea—long story, "my night in jail" (absolved eventually) too long (and rather funny) a story to put here! The best thing about Vassar was that at that time it was women only so I could argue as fiercely as I liked with anybody in class without feeling I was cutting down on possible dates. Also, with no men there was less vandalism and loutish drunkenness—boys do "lower the tone"—tho I feel that there is an advantage in having schools the way they are now—it early disillusions!

LH: *During your university years you were reading such poets as Elizabeth Bishop and Robert Lowell. What other poets did you find influential at this time?*

TL: At some point in my early adolescence I encountered a list of the 100 best books that an educated person should have read before going on to college—beginning with ancient Greek philosophers (in translation) and going on up through the 19th century. In addition an aunt, aware of my interest in great poetry, sent me the fashionably rediscovered works of Donne, Hopkins, and subsequently Thomas. Of course I read Browning and Dickinson and Arnold, and in college I took a course in great French poetry and a course in contemporary American poetry. I try to read the best there is, and sometimes have to content myself with translations, preferably with the original language on one side and the translations on the other—thus I became aware of Montale, Neruda, Rilke, Goethe, Tranströmer, Quasimodo etc. My desire is always to read the best there is when I can. I cannot say anything "individual" about the great writers nor can say anything sensible about the differences between languages, historical situations or aesthetic/spiritual concerns of these writers. I cannot define literary excellence.

LH: *You completed your M.A. thesis and Ph.D dissertation on Robert Frost. What you have in common with Frost is the importance of pastoral, that fine observation of nature, the drama of human characters, the wide scope of his interest—from the stones, plants, animals to the stars. What other aspects of Frost's poetry attracted you?*

TL: What continues to appeal to me in Frost's poetry is his understanding of the emotional sound of the sentence—to get that right without ever losing the sense of the language as normal rather than invented.

LH: *During your graduate studies at Cornell University, you were a section leader for the renowned literary critic M.H. Abrams and marking papers for the Russian novelist Vladimir Nabokov. Can you speak about any formative experiences there?*

TL: I much enjoyed working for Abrams and Nabokov but have no anecdotes about them—except that Nabokov wanted me to save really stupid answers on his tests so we could laugh about them. He said that nurses were his best readers and English graduate students his worst because nurses paid attention to the details the author wrote, but graduate student kept trying to find an abstract "meaning" and thus missing what was actually written! The Abrams and the Nabokovs were friendly and gracious and had us over for drinks.

LH: *Why did you come to Fredericton?*
TL: There were so many reasons—but this is one: my last two years of high school were spent at Clinton, Maryland near the Army Air force base where my father was stationed. My first year there—the high school (very small—graduating class about 30)—we had a history teacher who was absolutely marvellous and he encouraged me to do research in the Library of Congress (a bus ride away). But the not very good Home Economics teacher discovered that our history teacher had been some time ago on the Refreshment committee of the Communist Party in Pennsylvania, so she got him fired from the school and he was replaced by a fellow who placed firmly on his desk at the front of his room a book proving that the world was created in 3000 BC. This was one of the reasons I thought Canada would be a good place to live—but from time to time I worry.

LH: *When you emigrated from the United States in the 1960s with your husband, Dr. Lauriat Lane who accepted a position in the English Department at the University of New Brunswick in Fredericton was the transition difficult for you coming from New York State to New Brunswick, Canada?*

TL: Transiting from upper New York State to Fredericton was not difficult. We were made very welcome. It was restful in 1960 to abandon complex fictions of "the American dream" and the political hostilities of the time. We found Fredericton "laid back" and tolerant.

The real poets at UNB, Bailey, Gibbs, Cogswell (and later Bauer and Peter Thomas) admired my poetry, said so, gladly joined in readings with me, urged me to join the League of Canadian Poets, and knew I had published more than one book and had won the Pat Lowther prize for the 1980 collection. They were friends and very supportive.

LH: *You discovered a list of New Brunswick poets being taught in the department of English that had only one woman on it. How did you react?*

TL: In 1980-82 or thereabouts there was a chap who was teaching Maritime literature at that time who was not a writer, and apparently disinclined to discuss his subject with the local poets. He had printed out a list of Maritime poets for his students to read; my husband got hold of a copy and showed it to me asking what I thought. There was only one woman writer on the list: Betty Brewster, but there were several members of the current English department who had never published a book, but for whom Nancy Bauer had brought out a tiny chapbook. She had done chapbooks for a lot of folk in the English dept at that point. I went to the UNB library and collected a long list of women Maritime poets who had brought out books (not just chapbooks) and pinned that list up in the English department. I do not know if the fellow bothered to change his list.

LH: *You said, "I was once excluded from a list of NB poets on the grounds that I had not been brought up in NB."*

TL: The person who excluded me from a list of NB poets because I wasn't born here was not that chap, but a woman (and a non-poet).

LH: *Your house, which I was happy to visit on two occasions, is not far from the University of New Brunswick campus and close to the office of* The Fiddlehead *where you began to publish your poems and reviews. You have written over 120 book reviews, many of which have been reprinted in* Heart on Fist, *edited by Shane Neilson. Today there is a dearth of criticism and fewer outlets for it in newspapers and magazines. Why is it so necessary for you to review books?*

TL: More Canadian books of poetry are produced in one year than any one person can read attentively—and as you say there are very few places for reviews. I notice that some people use Facebook to report on books they have enjoyed, but I can't follow all 100 of my "friends" on Facebook. There are internet magazines that do reviews, but I can't keep up with them either. The best we can do, when we read a good book, is to let other people know how good it is. Share the joy!

LH: *We all know the importance of translation, from the Greek and Latin classical literature to the King James Version of the Bible, Dante, Cervantes to Flaubert, Tolstoy, and Czesław Miłosz. The development of our culture depends upon the translation of distinguished writers into English. Without these works, we would live in a limited world. You have reviewed a number of books of translation, among them Tomas Tranströmer, Nichita Stănescu, and Hélène Dorion. How would you characterize a good translation? What kind of translator is the ideal one?*

TL: A good translation ideally should be a beautiful poem in the language in which it appears, and, also ideally should convey the mood and meaning of the original—and this is not always possible due to differences of sentence sound, grammar, and literary resonances/quotations. Often we settle for a translation that leans toward accuracy in translating literal meaning and does not try to attempt the musicality and particular form of the original poem.

LH: *When I asked Al Purdy a question about the influence of writers on his work, he said, "Don't you ever wonder how you happen to be writing the way you are and who influenced you and whether you submerged those influences or not?" I'm curious what particular Canadian poets and international poets influenced you?*

TL: I wished to study and write about a major poet, a poet about whom I thought I could say something useful that had not yet been said—and whose style would not "rub off on me" in a way to make my own poetry sound stylistically derivative. A poet with a strongly unusual style is best not, however unintentionally, imitated. I chose to write my MA and PhD on Frost because I felt that whoever I studied that closely would very much influence my own writing. I did not want to find myself imitating. An imitation of the highly stylized and distinctive poetry of Stevens, Eliot, Thomas, etc. would be pretty repulsive.

LH: *Looking back now at your long and very productive career, all the ups and downs which are part of our existence as poets, can you talk about the turning point when you realized that you were accepted as a writer in Canada and you had an audience?*

TL: I don't know if there was such a thing as a turning point. Getting the Pat Lowther prize in 1981 was certainly cheering. Good reviews certainly help. The articles by Lynes, Zwicky, and especially Neilson certainly are wonderfully reassuring.

LH: *What was it like living among a community of writers connected to the English Department at the University of New Brunswick?*

TL: I taught only briefly at UNB, never taught creative writing, have only twice been asked to sit in on a MFA defense and have only been asked to address creative writing classes by Cogswell and Finlay, once each, at UNB, and by McConnell and Moore several times at STU. I like to go to poetry readings and book launchings, especially if they are not late and set in noisy bars, but I am not a member of a writers' "group" though I am a member of the Writers' Federation of New Brunswick and the League of Canadian Poets. I don't give or attend workshops. I have several poet friends, here and in other parts of Canada.

My community is mostly women: nature, gardens, history, conservation clubs, Presbyterian/United church, Voice of Women for Peace, Raging Grannies.

LH: *Alden Nowlan suggested that Maritime poets were cut off from the rest of Canada and were neglected. Do you think that this is still the case?*

TL: There are times when I think many people think that if you are a good writer you will naturally want to live in Major City where you will be able to give frequent readings and become acquainted with similar Major City poets. If you are really important you will lecture at Harvard and shop in New York City—if you can't do that you may have to settle for Toronto. Consider how many folks automatically refer to a Maritime city as "sleepy".

LH: *During the 70s and 80s there were many debates about feminist issues. Women were under-represented in the League of Canadian Poets. You once observed that there was only one woman* *represented on a list of Maritime poets at UNB. You felt the injustice of the exclusion of women writers. How important was the feminism movement for you? How has feminism changed over the last few years?*

TL: Feminism has been central to me—my father was a feminist and encouraged his daughters, hired women lawyers—my mother and her mother and her sister were feminist. Over the years the concerns of feminism have broadened to include awareness of and demands for justice issues for other previously snubbed, ignored, or denigrated genders, races, cultures, religions, disabilities.

LH: *You have suggested that the subject is not as important as the technical aspects of a poem such as syntax, metre, and sound. Why is sound so essential in a poem?*

TL: Many excellent poems constructed for the eye alone exist, but I tend to find them less appealing than poems which concern themselves with the sound and shape of language. The sound of a poem is language as language: i.e. sentences meant to communicate, not as bits and pieces—the echo and chime of rhyme or alliteration can be pleasing—but what matters is the emotional thrust. The English language involves not only stress, but also time (some short syllables are shorter than others)—and pitch. The dramatic situation, the sentence chosen—all will affect pitch. Syllable count is an amusement—but since English syllables are not all the same weight and length, counting syllables is irrelevant to poetic music in English. Patterns of stress, weight, repetition, syntax—all can be amusing or useful—but every poem needs its own sound, its own development—the words should be arranged as they are because that is the only way they can say what needs to be said.

LH: *The historical events in the poem "For the Cenotaph, November 11, 1983" are important to you. In the poem "For Brigid" you speak of Maritime life tracing the history of an abandoned house. There is an elegiac tone in this poem; the last line expresses this feeling: "We have lost our place." Do you feel that poets have a responsibility to preserve the essence of the past?*

TL: Recollection of the past is a very common theme in all poetry—also common, as in "For Brigid" is the theme of the past seen as past, not as remembered but as realized, alien, present, but no longer ours. Poets, prose writers, painters, historians, musicians—all may concern themselves with the essence of the past, but we are not obliged to.

LH: *Many of your poems are journeys or explorations. There is this sense of discovering, of moving or even leaping from one image or metaphor to another, which Brian Bartlett uses the adjective "gymnastic" to describe. Can you speak about this idea of poems as exploration?*

TL: A poem may explore itself—asking why does this image or this idea seem important, what does it suggest, should the original thought be questioned, etc. Such poems have no controlling argument, but are instead the record of discovery.

LH: *How does a poem come to you? Is it a thought, a phrase, a rhythm? From which place does the poem originate?*

TL: There are so many different things that might start a poem, and I don't always remember what starts a particular poem, nor does the starter necessarily stay in the poem. Occasionally I remember what started a poem, but usually I don't—and the start is rarely of great interest—I start lots, but not all hatch.

LH: *Sometimes your poems seem phenomenological. In the poem "Upon the Forcible Entry by Cat into a Poem Originally Upon Trilliums" you write with immediacy when the cat becomes an integral part of your thoughts about poetry. Does this often happen where the poem suddenly and in a surprising way becomes something else?*

TL: I want poems to be read as if existing in real time between real people—and thus they can be interrupted sometimes.

LH: *Poets find that the first draft is still far from the final form of the poem and they spend much time rewriting it. How much do you revise your poems?*

TL: I revise my poems often, sometimes for many years. *I don't* change my poems after I have got them to publishable condition and I do not save old copies of poems in process—the house is small and there would be no room for boots or canned tomatoes if I saved earlier versions. I do a lot of revisions. I do not know what I could say about how I know when a poem at last is finished—I do not keep old examples of works in progress.

LH: *"This is no wall or country that I weave/ but a plain language you can't read/ unless you bruise your knuckles," you wrote in "Gold Fleece." Your poems have many levels and I'm reminded of the poems of Ralph Gustafson and Margaret Avison in their richness and complexity. It takes time to read them. I find this process very rewarding.*

TL: I do not "make my poems difficult to read." Most people read poetry very little—and mostly prefer to read simple anecdotal poems giving a conventional take on a conventional subject. What makes a poem seem "difficult" is that it is not what the reader would have written or said—so it demands that it be paid attention to. I think people in the habit of reading major poetry are less often confronted by modern poems they think are "difficult" to read. Perhaps my attitude is not the attitude they think I ought to have!

Nabokov, talking about fiction, once said something that I think is also true about poetry—he said nurses were better readers than English graduate students because nurses paid attention to the details but grad students kept trying to "interpret". When I taught West Indian poets here at UNB one year to a batch of graduate students, I found them very peculiar. Twice on two different occasions I asked them what a long poem by Walcott, and then a long poem by Braithwaite, was about. They looked blank, and after an embarrassing pause, suggested "passion"—except the political student who suggested "colonialism." The Walcott poem was about the burning of a city, the Braithwaite about the burning of cane fields. There was nothing difficult about either poem. But there was something very strange about the graduate students.

I think that a poem that seems "difficult" may be merely not what the reader wanted, or had got used to. It is a little like music. I was astonished to learn in college that although my father loved the old spirituals, he did not like " the blues"— and I have a friend who loves fiddle music but can't endure that master fiddler Vivaldi! If the reader pays attention to the details, listens for the emotional sound of the sentences, and "gets the mood" he or she is understanding the poem. I am not writing to be interpreted. I am writing about how thought feels. The only way not to understand my poems is to resist the sound, the imagery, the viewpoint. Perhaps my allusions to other literature may make a poem difficult to those who don't recognize the allusions—if I refer to blind Pew's black spot or Porthos's cloak—this may be difficult for people who don't want to encounter anything unfamiliar (tho they could look up blind Pew or Porthos—what pleasures await them!) It is also true that some of the moods I explore are not currently fashionable—which does not mean they are not there, but only that they are not being noticed—the "headline" approach is pretty shallow—or if you don't like that phrase, how about "be sure to look under the chair?"

Sometimes problems can turn up when the reader's expectations and the author's intentions are not the same. In my three part "'Divinations" the first section "Nothing" is spoken by an adolescent who finds hell in the apple orchard regions of upstate New York. The third section, "The Book of the Thrones," is spoken by a middle-aged woman who finds paradise in Saint John. The middle part, "Red Earth," is spoken by a young woman who finds herself useless, and her life meaningless, while her husband studies the Indigenous practices of the people in a small reserve in northern New Brunswick.

Her life is perceived by herself as a sort of limbo. She is full of good intentions and misinformation, and does, in the course of the poem correct some of her initial misperceptions. She doesn't "fit in" the life of the community, and she perceives the community itself as not "fitting in" contemporary life. She fantasizes about the community and has a number of visions in which she imagines her neighbours somehow escape to a greater reality, and ends with an imagined escape (rebirth) for herself.

This limbo section of "Divinations" has been disapproved of by reviewers who find the opinions of the poetic speaker old-fashioned, out-of-date, prejudiced and the speaker's observations romantic and inaccurate. Well, of course! Just as "Nothing" is not an accurate description of upstate New York but instead a description of the speaker's perceptions, and "The Book of the Thrones " is not an accurate picture of Saint John, but instead a description of the speaker's state of mind.

LH: *In your poem "Reader" you say, "I am your reader, reader, write. / You write for me." Can you expand on this?*

TL: I think of the reader as someone close to me, sharing my feelings or at least listening to them, and I feel that my reader has something sometimes to say to me—the relationship is personal even tho I have no imagined one person to represent that reader—that reader is "you".

LH: *What would you like your legacy to be?*

TL: My poetry, what else?

June 25, 2018

Photo credit: Unknown

JOHN B. LEE

First Interview (1992)

Laurence Hutchman: *In 1987, you resigned from teaching. What prompted you to give up that position?*
John B. Lee: Well it's quite simple. When I was very young, I could be inspired whenever I wanted to be and then I finished university and started working. And I was young enough to burn the candle at both ends. We had no kids. Then our first boy was born and I could write at night and early in the morning; then the second boy was born and I couldn't write in the morning or at night because as soon as I stepped on the floor, the boards creaked and it woke him up. And I got to an age where I was going to have to give up expending some energy in one direction or another direction. And we were at a point in our lives where we could afford for me to quit teaching. So I quit in order to dedicate myself full time to writing, see if I could make a go of it.

LH: *Why did you begin to write?*
JBL: The Beatles! As simple as that. I remember 1964, the first time I saw the Beatles on television. I had never heard of them and my uncle said, "The Beatles are on Ed Sullivan. Aren't you going down and watch it?" And I thought who needs another Topo Gigio. And it was like somebody had lifted the veils from my eyes. I was born.

LH: *What about them triggered you?*

JBL: The words, I think. And the energy … and I felt like I was becoming part of a movement. There are a lot of things mixed up together. Puberty was hitting me at the same time. I started getting interested in girls. But, I think they were just incredibly inspired, energetic people and I wanted somehow to get attached to that.

LH: *While you were an undergraduate at the University of Western Ontario, you took a course with James Reaney. Did he have any influence on your perception of your region and on your writing?*

JBL: When I took Reaney's course the second time, I took it at a graduate level and he was telling us that what he was trying to develop in us was a sensibility. And I think maybe the reason Reaney had an influence on me was that he was talking to somebody who was already one of the converted. What he did for me was give me another way of making legitimate what I was already doing. He reminded me that there were other writers out there in touch with the land—everything comes from the earth, digging down, looking out. Reaney's course drew in music; it drew in the sound of thunder. Stan Dragland read a poem in class one time and the rattapallax of the thunder came through in the background. Everything was game for the experience of the poem. And that's what I liked about Reaney's course; it's all connected with the land, with the earth, and it all comes out of somewhere. Poets are living, breathing human beings.

LH: *Also, while you were at Western, you met Stan Dragland.*

JBL: Yeah, Stan was the tutor that I had when I took Reaney's course. Stan is one of those incredibly gentle people who is brilliant and yet is able to put his insights into such simple language and I found him incredibly appealing. Stan is one of the best teachers that I ever had; James Reaney is another, and Don Gutteridge, a poet over at Althouse College. And I would say those are the three best teachers that I ever had. They certainly had the strongest influence on me, and not on me as a writer as much as on me as a reader, and on me as a thinker, and a teacher of other people because they had such generosity of spirit.

LH: *In your poems you refer to Dylan Thomas, Al Purdy, Irving Layton, Milton Acorn and Margaret Avison. Did these writers influence you?*

JBL: Oh, definitely, and all of them in different ways. I suppose I should have mentioned Michael Ondaatje too, because *The Collected Works of Billy the Kid* had a very dramatic and remarkable influence on me. In fact, I think it irked me on to do, to go … not to go one better, because how does one go one better than that book, but to try to accomplish something of the same. The first influence was Dylan Thomas. What really impressed me was the first time I read "Fern Hill." That poem just made the hair stand up on the back of my neck. So I immediately went out and looked in the library to find anything I could on Thomas. I discovered his *Collected Poems* when I was about seventeen. Then I started reading everybody I could discover in my high school library. Layton was there. Layton was full of things that were surprising to me. I don't think I liked the obvious vulgarity in some of his work—the imitation of Catullus and that kind of thing. But I remember reading "Keine Lazarovitch" and thinking, "Wow, this is brilliant. I want to do this."

LH: *How about Al Purdy and Milton Acorn?*

JBL: I discovered that there's a lot of common ground between Purdy's work and my work. I remember being influenced by

Owen Roblin. There's an image in Owen Roblin of the ghosts of the builders of the barn. There's a beautiful poem that he wrote about a girl and lilacs and the twenty-third of May, and "Caribou Horses." All these poems are wonderful, but I came to Purdy when I think my own voice was already developed, so I wasn't really so much influenced by him as an admirer of his. And likewise Acorn. I came to Acorn fairly late, around the time of *More Poems for People*.

LH: *Margaret Avison is a different case for you.*
JBL: Yes, Margaret Avison was a wonderful example for me. She was writer in residence in '73 at the University of Western Ontario and I think I was at that point just writing some of my first poems. I was on the verge of discovering my voice and she was incredibly generous with me. She was very complimentary and careful. She said what she liked and what she didn't like. I was like all young writers, full of hubris, full of myself thinking, "I'm doing *it* now. I'm really doing it." At the same time, it was an incredibly fragile hubris, like all hubris, and I suspect hubris is always fragile and hollow. I could have been devastated if she had been a different kind of person.

LH: *I'd like to move now to some questions concerning technique. How does a poem begin for you?*
JBL: There are several ways in which poems begin for me. My favourite way that they begin is with the first line. I really like it when the first line comes to me, because then I know that it's going to be an inspired thrill from beginning to end. Usually, that's what happens when I get the first line and it just makes my ear sit up and pay attention—there's music in that first line. "The swallows used to swoop the cats, but all the cats are gone." I heard that in my ear and I saw the image of that in my mind's eye. Sometimes it's more journeyman-like

than that. I sit down and I have an idea of what I want to write about. For instance one of the recent pieces I wrote concerned a story that came to me after I'd finished *Variations on Herb*. My father told me a story about when he was driving my grandfather away from the Canadian National Exhibition in Toronto and he was in a bumper-to-bumper traffic jam. They were packed in this car, three in the front and three in the back. My grandfather, sitting in the middle of this traffic jam said, "Stop this car, George, I wanna git in the trunk and git myself some cheese. I'm feeling kind of hungry." And he was serious. He was that kind of selfish person, oblivious to the whole world, a genuine eccentric. Not only do I like the story, but I like the lilt of that line. So that was a gift that was given to me. Now, rather than it being inspired, I've got a kind of journeyman's task of sitting down and writing it and hopefully it will come. I didn't know whether it was going to be a poem or a short prose piece. It ended up being like a snapshot fiction piece.

LH: *Does it ever come in another way, such as a visual image or an idea?*
JBL: Usually when it comes as an idea, it's bad. I'm unsatisfied with it because I don't like the poetry of ideas. Not that my poems aren't about something, but I'd rather that they suggest their theme based on an image or a metaphor or a brief narrative rather than an idea.

LH: *In your work, there's a special concern for dissonant sound, onomatopoeia, unusual diction and unpredictable imagery. What are the important elements in the poem for you?*
JBL: Well first and foremost in all the poetry that I read and in all the poetry that I write, I want the ear to sit up and pay attention. I love the way language sounds. In a book called

When Words Sing a child was asked to define poetry, and the child said, "Poetry is when words sing." Joe Rosenblatt, I heard him say in a classroom one time, that "if there's no music, there's no poetry." Now, you mentioned imagery as well, or startling imagery. I can trace that back to something that my English teacher said in Grade 13. It was an epiphany for me and I think it pushed me to make my poetry better. It also made me recognize what I liked best in other poets of the time. It didn't occur to me until this teacher said it. Commenting on Leonard Cohen, he said what he liked about Cohen was the unusual nature of his imagery and the unusual connections he made between things. He was talking about metaphor.

LH: *What about rhythm?*

JBL: I come at that through the ear too. When I came across The Beatles, about Grade 7, I wrote rhyming verse. Most of the poetry that you read when you're in grade 6 to 10, even Grade 11, most of it is rhyming verse. So I wrote a lot of rhyming verse and I wrote a lot of imitations. I discovered I had a real ear for it and a facility, almost a felicity for a natural rhyme and a natural sense of rhythm. When I teach rhythm to young people, I always come at it from da-da, da-da, da-da, da-da point of view. You don't count, you get it in your heart and in your head. You don't have to count the sounds; you know when it's wrong because it sounds wrong, not because you've counted out the fact that you need five iambs in a line. I even talk to my students about rhythm in conversation. They think that if it's not metric, if it's not regular, then it's not rhythmical.

LH: *Do you find that often when it sounds right, then the rhythm and the image and the idea are right also?*

JBL: Well, hopefully I get better from book to book. I don't want there to come a point when I've stopped developing. I guess the very first book that I think was fully realized as a book was *Hired Hands*.

LH: *I think* Hired Hands *is a turning point for you. I think it's more focused.*

JBL: Yes. Tom Sheil Malott, the subject of the book, was my father's hired hand, and had been there on the farm since my father was a boy, and was still there after I left home and went off to university. I realized about the middle of that book that it was going to be something quite special. For another thing, it was a story. To quote Margaret Avison who wrote me a letter about it, "It was a story that just had to be told." It only occurred to me about halfway through how it was such a startling thing to me. Why didn't I realize that this man needed to be written about, I mean, it's so obvious. It's to legitimize the fact that I would write about my childhood, write about the farm that I grew up on.

LH: *You said something interesting there about the microcosm and the farm. Don McKay frequently interchanges the urban with the pastoral and gets striking effects. The same thing occurs in* The Pig Dance Dreams *where you bring the larger life into the farm in different ways.*

JBL: I've written a poem since the Black Barns trilogy called "These Are the Days of Dogs and Horses" and I've come to the conclusion that because this is an increasingly urban society we have to maintain our contact with the soil and with the animal world in order to keep us sane, in order to hold us to those things that are eternal: the earth and the sky and the natural world. It's important and it's important beyond the urban pets and domesticated animals in that actually some of their nature is changed, and you see awful things like the Disneyfication, anthropomorphising of the animal world. Well I do that to a certain degree in the Black Barn's trilogy by turning it into a fable, but it's with a very different intention and with a very different vision of the world of animals and the world of human beings in mind. I think that there's really a lot of nasty things happening to the human race because we've lost touch with the land. And I don't mean that everybody should go back the way they did in the sixties to the farm and flirt with that because there is a dullness in routine and country living that I wanted to escape desperately. I think Purdy's "Caribou Horses" is about the way in which we have to maintain touch with the animal world and the natural world.

LH: *Can you give an example of the genesis of one of your poems?*
JBL: Sure. One of my favourite poems that I've written is "Events Have a Way." It's a poem about the sixties. An old Polish fellow got it all started when he told me a story about being out in the channel behind his cottage in Turkey Point and catching a dogfish and the dogfish pulling the boat along. So there's this image of being pulled by the dogfish that I knew happened in the sixties. There were the Beatles landing in New York City with smiles on their faces, waving to the screaming crowd and Murray the K talking a mile a minute about the Beatles' arrival in New York. There was another fellow I met at a Dresden fair, this young fellow named Philip who was a friend of a friend, an American. He was eighteen and he was just going off to boot camp and then he was off to Vietnam. And I think to myself: "Here's this little isolated world, Southwestern Ontario, Dresden, the fair. Here's Turkey Point, the dogfish. Here's Vietnam, here's New York City, here's a concert in Detroit." Another thing that came into the poem … (*a bird just hit the window and died while John*

is talking). You know, that's what I mean. I wanted to see how it all connected, the private and the public, the personal and the universal, so I sat down to write this poem called "Events Have a Way."

LH: *Your work sometimes has multiple perspectives, as you try to empathize not only with people and animals but things.*
JBL: I think every event that happens to a person needs to be turned over and over and over and thought about. For instance, in *The Pig Dance Dreams*, there's an image that I keep thinking of and that is the connection between the Sunday dinner ham and the family celebration and the killing tree. For most people, that inability to isolate the horror of the one image from the beautiful reality of the other image would drive them mad. So much so, that many people resent the vividness of my work and think that I'm trying to drag them into the abattoir all the time.

LH: *But that's what Conrad says a writer's role is, to make us see.*
JBL: I think so. And actually that's one of the things I am grateful to poetry for. I don't mean just from the point of view of reading it, I mean from the point of view of writing it. Writing is a discovery and a rediscovery of things that I already knew, but forgot, or that I never knew or that I didn't really know that I knew. Poetry is more profound than conversation.

LH: *You mentioned the book* Variations on Herb. *You create unusual perspectives of your grandfather. It reminds me at times of an ironic elegy, the sense of Purdy's elegies for his grandfather.*
JBL: Yes, and at the beginning of the book, I admit quite frankly that when my grandfather was alive, I could hardly wait for him to die. At the end of the book I talk about missing him despite it all. And I realize that he was fully alive,

warts and all. My mother has put it quite simply. He was already too old when I was born, which is one of the reasons why I didn't make the kind of connection that you usually associate with a grandfather.

LH: *You give a wonderful celebration of him, a recreation of him.*
JBL: Oh yes. That's what I think is similar to *Hired Hands*. I think you have to be totally honest about the people that you portray, especially if they're real people as opposed to fictional people. Now, of course, in both cases, even more so in *Variations on Herb*, I've had to make things up. I've had to invent. I think it's the case that some of my relatives won't forgive me because they'll miss the celebration. That story in *Variations on Herb*, about my grandfather being thrown in jail, I heard that from my eighty-year-old cousin in Regina. I wrote her a letter and I said that my father had already told me a few quaint stories, but he's not really telling me any of the stories to show me the fully rounded Herb. And I said, "Do you have any letters around that your older sister had in correspondence with Herb?" She told me a couple of stories, one about him singing to the sheep after he'd had a few jars and people starting to gather and watch this man singing to the sheep at the Royal Winter Fair, and the other story about my grandfather being thrown in jail. That's the kind of story that I think some people would have repressed or hidden.

LH: *You deny the history then.*
JBL: Yes, exactly. I think we do that. I think we Canadians have a tendency, if we're looking for a folk story, to sit around in conversation in a living room and with a big grin on our faces, tell one another stories. But it mustn't go outside of the family. It can't be put in a book.

LH: *It's the whole suppression of memory.*

JBL: Yes, suppression of memory, except for those things that are flattering to the family. My great grandfather was an M.L.A. That's all I know about him. The only thing I know. Or so and so had his picture hung in the Agriculture Hall of Fame. That's all I know about him. If I hadn't known my grandfather, that's all I would know.

LH: *So, you're exploring the more interesting side of him.*

JBL: Yes. And I was also exploring my own contradictory feelings about my grandfather. I think that's true of everything that you write. It kind of blends an exploration of self in with an exploration of somebody else's story.

LH: *Even though you have long since left, the farm it has remained the vital source of your poetry. You have devoted individual books to specific domestic animals:* Rediscovered Sheep, The Bad Philosophy of Good Cows, The Pig Dance Dreams.

JBL: And even something like "The Beatles Landed Laughing in New York," which is about The Beatles, about the sixties and about art, and music and literature and events and movies … When I first started writing that I was trying to write something that would be a grand commentary on the sixties, and it wasn't going well. Then I wrote a poem called "Jimi Hendrix in The Company of Cows." And I realized that it was another occasion when I was going back and mixing all these apparently disparate elements together.

LH: *How old were you when you began to realize how important the farm was?*

JBL: *Hired Hands!* It was 1986. It was written in '85, so it wasn't so very long ago. I was over thirty. And it was *Hired Hands* that gave me that gift. I'd always written a little bit about the farm.

LH: *When I think of the books in the trilogy* The Pig Dance Dreams *most effectively integrates the outside world with the farm.*

JBL: I think it's a combination of two or three things. It makes a greater leap out of the barnyard than the other two books. It's because it's about pigs. And I think pigs work that way best as a metaphor because pigs are brighter, and closer to human beings. That's one reason why I think it makes a greater leap.

LH: *You know that Winston Churchill liked pigs?*

JBL: No, I didn't.

LH: *He thought they were the most egalitarian of animals.*

JBL: I hated pigs. You think about it when you're living with animals on the farm. You would think, based on this example, that I would like sheep the best, because they're the least amount of work. I always liked cattle the best of the three animals. I found myself more affectionate towards cattle than any of them. But I disliked pigs because, for one thing they're very smart and they can outsmart you. For another thing, they're a lot of work because you farm them more intensively than you do the other two. So I wasn't a big fan of pigs back then.

LH: *How did the Black Barns trilogy come about?*

JBL: It's really quite a bizarre story. I was just finished writing a manuscript that eventually became the book *Small Worlds*. I was between books.

LH: *In fact, "Pig Dance Dreams" is in that.*

JBL: Yes, the original copy of the poem "Pig Dance Dreams" is in *Small Worlds*. I was a graduate student at the University of Western Ontario. I'm walking down the road, and all of a sudden the words "rediscovered sheep" seem emblazoned on the sky. The *Rediscovered Sheep* book was finished in manuscript form, submitted, and accepted before I even thought of the Black Barns trilogy as a trilogy. Then, I was down on the beach here at Peacock Point with my friend Roger and he said, "What are you working on now?" I had written a poem called "The Bad Philosophy of Good Cows" along with a lot of different poems. I was making this up as I went along. I said, "I'm writing a book about cows." It was almost a discovery to me when I said that out loud. He said, "Oh yeah, what's it called?" and I said: "It's going to be called *The Bad Philosophy of Good Cows*. In fact, I'm writing a trilogy."

LH: *Another beach epiphany.*
JBL: Yes, another beach epiphany. Where's the bird girl? And that's basically how the whole thing got started. Then I was writing about pigs and I remember that I'd written this poem about pigs in *Small Worlds* and I lifted it out, put it in the book and I thought, "That's a great title for the book, *The Pig Dance Dreams*."

LH: *Could you talk about one of the poems in* The Pig Dance Dreams, *"Pig Roast."*
JBL: Yes, I really like that poem.

LH: *It's a very structured poem.*
JBL: That structure occurred to me quite naturally. I can remember as I was writing it liking the repetition "And the door clapped once/ and the door clapped twice/ in the house on the hill near the field by the road …" and those prepositions. Afterwards, when I looked back, I realized how intricate and lovely that image was. It wasn't as if I was constructing it on any conscious level. I just remember as I was writing it thinking about those images occurring quite naturally. It's like the

way the sound clap of the clap of the door travels. The door clapped once and the sound travels out, and the door clapped twice and the sound of the door clapping. It's a really beautiful sound, the sound of a wooden screen door clapping shut. Somebody is either arriving home or somebody is going out.

LH: *You try to imitate sound.*

JBL: I also wanted that kind of peaceful, soft, breathy feel that you have when you eat outdoors. If you eat indoors, it's usually wintertime and the windows are all shut and it's a quiet room and it's a dining room and you're after certain things when you write about them. I think there's something very different about eating out of doors. But also involved in that, the whole poem, is the fact that there was a woman who committed suicide who wasn't at the pig roast, and I felt the presence of her ghost, the presence of the tragedy that led up to that. There's a very grotesque aspect to a pig roast, the pig with the sharpened point in the heart of his head coming out through his mouth and turning on the spit. So there's this whole celebration in the quiet little clicks and clinks and conversations taking place everywhere. And the breeze blowing. There's a ritual there like "a priest / who bends to blow a candle out" in that line. And the fact that it's haunted by the ghost of this woman and the tragedy of this woman and in a sense, everybody is there celebrating on this particular day in one way or another escaping the fact of her death, but for me it was there, that ghostly presence. It was a like a softened gothic.

LH: *Another source of your poetry has been your ancestors. In* Love Among the Tombstones, *you write, "I am a house people live in."* *It's an important phrase for you.*

JBL: Yes, and I think every person is inhabited by the generations of people in their own family and in their own community who came before them and I feel it's my responsibility to sing their stories and I'm grateful for the fact that I grew up with people who valued story. When the tractor was shut down and you were sitting in the quiet field under the shade tree, people told stories. When you sat at the kitchen table, people told stories about one another, about the war, about their fathers and mothers and the generations that came before them. And with the JBL family especially, there is this sense of a tradition; it goes back to the century farm and a legacy there. That land has been in the family for five generations. So, there's always the sense of the people that came before you and the people that came before them, and the people that came before them, etc.

LH: *Let's move on to a different subject. Thomas Kinsella and other writers have written with originality about baseball. What qualities of our national sport did you want to express in* The Hockey Player Sonnets?

JBL: Maybe "aspects" would be a better word because qualities suggest that there's something to be admired. I think there's a lot to be admired in the sport of hockey. I love to play the game of hockey and always have loved to play it. So, I want to capture that. I want to capture the idea of being an outsider from the point of view of playing the game. I was never very good at it. I'm still not very good at it, but I love to play. I'm outside of the lucky circle of blessed people with grace in their bodies, and who are fascinating to meet.

LH: *Not like that other Brantford native.*

JBL: (laughter) Yes … Wayne Gretzky. Unlike Wayne Gretzky. The people who have grace in the game. They amaze me. I played one game with the NHL Old Timers.

LH: *That must have been a highlight.*

JBL: It was. I was tripped by Andy Bathgate. We were well away from the play—the play of the game—and Andy Bathgate was standing beside me. I mean, Andy Bathgate was a name that I knew as a child. And Andy Bathgate was standing there, very handsome, and skates on and we're away from the play.

LH: *Jack Palance of the ice.*

JBL: Yes, exactly (laughter). And he puts his stick between my legs and pulls my legs out from under me, looks down at me and says, "Keep your head up!" (laughter) And, I mean, that made the whole game for me. It made my life in hockey worthwhile ... just to be tripped once by Andy Bathgate. But there's another aspect of the game, an ugly aspect that I don't like and I was trying to capture that too and that is the people who use the game against you.

LH: *So hockey becomes another dialectic, another series of metaphors, complementary metaphors.*

JBL: Yeah, I hope so. Just as the Black Barn's Trilogy tries to leap beyond the farm and make the farm a metaphor for something much larger than what it is. I hope that what I have achieved in *The Hockey Player Sonnets* is something that will be interesting to someone whether they are interested in the game of hockey or not. It was interesting that you mentioned Kinsella's book. I don't have any interest in baseball as a player, or spectator at all, but I think *Shoeless Joe is* pure magic ... *The Thrill of The Grass* is pure magic. I loved those books.

LH: *I like the magic that you capture in the first poem about the time you finally hang up your skates.*

JBL: That's the sonnet, "Where will I winter when I'm old?"

LH: *Maybe it's because I just hung up my skates last winter.*

JBL: (laughter) Yes … Winter is my favourite season. Hockey is one of the reasons why it's my favourite season. The interesting thing I discovered when I wrote that book, I realized as I was piecing it together there's a different tone to the beginning and the end of the book. I realized afterwards one of the reasons for the tonal difference is because many of the earliest poems and a couple of the latest ones are about playing hockey outside, which is quite different. As I wrote in one poem, "When I was a Boy and the Farm Pond froze," "we'd go down with skates, puck and stick / and play in the burning wind for days." You're only limited by the size of the surface of the ice. Whereas if you play indoors, there's a sense of the game being confined and there being rules and you actually keep count of the number of goals that everybody scores, whereas if you just throw a couple of boots on the ice and …

LH: *In* Voices in the Peacock Stone, *you are concerned with history and place. How did this interest come about?*

JBL: Actually, I'm not concerned with history. I'm concerned with what history ignored or what history suppressed. I'm concerned with this story of the losers. I've discovered much over the course of doing the research for the book and I've come to the conclusion that recorded history is the story or the biography of the winners. How did I come to this story? I just lucked upon it. Peacock Point is where we have our cottage, where we're sitting right now. I always wonder wherever I go, I want to know about the names of the place. I wondered how did this place get its name. And I ask around and nobody knows! Everybody speculates. I hear from one person: "Oh, I hear there were wild peacocks around here." A couple of people suggested that somebody was a spy, or a rum runner, or a pirate way back in the early nineteenth century. That intrigued me. I said to myself: "Why wouldn't these people know what's behind the name of this place?" It was very exciting to uncover little bits of a story that in some ways is so awful. As it turned out Peacock Point was named after a squatter, George Peacock, whose son, George Peacock Jr., was one of eight men hanged, drawn and quartered for the crime of High Treason during the war of 1812. I think it was repressed because we were ashamed of what we did to those men. The people at one time saw it as necessary, but then we buried it. It became a forbidden story. It's really a story about men with no land. And I think that, finally, almost every conflict in human history has been about land.

LH: *Although your poems are often concerned with tragic events, there is also in them a strong presence of humour, compassion, and vision. Can the poet be affirmative in today's world?*
JBL: I don't think a poet can be otherwise. You celebrate life. You see, I think of myself as a person who happens to be a poet and it's as important to me to live a life that's positive and life-affirming as it is to write well. And I think that's what is reflected in my poetry. It couldn't be otherwise. This is a celebration of who we are, warts and all. This is a celebration of ancestors, a celebration of self, a celebration of the people that I love. I had no intention of even flirting with anything less.

Peacock Point, Ontario
July 23, 1992

Second Interview: May 14, 2020

LH: *The last time that we spoke in our first interview, we were both younger and looking to find new means of developing our poetic voice. You have published more than 70 books, won 80 literary awards, including the prestigious CBC Literary Award (twice). The People's Poetry Award, (twice) and published in over 500 magazines. Could you tell us what was the biggest challenge in your writing career?*

JBL: *1) Waking up to Wordsworth*

> *Yes, my guard stood hard when abstract threats too noble*
> *   to neglect*
> *Deceived me into thinking I had something to protect*
> *Good and bad, I define these terms quite clear, no doubt,*
> *   somehow*
> *Ah, but I was so much older then I'm younger than that now*
>   From the song *"My Back Pages,"* Bob Dylan

The biggest challenge for me as a writer—is now, was then, and has always been the obstacle created by living in what is an essentially anti-intellectual culture. As a writer, as a person, I have changed and evolved and become someone other than the person who wrote the poems I wrote at the time they were written. If aging involves a dulling of cognition, as it is with a weakening of the eyes, a dampening of the ears, a numbing of the senses of smell and taste, thereby making exigent the spicing of food and the giving of Scotch as a gift to the palate, and the desires of the flesh become less sharp when the lasciviousness of youth fades into old desire more easily satisfied and less frequently felt. If that is the case, then there's also the consolation of memory as a profound reward taking precedence over plans for the future. Imagining the past in service of deep need takes the place of anticipating the wonderful things yet to come. As Faulkner once wrote: "The past is not dead; the past is not even the past." I suppose I might describe what is happening within me as *waking up to Wordsworth.*

This past summer, my wife and I made a journey to England beginning in Liverpool thereby fulfilling a lifelong dream of walking the streets of the city where John, Paul, George and Ringo spent the halcyon days of their youth. We travelled from there to visit Wordsworth's home at Dove Cottage on the edge of Grasmere in the Lake District. And I woke to the walker. I woke to the contemplative reflection of a man who had seemed rather dull to my younger self, as though for the first time I began to understand what he had meant when he wrote "Poetry is the spontaneous overflow of powerful feelings: it takes its origin from emotion recollected in tranquility." And for my part I wrote a couple of poems inspired by the experience of waking to Wordsworth. The one written at Dove Cottage, the one with smoke and damp fire in the words began:

> *I have stood*
> *in the living light*
> *of a common day*
> *considering the small darkness*
> *of Dove Cottage*
> *wishing upon the flagstone floor*
> *and contemplating*
> *the hard-to-see*
> *spirit of Wordsworth*
> *dead these many years ...*

> lines from my poem "In the Living Light of a Common Day" in the book *My Sister Rides a Sorrow Mule (Beret Days Book, 2020)*

However, to return to the culture into which my poems fall as created in need of the educated imagination of a reader/re-creator, this culture and the readers it produces are increasingly problematic when the twin toxins of the dumbing down of formal education and the dulling of the mind that occurs with the increasing time spent surfing the internet, these trouble me. There's a joke I like. The question "What is the problem with instant gratification?" is answered by: "It just takes too damned long." And when people flip open their phones to seek an answer to some trivial question, the entire point of inquiry is missed. The peripheral, the incidental, the accidental, the random discovery of things along the way, these things that reward the searcher, like going to the stacks in the library, or thumbing through a dictionary, these aspects of discovery are lost by the Pavlovian reward of the right answer. We salivate when a bell is rung. What about the wonderful meandering that comes with simply wandering in the wilderness in search of whatever comes your way. And of course, Frye was correct when he wrote of the educated imagination. When poetry is not taught in school poetry may well still produce a new generation of poetasters. But I'm not interested in appealing to someone who hasn't read the poets from Gilgamesh to the Nobel Laureate Robert Zimmerman. That is the great challenge. How to awaken the deep reader in a culture that doesn't read.

LH: *The style in your poems is very recognizable: the enjambment of lines, the use of nouns as verbs, the appearance of exotic words in unexpected places, startling lines, startlingly original metaphors. Why did you move away from more traditional forms of poetry? How did you develop your unique style?*
JBL: All the Work is in the Style

Susan Sontag wrote "all the work is in the style." As for my own style, there has never been anything like a self-conscious creation of style. As a youth I was very much inspired by Dylan Thomas who taught me that poetry appeals to the ear. It's what I call dictionary music. When the language doesn't sing, then there is no poetry. As for my own style, I've often thought that in the case of my two favourite songwriters, John Lennon and Paul McCartney, the melodies they wrote were often the result of the voices they were given by nature. McCartney's musical imagination seems inspired by the notes he can sing. Lennon's voice, that wonderful voice, is far more limited in range. He's more likely to write a melody along a flat line whereas McCartney's vocal range dips and soars. Think of the two-sided single "Strawberry Fields" and "Penny Lane." Look at the melody line, how McCartney's piccolo trumpet composition at the end of the song imitates the sounds just beyond the upper limits of his voice. They write the music they hear, and they hear the music of their own individual voices. That is what inspires my own style. I hear my own voice as it vivifies the language the dictionary makes available to my work.

LH: *I think that one of the qualities of an excellent poet is to be able to empathize with nature. Keats' "Ode to a Nightingale" illustrates this idea of his idea of "negative capability." I think that your metaphors are some of the most original in contemporary Canadian poetry. In your poems you master metaphors, letting them speak as if nature could speak. How did you develop this sense of empathy, this Orphic voice?*

JBL: I don't know. It's a mystery to me. I try my best to vanish into the work. To plunge into the deep wells of the self where the writing is done. As for empathy, I was given the gift of being born to a father with a brilliant mind and a mother with an optic heart. The Lees were bookish and the Busteed clan was blessed with kindness. I read somewhere recently "nature enables; culture denies." And I'd say that although I have always loved books and reading, I have also always been profoundly aware of the fact that books were not born in libraries. I said in a previous interview "sometimes it's the dog in the library who sees the ghost in the door." As a farm kid, I've always had a profound respect for the natural world. I husbanded sheep and cattle and I've always had a dog to teach me the beauty of loving and loyalty. Thus far I've lived a five-dog life.

LH: *After travelling to Ireland, the land of your ancestors with your father and your wife, Cathy in 1995, you published* Tongues of the Children *depicting the suffering of the Irish people during the potato famine. Why did this period in history touch you so deeply? How did the idea of this book begin?*

JBL: I suppose that book began with the first phase of exhaustion arising from the mining of childhood. I've always loved history. And I've always thought of the place where I stand as a tel into which I might dig. As a fifth generation John born on the farm I was born to, I've ever been in the company of local ghosts, and I've always been conscious of ancestry and I've felt for a very long while that writing is in no small part a form of ancestor worship. So, conscious of my own Irish ancestry, and very aware of the connection between Souwesto (Southwestern Ontario) and the past, it is quite natural that I would begin where I stand. And one need not go very far into the past to see the presence of Irish ancestors, tales of the underground railroad, victims of influenza, and cholera, soldiers and militia serving in the war of 1812 and so on. And in my case, I decided to attend to the history of the forgotten and the maligned, rather than the obvious folk whose heroism is relatively common in history books written by others.

In my case, the Lees came from Skibbereen in County Cork. Although there is no family lore relating to the great Famine, the town where my great-great grandfather Irish John Lee came of age is the epicentre of the worst starvation in the Great Famine. So, my interest started there. And digging around in local primary texts, I unearthed the five stories I wrote in that book, *Tongues of the Children*. The threads I found in doing research for that book yielded years and years of material of great personal interest.

LH: *Al Purdy took a trip to Pangnirtung in the Arctic and wrote original poems in his book* North of Summer. *You also took a rigorous two week trip to this place on Baffin Island with your son, Sean, which inspired you to write your chapbook,* The Echo of Your Words Has Reached Me. *How did the uniqueness of the Arctic find its way into your poems?*

JBL: In my writing I've always taken pleasure in the beauty of being elsewhere. On my travels I've visited four continents, and wherever I travel I try my best to be a traveller rather than a tourist. The opportunity to visit Baffin Island presented itself thanks to the invitation I received from a friend who had been my elder son Dylan's Venture Leader at the end of his time in Scouting. That friend, Walter Soroka, had been to the Arctic on a previous occasion and he and a lawyer from Port Dover, Ash Winter, my son Dylan and I flew to Pangnirtung and travelled by boat from there to the base of a trail running along the Weasel River where we camped and trekked north to Summit Lake. Along the way I kept a journal and wrote the poems that appear in my chapbook *The Echo of Your Words Has Reached Me* (Mekler & Deahl, 1998). Of course I was familiar with Purdy's *North of Summer* and he and I corresponded briefly about the connection between his experience and my own. However, in preparation for the journey I read a great number of Inuit poems in English translation, one of which gave me the inspiration for the title. "Little man!" the mountain cried./ "The echo of your words has reached me!/ Do you really think I can be contained/ in your song?"

What I wanted to capture was the wind and the weather howling through the landscape. When our guide who took us by boat to the start of the trail asked us how we liked out journey and I told him I found it to be wonderful, he responded by ejaculating disgust and waving his hand in rejection of the place from whence we had just returned. I realized that what I had found beautiful, he found repugnant because there was nothing there in that landscape that would sustain life. The water was too cold for fish life. The caribou had disappeared forty years before. We'd seen only one arctic hare gnawing at black lichen. One paw print of an arctic fox having passed that way, a few arctic bunting nesting in the high rock, and ravens in flight above us inspiring me to write: "those black-winged angels/ visit like death-bed priests/ and you can almost see/ in their hungry eyes/ how they wish we were dead/ or dying."

In the past I'd been to every province in Canada. So, travelling to the far north and crossing the Arctic Circle on foot brought to completion my intention to know my nation. Prior to this journey, I'd written an unpublished manuscript called *Infinite Solitudes*. Although I abandoned that project quite some time ago, I had completed the work before setting it aside and moving on. I think I wrote those poems the same year I wrote the poems which would become my book *Hired Hands*.

LH: *We were growing up in the shadow of World War II: the wartime cards we traded, the guns we played with, and the combat movies we watched. Yet beyond this, we also saw the devastating effects of the war on our relatives and our neighbours. Why were you compelled to write poems like "what we might learn if* *we listen" and "tainted music" from* dressed in dead uncles *about people who had suffered during the war?*

JBL: I grew up inspired by cowboy culture and by war stories. There was a program on TV called *The Twentieth Century* sponsored by Prudential and hosted by Walter Cronkite airing every Sunday afternoon. World War II footage often dominated the broadcast. And though I was born six years after the war was over, I knew that my Uncle John had served in the navy, and that he had been in peril in the English Channel during the build-up to the D Day invasion. My mother's favourite cousin had been wounded in the war. German prisoners of war had worked on our farm. My grandfather Busteed had served in the local watch. There were two dramas on television during the sixties. I watched both *Combat* and *The Gallant Men.* The protagonist in the latter of these two programs was a war correspondent. I remember typing a poem and smoking my first cigarette pretending to be that sort of writer, that war correspondent, when my mother came into my room, drawn there by the smell of cigarette smoke. I was caught smoking. I never told her I'd been playacting at writing. That would have been far more mortifying than being caught smoking. Writing remained a secret vice for a long while after that moment of shame. Then along came the Beatles, and twelve-year-old Johnny Lee was lost to soldiering forever. That said, I'm still drawn to writing about wars and wars and rumours of war.

LH: *In order to write we need to be constantly nourished by new ideas and experiences. Our poems are shaped by a close interaction with nature and by travelling to different parts of the world. Do you think that by being open toward the uniqueness of other cultures, we are able to extend our perception of the world, even when some subjects seem to be "taboo"?*

JBL: I'm not only open to other cultures; I crave understanding. In university I studied both French and Spanish literature. When I was quite young I read Homer's *Iliad* and *Odyssey*. After reading Layton in the high school library, I sought out Catullus. I read Caesar's Conquests in Classic Illustrated comics. I read Remarque's novel *All Quiet on the Western Front,* and after discovering Pasternak, I read Dostoyevsky and Tolstoy. I was intrigued by ancient cultures, most especially Hittite culture, and I read *Gilgamesh,* and of course the many cultures of *The Bible.* As for 'taboo' one of the two things I learned from my mentor Margaret Avison was her caveat "find out what your taboos are and then break them all." I have no taboos when it comes to writing. Only write well and be true to your muse.

LH: *You previously mentioned that one of your favourite trips was to Israel. Growing up in a Christian tradition, you undoubtedly inherited powerful images of Israel in Biblical times. What did you feel when you travelled to such places as the Jordan River, Masada, and Bethlehem when you stood there at the crossroads of three powerful religions? What did you find particularly memorable?*

JBL: I suppose the best and only answer to this question would be to say "read my book *Let Us Be Silent Here,* (Sanbun, 2012)" because the experience of travelling in the holy land was so profound, so life-changing, that short of reprinting the entire book here, nothing would suffice to capture how it felt or what I learned. To stand under the night sky in Jerusalem and look up at the moon and the stars, or to stand in the blue of the day and look at the sun, and to feel the heat of that sun and the soothing elixir of the shade of the Holm oak near the home of Peter in Capernaum, or to travel by boat on the waters of Galilee, or to observe the baptismal waters of Jordan, well for a boy weaned on Bible stories, a boy who had once imagined he might become a man of the cloth, these experiences rang deep. And what might be more powerful, more profound, more moving than a reverential visit to Yad Vashem where I wrote these words "softly, softly, let's be silent here/ oh reverent grief/ that war is done/ those lives/ have lined the earth with bones/ the rootwork of a thousand-thousand-thousand/ wind-broken trees/ the soul of man/ grimes over/ like a lamp of oil/ and shame shines through/ the tainted light we touch."

LH: *In "Linen and Wool" from* Let Us Be Silent Here, *you wrote about the Jewish novelist Yehuda Amichai and the Palestinian poet Mahmoud Darwish. You introduced the poem with a quotation from Deuteronomy, "you must not wear a garment woven from linen and wool." What kind of reaction did you receive from Jewish and Palestinian readers in bringing these two writers together in the context of this poem?*

JBL: I've been published in several issues of *Voices Israel*. Through that journal I came into contact with Israeli poet Helen Bar-Lev whose watercolour painting of the old city of Jerusalem appears on the front cover of my book *Let Us Be Silent Here*. Prior to publication of the book, I sent her a copy of the manuscript soliciting her opinion of the poems. She immediately expressed reservations about the poem "Linen and Wool," wondering if it might be too controversial a poem. She requested permission to show the poem to her friend, the Israeli novelist Yosef Gotlieb. Not only did he not share her reservations about the poem, he found it enlightening. He had only recently been appointed president of an organization dedicated to the peaceful co-existence between Arabs and Jews within the boundaries of Israel. And it had never occurred to him to reach out to Palestinian poets living within the borders of his beloved nation. He told me that my poem had inspired him to reach out. In my poem I had sought to find common ground between Jewish novelist Yehuda Amichai and Palestinian poet Mahmoud Darwish. Like the forbidden blending of linen and wool, I interwove the dreams of Darwish and Amichai, ending the poem with a quotation from Darwish where he wrote "who is the owner of the language of this land? Who loves it more? Who loves it better?" and through this poem, inspired by my poem, Yosef Gotlieb stated an aspiration of inspired peaceful cohabitation of two peoples. He also saw fit to write a very positive review of my book. He concludes his review writing:

Let Us Be Silent Here is a highly laudable contemplation of this world where "blue heaven blooms" in the sunlight, which masks the stars and their constellations, the interface of what is known and what might be. Lee's poems resonate with transcendence. The collection chronicles the existential probing of a poetic spirit as he moves across a landscape that is both mythic and true. **The Mythic and the True: Poetic Contemplations on a Visit to Israel and Jordan A review of John B. Lee's** Let Us Be Silent Here **By Yosef Gotlieb**

LH: *You have been to Cuba numerous times as part of the Canada Cuba Literary Alliance and met a number of writers, including Miguel Angel Olivé Iglesias, Jorge Alberto Pérez Hernandez and Wency Rosales. In addition to writing poems influenced by the Cuban people and nature, you worked on an anthology of translation of famous Cuban poets* Sweet Cuba: The Building of a Poetic Tradition: 1608-1958 *with Manuel de Jesus Velasquez Léon. What fascinates you about Cuban poetry?*

JBL: I'm interested in everything; and I'm fascinated by everywhere I've ever been. I first visited Cuba on holiday in 1991 during what would come to be called 'the special period.' As a tourist I was totally unaware of how the people of Cuba were suffering, though I should have known. I wrote a series of poems about that first trip under the title "Cuban Journey" published in *Matrix Magazine* having been named winner of the Travel Writing Award as judged by Charles Foran. Then I was invited to return to the island by Richard (Tai) Grove. My wife Cathy and I stayed in a resort at Guarda la Vaca, near Holguín where I read poems at UNEAC along with fellow Canadian Ken Mitchell. It was there at that reading where I first met Manuel Léon and his former student Wency Rosales. I was enthralled by their warmth and hospitality. Little did I know then that I would become close friends with those three wonderful gentlemen. The Cuban professor Manuel, his protégé Wency and the Canadian founder of the Canada Cuba Literary Alliance Tai Grove have become three of my closest and most beloved friends.

The credit for the inspiration for *Sweet Cuba* goes entirely to Manuel. He did all the spadework for that translation. I am eternally grateful for the fact that he saw in me a poet who might have the talent to work on the translations. At first I cautioned him that he might seek a collaborator elsewhere. We talked for many hours on the steps leading up to cross on the hill above his home city of Holguín. I acquiesced, and the rest as they say, is history. I've returned to Cuba at least a half a dozen times. I've written two full books of poems inspired by Cuba. I'm involved in two projects, one as part of a Bridges series with two Cuban poets and Richard Grove, and of course I'm one of the four poets you're included with in the four Canadian poets being translated by Miguel Angel Olivé Iglesías.

LH: *Many of your books pay homage to your days on the family farm. You return many times trying to understand the complexity of life there, your interaction with family and people working on the farm, bringing both disturbing experiences and experiences to be celebrated. It looks as if this engagement with the family farm there will never end as you wrote in a recent book* The Widow's Land: *"I am making the world I am made from."*

JBL: Manuel gave me the gift of a phrase I have used often. That phrase "so, this is a place of places" applies to the farm on which I was born and raised. That farm gave birth to a member of parliament and three men who went on to be named to the Agricultural Hall of Fame. And when I was writing *Hired Hands,* my book of poems and stories inspired by the life of our hired man Thomas Sheil Malott, a visual artist named Michel Binet was on a car journey through Kent looking for subjects for his paintings. He was so struck by the beauty of our farm that he drove up the lane. Tom stopped him right there at the crest of the hill. He was so impressed by Tom that he took his photograph and from there went back to his studio to paint his subject. When I first showed my manuscript to my mother she said, "You know there's an artist from Quebec living near Thamesville who is working on paintings of Tom." That synchronicity is so common of that farm, there is something that cries out to be conserved and preserved in literature and in art about the place. It is, in the words of Manuel, "a place of places." And it has been visited by photographers, poets, writers, journalists, supreme court justices, politicians, and until it was sold out of the family it inspires everyone who has been there. And it continues to serve me well, even though the barns are gone and the house is a dwelling of strangers.

LH: *From your poems we learn that your grandfather, Herb Lee, who owned the farm was a complicated man. He became the central character in many of your poems. What kind of relationship did you have with your father? You worked with him on the farm when you were younger. How did your relationship change over the years?*

JBL: After my father passed away, my son gave me a copy of a letter he'd received from Dad when son Sean was attending university. In that epistle my father told my son that he considered me to be his best friend in the world. I cherish that sentiment. My father would have called himself a farmer, though he was also president of an insurance company, and he was a qualified and practicing insurance adjustor. He and his brother were both named to the Agricultural Hall of Fame in Chatham. I said at the dedication of my late father, if someone had mentioned his achievement he would have said, "Never mind that." He was a brilliant and humble man. Like his father before him, he was a world-class herdsman. And he sired a son who felt himself to be something of a foundling. I had no interest in farming. I had no affection for most of the things my cousins favoured. I didn't like cars, machinery, tools, and once I'd seen the Beatles on television, I had little interest in anything but music and literature. I once said that I started writing because I wanted Paul McCartney's attention and my father's approval. The first of these two motivations remains an unlikely impossibility. However, by the time of his passing, my father was one of my most avid readers. When Marty Gervais told him in the last week of his life, "George, your son is a very fine writer." My dad patted him on the hand saying, "I know." As though it were a given.

LH: *As Poet Laureate of the City of Brantford and in your role of teaching creative writing workshops and readings in high schools and universities, what advice would you pass on to younger writers? Is there some kind of creative vision you would impart to give them?*

JBL: First and foremost I would ask them "who are you reading?" because it is my firm conviction that if you do not read, you will not write. I would also say to them, wake up and be alive in the world, be interested in everything, I often put it this way "be the dog." By that I mean, be so awake and alive in the world that you are like the dog who has been absent from a room for two minutes and upon returning he sniffs and snoops in every corner just in case something has changed while he was away. And I would advise them to get as much formal education as possible in order to reawaken the curiosity that is ironically the first victim of formal education. And I would say, learn your craft by practicing your craft. Read. Write. Be awake and alive. And be true to your inner life. Poetry encourages lingering. It requires a kind of studied attentiveness. And strive to include the mind, the heart, the body, the soul and the spirit in everything you attempt. And do not fear true sentiment. Do not fear confusion and failure. These are very good teachers. There's a kind of accidental brilliance that makes itself available only when you vanish into the work. Certainty of conviction is a honey trap for those who come to a false understanding of complexities. Paradox. Ambiguity. Complexity. Irony. Entering the mystery carrying a light where you go. Muddy waters need not be deep, and clear water in limpid darkness reveals itself when you carry a light where you go. And, as Margaret Avison once cautioned me "mind your prepositions, everything can turn on the smallest of words." So, in that precision consider Neruda's poem, "I want to do with/ to/ for you, what the springtime does with/ to/ for the cherry tree."

LH: *In recent years you have worked with Richard Tai Grove at Hidden Brook Press, publishing writers in the John B. Lee Signature Series. Why was it important for you to undertake this venture?*

JBL: That's an easy question to answer. Tai conceived of the series. He presented me with the opportunity to participate in the selection. I chose the first three, then the next three, then the next. And what an opportunity it has proven to be. What a chance I've been given to honour writers. I'm so thrilled when I have a chance to participate in a project that brings writing to the attention of readers.

LH: *Your latest and, in my opinion, one of your most original books* Into a Land of Strangers *you once again return to a favourite subject, your family. This time you dedicate most of the book to your Great Aunt Ida, who was a missionary teacher in China in the period of World War II. Never having known her, how were you able to create such a powerful portrait of her and her time?*

JBL: I've always known about her, and my cousin Dorothy Kay, who is something of a family archivist when it comes to ancestry, produced a hundred-page document on the life of our great-aunt Ida. So, the spadework for the facts of her life was done. I read dozens of books on the history of China, many of them focusing on the period of her lifetime. I read hundreds of poems written by Chinese poets over the last thousand years. I visited China with my wife. We travelled there for two weeks. The closing section of the book called, "Counting Cranes," was first published as a chapbook, then republished in *This Is How We See the World* (Hidden Brook Press, 2017). I suppose I was simply ready to write the book when I wrote it. From conception to completion, I felt it was time.

LH: *Recently, at the end of the interview I'm conducting, I am asking poets the question: What are you working on now during the Coronavirus epidemic?*

JBL: I'm reading Faulkner now, catching up on the novels I've owned for years, but haven't read yet. I just reread *Go Down*

Moses, and in doing that, I watched a few bios on YouTube and it stunned me to learn (or to be reminded) that he was only 64 when he died. When I read *The Sound and the Fury* as a young undergraduate at age 19, I saw him as a very old man indeed. Of course, I was amazed by his writing. Indeed, his opening chapter in that novel gave me the inspiration and the courage to write *Hired Hands*. And on re-reading *Go Down Moses*, in the closing chapter of "The Bear," I was struck by the brilliance of his description of the train. It's two pages of the best writing it has ever been my privilege to read.

I am brought to this point in my writing career to have it reconfirmed that in description, in capturing experience, as it in in painting, and indeed in Marty Gervais' photography, the masterpiece involves capturing something so beautifully as to make it come true in a way that water is true in a river, a lake, an ocean, a well, and a cup brought to the lips for slaking a thirst, and the water within the thirst or the thirster. This whole thing … That is writing!

May 14, 2020

Photo credit: D.A. Lockhart

DANIEL LOCKHART

Laurence Hutchman: *You are a citizen of the Lenape nation. This nation did not have its origins in the Windsor/Detroit (Tùkhòne) area. Where did the people come from, and how did they end up in the Windsor/Detroit area?*

D. A. Lockhart: Originally, Lenapehoking was situated around the current America Atlantic seaboard. Being descended from Unami clans of the Lenape nation, my ancestors were from the south-central portion of what is today New Jersey. As you can imagine, we were part of the earliest sustained contacts with the Europeans. Our ancestors had a vision during a gamwig, or Big House Ceremony, that foretold the arrival of the "white" people from over the ocean. In that vision those ancestors perceived the danger and told a good portion of our ancestors to get inland and be safe while they stayed and sought to work with the newcomers. A portion of our ancestors went inland, going with our Three-Fires relations. After that my ancestors began a long and painful inland migration that brought them up the Ohio River Valley and into what is modern day Indiana. They lived at Prophetstown with the great prophet Tecumseh and followed him north to fight the Americans in 1812 alongside the British. A few decades earlier the Moravian Missionaries that helped to work with other refugees from the homeland had arrived at the Dishkan Zibi just outside Thamesville and established Fairfield. It was there that Tecumseh was murdered by the American army in 1812. It was there that our ancestors settled.

To put it most succinctly, our homelands and nations were shattered by the genocidal practices of the Americans and other European settlers. Wall Street in New York City was named for the first wall built to keep us out of our lands. The survivors moved in pulses across the continent and the pockets of survivors ended up in surviving nations that welcomed them. My ancestors followed others that fled before them. They ended up in Moraviantown here in Ontario. But the majority of Lenape survivors were forcibly relocated to what is contemporary Oklahoma with some landing in Wisconsin. My Grandmother, Pearl, was a residential school survivor that lost her status. She was part of the early and generally unrecognized surge of urban Indigenous peoples that landed in cities. She settled in Windsor, not far from Turkey Creek in South Windsor. My mother's father was another non-status Indigenous man who had settled in the areas around Windsor, in Ford City, and had spent his early working life on the Great Lakes freighters and then in the military during WWII. He wasn't Lenape, spoke French as his first language, and was no fan of the Catholic Church.

LH: *You often use Lenape in your work and your readings. Did you grow up with that language? Are you conversant in other Indigenous languages?*

DL: Honestly, I grew up understanding fairly little about my Indigenous heritage. That's not to say that we weren't busy being Indigenous. We spent a lot of time with our Indigenous relations in the City of Windsor and around Bucktown. Which most clearly make our experiences decidedly Indigenous, just perhaps not in all the romantic ways that non-Indigenous folks perceive as living. We went to see *Star Wars* in the movie theatres, we biked to Becker's for candy and baseball cards, and watched the Detroit Tigers on rabbit ears. But languages and ceremony were pretty distant in our daily lives.

My brother and I, as well as my father, were all raised in Anglophone households. My mother's father spoke primarily French, although my mother was raised speaking English. By the time of my father's childhood, and in fact for at least a few generations, speaking English was the norm. Speaking our traditional languages was an absurd thought amongst so many of our relations. And even the French speaking heritage of my mother's line has been somewhat looked down upon. Assimilation was a survivor's technique, particularly in eras in which anything else was likely a death sentence. And if I can say anything about my ancestors is that they are very good at surviving.

The first time I actually got down to learning a non-European language was during my time as an undergraduate at Trent University. The Native Studies program there was the first massive steps I took in coming to understand the rich heritage linguistically and culturally nations such as mine had. It was there that I took Ojibwe as a student of Shirley Williams. There were no Lenape (Unami nor Munsee) courses, but seeing as I had grown up on lands where a similar dialect of 'Nish was spoken, I figured it a solid choice. I am a bit of a language nut, to be honest. I've studied French, German, Old English, Latin, and Ancient Greek at the university level. I even held a Foreign Language Acquisition Scholarship at Indiana University for Norwegian. Spent a good number of years as a research consultant in French and Norwegian after I moved back to Canada.

And why languages? Well, there is a slippage of meaning between different languages that fascinates me. The metaphors that these culturally constructed clusters of sounds draw from in terms of what they are trying to communicate are so very interesting. They are worlds unto themselves. And the fact that there is no one-to-one relationship with linguistic metaphors makes this whole pursuit of languages so interesting for a writer, let alone a writer that kicks at the edges of decolonization. There is a great deal to learn from the space between languages.

LH: *What were the circumstances which inspired you to start writing?*

DL: I recast *Star Trek* as *Spy Vs. Spy* into hand drawn comics in grade school. They were parodies of the movies that my closest friends and I adored. But my grade seven teacher took them away from me one day and trashed them. There was nothing offensive in them. In the closed-minded world of a grade seven Catholic school teacher, there was no room for creativity or honouring that spirit. Perhaps this is the first real literary critic I encountered.

However, by the time I reached senior high school we were allowed and encouraged to create. My senior English teacher at Catholic Central, Stephanie Cosgrave, was, in fact, the first adult that encouraged me to write creatively. Particularly poetry, but also plays, and a little bit of short fiction. Myself and a group of students did writing workshops with her. She encouraged reading outside the classroom reading lists, the stuff that a Catholic Schools Board in Canada wouldn't have thought valuable. Texts like Henry Rollins poetry and Leonard Cohen fictions. She really opened the door to habits that I would carry with me until today. Things like daily writing, journaling, and reading the "classics" that often failed to materialize on my university syllabi over the years.

It was during my sort of cultural awakening at Trent University that I began to see writing as a possible outcome to my education. Professors like David McNabb from Walpole Island and that quintessential Canadian studies and Bioregionalism scholar John Wadland encouraged my writing, even though I was still far from the student I would become later. Their belief in my ability to craft with words mattered.

I had written a biography of Latvian-born Canadian painter Andre Lapine for the Agnes Jamieson Gallery and had taken real pleasure in its construction over my senior year at Trent. A project that, without doubt, left a lingering sense of joy of writing in me after I graduated and relocated to Metro Detroit in search of the ever-elusive career and real life after university.

Fortune had it that, after a brief stint at Schoolcraft College in Livonia, MI, I was admitted to Montana State University. It was there in Bozeman, in the Valley of Flowers, that I would really say that I came into writing. My major this time around was English Literature and I had taken on student employment as sports and features writer for the student newspaper. Those were my first paycheques from my writing. It was through a group of fellow student writers that I really began to return to poetry. Three of us from that group went on to get our MFAs and I was truly blessed to have received that spark from them. Alison Bailey and John D. Powers introduced me to Seamus Heaney and Richard Hugo and from there we all just wrote our early work and pushed each other to create. A short-lived lit magazine, READ THIS, came out of that group. It was my earliest foray into publishing and, needless to say, I am fairly certain it was a good start. From there I was fortunate enough to be admitted to Indiana University-Bloomington's MFA in creative writing. And daily writing and editing and reading practice became the thing I did.

LH: *How do poems come to you? Can you describe the process of writing your poems?*
DL: For me they come in glimmers and experience. Meaning that everything for me comes as the opening up of a concrete image that needs some further thought or exploration. And these images come as a simple gift of living in creation. For *The Gravel Lot That Was Montana,* it was the truck stop sign

burning the night alive in southern Wyoming. *For Go Down Odawa Way* it was a taxidermized iguana in the back of a guy's car. For *This City at the Crossroads* it was witnessing pigeons move between the buildings of downtown Indianapolis from the ballpark. These were images that became lodged in my mind and that needed unpacking to witness how the emotions started and continued.

It was Snyder and Kerouac that first illustrated this process for me. And they did so pretty early along for me, during my early days in the 'States. And hence why so many of the poems in collection like *The Gravel Lot That Was Montana* are built around those. But it was in graduate school that my instructors like Maura Stanton and Tony Ardizzone spoke about the importance of the glimmer and opening those glimmers up to an audience and to specific forms. And most clearly the satori-notion that lies at the heart of *haiku* fascinates me because of this. I suppose I did write a whole book of haiku and haibun and that might speak to that. But I'm a strong believer in the experiential aspect of the haiku and in most of my work, the poems start there and opens up consciously from the moment into something so much larger. It's a principle of building the creative process of the whole Blakean concept of seeing the universe in a grain of sand. That's what drives my process from that first glimmer to the poem.

LH: *In the introduction to* Tùkhòne *you wrote: "I trace my roots as an ecologically-centred writer through the works of notable American poets such as Philip Whalen, Gary Snyder and Gerald Vizenor." Were there any other poets who significantly influenced you?*
DL: I was fortunate enough to work with some particularly gifted and passionate regional and national poets during my education in the US. You could say that it starts with my time at Montana State University, working with Greg Keeler as

an undergraduate. He is part of that whole Western United States group centred around his old friend Richard Brautigan. I took a fiction class from him, although he is more renowned for his poetry, and memoir, Keeler was my entry to point to writers that really pushed me into my current direction as a poet. Between him and a former aspiring poet friend John Powers, I was introduced to Richard Hugo. Whalen, Synder, and Vizenor played the role of early embers to my poetic journey. But it was during my reading and engagement with Richard Hugo's *31 Letters and 13 Dreams*, *Lady at the Kicking Horse Reservoir*, and *What Thou Lovest Well, Remains American*. It was his work that *Devil in the Woods* emerged from. I suppose you could argue that *This City at the Crossroads* was strongly inspired by *Lady at the Kicking Horse Reservoir*. Everything is rooted in the place in those works, and poetic self tries desperately to add themselves to the history and fabric of that place. It's a metaphysical connection point. Like all poetry should have in its heart. As was mostly clearly, *The Gravel Lot That Was Montana*. If anything, the title is a small homage to Hugo's poem "Driving Montana" in its title. I spent a lot of time reading his work with clear vistas of the Bridger, Bangtail, and Tobacco Root Mountains. These are haunting memories that linger in every line that I have written and will write.

Obviously, my time in Indiana informed my poetry in much more concrete and readily observable ways. I spent considerable instructional time with well-known poets like Maura Stanton, Catherine Bowman, and Campbell McGrath. Stanton taught me myth-making, Bowman line control and traditional poetic forms, and McGrath the path to unit criticism, philosophy, pop culture, and poetry into readable and approachable forms. If Hugo, Snyder, Vizenor, Keeler, and the like were conscious underpinnings of my work, these were the refiners. Fellow graduate student and poet Michael Dauro really helped guide me into the pathways of haiku and traditional Japanese forms. And yeah, I read widely still today. Al Purdy comes to mind. Been working a lot with his work lately and really connect with his voice from both the land and the people. Eugene McNamara's work has been fairly important to me over the last few years. I find a touchstone in his work, as another poet and writer who relocated to Waawiiyaatanong from the American Midwest. His work has been an interesting intersection of Canadian lit and American lit. And to be honest, most everything I do here in Waawiiyaatanong I feel is done under his shadow.

LH: *You have worked at many jobs in your life in various parts of the United States, as well as closer to home in Detroit and Windsor. Did the variety of jobs that you've worked provide you with material for your writing by offering you different perspectives of people's lives?*

DL: One of the greatest challenges to any society has been the class struggle. I might argue it's the only struggle. The notion at the heart of this struggle is that the vast majority of people are working class, meaning that we actually produce the goods and services that are fundamental to our existence. Naturally, there are grifters that come along, take the wealth that these people produce, hoard it, and vilify those that they've stolen from. My goal has always been to understand and move within the circle of those that work and produce, and because of that understand the land. These are the working class. From directing truck traffic at the Ambassador Bridge to shuffling medical records at University of Michigan Health, to slinging coffee and beer at Bridger Bowl Ski Resort, these were the real school to understanding the world we live in.

Honestly, these types of jobs have often been my saviour. They have tended to be a lot less abusive on either myself or other BIPOC folk than academia or more white-collar jobs. And in honesty BIPOC folks don't tend to be particularly present in those less than working-class oriented jobs. At least we weren't in the first two decades of the century, and because of that the work culture in those environments was less than comfortable for me. Less comfortable but not less recognizable. Workers are the model for our future. They are the successful model that followed us until very recently. They are so much more true to our essence as a species than the aforementioned grifter class. When you grow up in the metro area of a city like Detroit, with its unionism and industrial work, you come to understand the ones that do the essential work, the building of freeways and infrastructure, those folks that handle the freight, or work in the kitchens and bars and grocery stores, those are the people that matter most. And there is an honesty in committing one's self to the work that every person on this planet should recognize and celebrate. My work tends to follow this basic underlying principle, it's the filter that I chose to find my aforementioned glimmers and the process by which I unpack them.

LH: *You often talk about borders in your poetry and why you don't like them, seeing them as not only physical but also an emotional division between communities. In the interview conducted by Will Johnson in* The Malahat Review, *you express this strong position on the subject: "As a Jay Treaty person, there is no border for me in some sense in North America. And it feels absurd that there is one running right through my community." Can you elaborate?*

DL: Borders have always been a way that those greedy for wealth and material gain, the aforementioned grifter class, have utilized in lieu of other techniques such as indentured servitude or more overt slavery, to control and corral the vast majority of working class or everyday peoples. When one is

tied to a specific piece of land or place that is owned by some-
one else there becomes issues of control. A prison is a prison
still a prison, regardless of size, when you have limits on where
you can travel to and stay. Borders are contrary to our essence
as living beings in creation. Look at the history of humanity
on this planet, it's about migration and movement. We are
more akin to birds and caribou than we are to the capitalist
close-minded vision of materiality and wealth.

And it's universal in so many ways to be able to move
freely across creation. Countries like Norway, Scotland, Ice-
land have this right to roam, meaning that one has the right to
engage with the land, to wander it, be natural in creation that
you were born to. No one person can own the world and limit
you or anyone else's ability to walk upon it, share its universal
gifts. Borders naturally limit this right to roam. This is the
best-case scenario with borders. It's best case because we don't
end up tying ourselves to some ridiculous clannish notion of
the political state. If we move freely we see creation as one col-
lective whole. The planet is not a carved-up bit of real estate
to be owned by a small percentage of people. And we should
own little allegiance to one cadre of bureaucrats or politicians
proclaiming province over people that never asked for it.

As for the Jay Treaty bit, well that refers to one of the semi-
nal pieces of treaty law on Turtle Island that permits recognized
or treatied Indigenous folks the rights to move and live and
work and hunt and fish in ways that predate the xenophobia
of newer states like the USA or Canada. Me and my relations
are covered under it. A pretty useful thing when you grow up
pushed right against this ridiculous border between the com-
munities of Waawiiyaatanong.

LH: *Your second book* The City at the Crossroad *seems to be an
exploration, or a search for meaning, and a deeper understanding*

of familiar places. By being an explorer, you have to let not only curiosity guide you, but to involve your being to seize something essential to providing answers to your questions.

DL: When we lived in Bloomington, we were very fortunate to study Buddhism at the Tibetan Mongolian Buddhist Cultural Center and Kumbum Chamste Ling Monastery on the city's south side. Fundamental to this study was the concept of mindfulness, slowing creation down enough to witness the myriad of important nuances that make up our lives no matter where we live. I often refer to this in terms of satori, or the moment of enlightenment that comes from defamiliarizing the familiar and then seeing the importance and interconnectivity of that moment. These are the teachings that came to inform my poetic and literary explorations. And after living in a crushingly beautiful place, perhaps sublime might be a better choice, like southwestern Montana, one grapples to find beauty in new, more manageable ways. The essential is that beautiful spirit that lies at the heart of every place, everything. And finding that is critical to living in a place and understanding and properly loving it. This essence comes in hard concrete ways, like the call of a cardinal from a sycamore tree in an Indianapolis eastside neighbourhood, or the dance of bluebirds in a Morgan County forest, the crunch of a hot tenderloin sandwich on a fairground midway. Perhaps it is easiest to say that the essential that I have been exploring my spaces for rely upon the small and the, in a sense, mundane aspects of our lives. I don't know if I would call it the joy I am looking for. But that is at least part of the sentiment. Probably because there is joy in those aforementioned things. And maybe that joy comes from shared experience. Like how many more people living in a place like Indiana have eaten a tenderloin or just listened to birdsongs and that framed some great happiness in their lives. This is the simplicity of connection, of understanding the myriad of ways that we share our time in any of the places that we inhabit with other souls is that essence that any one worthy of undertaking any exploration for the essential would understand. What is essential is what is shared.

LH: *In Bruce Meyer's interview, D.G. Jones said, "for English Canadian writers at least, there is a tremendous investment in space." Is the idea of space and particular place important to you?*
DL: It is. That idea of space is important to so many English Canadian writers because of their need to claim land and space that was not originally theirs. I might argue that the origin of contemporary Canadian lit stems from this. Look at how much the Canadian public holds the Group of Seven and the visual depictions of the land of Canada in their work in reverence. I would also argue that the centrality of the land works for everyone, Indigenous and Non-Indigenous, here on Turtle Island. It was Dr. John Wadland that often said we are nothing without the land. And it's that spirit that I see in the work of the truly great artists in Canada and North America. One can connect with space and land in a way that say a poem about one's self in terms of sexuality or mental illness in one's space cannot. Space and place can and should reflect internalities for aspects of existence such as the aforementioned. We all look for the recognizable and the concrete thing that is particular place holds the spot of the recognizable. Speaking about sexuality or disability or mental illness or even one's dead grandmother can be important and beneficial to others. Connection is critical in what we do as poets and writers. And place is the most visible and easy way to connect to.

LH: *Your book* The Gravel Lot That Was Montana *is very much concerned with physical place, which you evoke through a variation in rhythm, surreal imagery, as well as by making many* *historical, musical, and sports allusions, etc. Can you tell me more about this process?*

DL: Poetry needs to be more than narrative cataloguing. I believe it to be a nexus point of experience and creation. And as such rhythm, surreal imagery, history, and music all play a role in that. A poem should be an experience. And that is the hope with a collection like *The Gravel Lot That Was Montana*. It does have that narrative arc of the poetic self-crossing a nation to find something. Not an unusual basis for a literary collection by any standard. But the process matters. Hence the talk and song of sleeping in truck stop parking lot, or the cruise through Detroit to reach the gates of Zug Island. Physical place is one thing. So, we can talk about sunsets, and ice on the river, but they are only part of the experience that occurs on that land that is our central point. The taste of cheap slider, the music that fills the white noise of urban and rural environments, the steady motion of how we move atop it is all the central part of poetry as experience. And one should feel the history of the place in that experience.

And what poet or writer doesn't have some affinity to William Blake? I believe in seeing the universe in a grain of sand. Poetry, or at least good poetry, is about building an experience for the reader. So, it comes naturally that one must mix so many levels of being and sensing and experience into a work as possible. Shakespeare did this with the high-low aspects of his plays. The aristocrat, the barkeep, and the manual labourer all had something of common or recognizable form in the work. I reckon that my primary aim is along those lines. Crafting a work that speaks on multiple levels, opens dialogs between disparate groups, crafts experience, shares it, all the grander notions one can try and breathe into writing. My work might not always hit that level. But at least the aim is there.

LH: *You start your book* Wěnchikàneit Visions *by referring to the visions of the male speaker—an important part of Lenape culture. By adapting a kind of narrative structure, you write about various places in a spiritual manner that is situated in a contemporary context. How did the idea of this book originate, and why were you compelled to act as a speaker?*

DL: Ceremony is everything. And this particular collection comes from this fundamental belief. The entire notion of the book comes out of the ceremony that is the gamwig, or Big House Ceremony, of my Lenape ancestors. It has been one of the centralizing ceremonies in our lives. This is grand fall ceremony in which we gather to share visions of the previous year and celebrate the gifts of community, our ancestors, and creation. What the reader gets here is basically a lyric revelation of the "visions" held by the poetic speaker over the previous year. It is a part of ceremony with the word *Wěnchikàneit* identifying the pieces as being specifically to a male speaker in a specific part of that ceremony. You can witness some similarities in the roots of these pieces as testimonials of living closer to the everyman's experience, except the view and ceremony becomes transformed into a contemporary urban Indigenous experience. Deer and forest spirits become intertwined with bus trips, slow rolls in family cars, and parties in abandoned hotels. Maybe I can say this is a little bit what contemporary urban Lenape ceremony looks like. We share this belief that visions of the previous year are gifts from creation and gifts that are meant to be shared.

And this book and the reframing of the ceremony grew out of the belief that our contemporary and traditional Indigenous lives coexist in this moment. The sacred is the everyday. And it is sacred aspect that is not driven by "noble savage" stereotypes such as speaking animals in the northern woods. The hope with these lyric essays was to capture something truthful about the world we've come to inhabit and are gifted by creation. The poet is naturally the speaker across so many cultures. So, it was natural to assume the role, one must find their way into situations that one wants to discuss. And perhaps by miming the role of the speaker in this ceremony, there because a written record of how this part of the ceremony can unfold. This is a testimonial to the truth and beauty to being part of the contemporary urban Indigenous experience. And it's only one take on that multifaceted experience, for good or bad.

LH: *In the opening poem "Devil in the Woods: A Preface," you wrote:*

> *Between descending honour beats*
> *let us too sing defiance and become*
> *the devil that may overthrow*
> *the order which brought silence*
> *to our voices, tore at our clan*
> *lines, and jarred us from our mother.*

The title of your book Devil in the Woods *acts as a powerful statement in itself. Why did you choose the devil as a symbol of rebellion to "overthrow / the order which brought silence / to our voices"?*
DL: So many of the settler cultures that moved to Turtle Island brought with them this innate terror of their own fabricated devil figure. A figure that manifested itself often as demons in the forest or the darkness beyond the light of their tiny settlements and encampments. There was this notion that the devil was the other, the creature of evil and chaos, just outside the periphery of their lives. The devil of their making was the very entity that was antithetical to their very existence. As a Lenape kid, educated in the Catholic education system in Ontario, it was this sentiment that perplexed me. We were

195

taught, at home, that there was a balance of good/evil in the twins of our trickster figures. Both were part of the wonders of creation. Not to mention that the devil's home in the woods, the natural world outside of our cities, towns, and communities, were the places we drew out strength from as a people. Perhaps the first real notion of how non-Native Canadians saw us Indigenous folks developed out of this disparity. If we were people of creation, the ones that the forests and natural world formed our basis of life and understanding, then we were in fact the quintessential devil, the other that represented chaos and evil in the colonial world.

And this has been reflected in Canadian canonical literature. Think of *Marie Chapdelaine* or Atwood's *Journal of Susan Moodie*. Nature is the thing that drives you mad, makes you into a murderer. Purdy's work may have been the first real digression in non-Native writing that turned the view of nature around. The guy was rooted to the land in way no other blue blood type poet was around him. Yet still, the image of the devil in nature prevailed. There is a fear of nature in Canadian colonial thought that isn't there in say Norwegian or Icelandic thought. And it is what lies at the heart of a farmer being able to legally murder an Indigenous kid on their property. Your enemy's enemy has the strong potential to be among your best allies.

LH: *This collection contains two alternating types of poems, which are poems that are critical of famous Canadian figures, while at the same time they acknowledge their contributions to Canadian culture and history. The other poems are prayers or invocations to the Creator that have a hopeful tone. These poems are on opposite poles, yet at the same time, they are complementary. Do you see them in this way?*

DL: In terms of a rounded-out discussion of history and possibilities I think alternating styles work this way. It's rather similar to Hugo's book that the entire collection was based on. Rather than dreams it becomes prayers in *Devil in the Woods*. I mean, this works against the stereotypes held about Indigenous folks, going with the prayers. Suffice it say that, be it prayers or dreams, both operate in the metaphysical. Key difference between the two being agency, or the operation of the conscious versus the subconscious. Prayer comes from the active positioning of the self. One thinks and acts and speaks the metaphysical hopes and wishes into the world. The prayers in *Devil in the Woods* act as realistic metaphysical engagements one, as an Indigenous person in a colonialized world. Profoundly personal, these prayer poems are the added exploration of the lyric consciousness of the speaker and the collection. Whereas the letter poems are the very public and more controlled engagements with life under the contemporary settler colonial system. They might not be as friendly or neutral as polite Canadian culture generally call for. But they actually are for a survivor of colonialism that is the speaker of the collection. The hope was to speak truth to experience, point out all the facts that could be objectively illustrated as history. Somewhere between the two is a truth and honesty that has been rather absent from Canadian textbooks.

And together the two are hopeful. This is the major divergence from the spirit of Richard Hugo's collection. Life without hope is nothing but unrealized tragedy. Not exactly the sort of space I personally wish to inhabit, nor one that I feel is safe for people to inhabit from a mental health perspective. And if anything could be said of actual Indigenous folks is that we are survivors. Surviving is something to be both happy and hopeful about.

LH: *In this book, you seem to be trying to deconstruct stereotypes created by colonialism. One of the problems that you are facing when writing is that much of Canadian history was written by non-Indigenous writers. Based on my own experience of teaching history at the Protestant School Board of Montreal, I've observed that there were different interpretations of Canadian history from the French and English perspectives. How do you suggest that we change this stereotypical teaching of history?*

DL: One of the most central portions of our Big House Ceremony is that of sharing and listening to the visions of our community members over the previous year. This sharing of multiple voices and experiences over our shared time in our shared spaces helps the community to craft a rich, textured, and nuanced approach to our past, our present, and our future. No one set of voices or experiences dominate. Each clan and subclan speaks, we come to know, if not understand, the crosscurrents of individual experience that make up collective experience. Just like there is no one true English or French language, there is no one true history. There are facts that can't be ignored, like attempted and ongoing attempts at genocide of Indigenous peoples and our cultures. We need something more. I don't hold all the answers, but I know that honest conversations, listening and sharing, and doing so without all the malevolent considerations of power and who pays who is such an important step. We can deconstruct a lot of the harmful stereotypes and misinformation by allowing for more marginalized voices to be heard and listened to. Not all voices are equal and not everything being said is of value, one needs only to spend a few hours on Twitter or other social media platforms to see this. Yes, it's a post-modern seething pool of raw words and experiences there. Perhaps teaching people to listen. Deplatforming hateful divisive half-truths. Our path forward is a difficult one. My most fundamental belief is that a positive step forward is to focus on our old ways, the ways that predate the Capitalist and Colonial power systems that enriched so few and murdered so many.

LH: In the poem "Letter to Kane from the Agnes Jamieson Gallery, Minden ON," from Devil in the Woods, *you wrote:*

> *Funny how one*
> *shapes the world in the manner one wants it to be.*
> *Dramatic theatre lighting and buckskin buffalo killers*
> *found homes in places we know about from Knowlton*
> *Nash.*

Then you present a contemporary image:

> *I've always maintained neither one's anything*
> *near how a real Anishinaabe guy waits for an Interac*
> *payment to go through at Foodland for mastery*
> *of form. We're all images of some true self.*

Why did you juxtapose the paintings of Paul Kane, the 19th century Irish-Canadian painter, to an image of the Anishinaabe guy waiting in line at Foodland while entering his pin number?

DL: Simply put I juxtaposed them because one is an act of romanticized and highly regarded fiction and the other is the harsh reality that those romanticized fictions landed us in. Kane's paintings depicted a world that led to Indigenous peoples, who once drew their very life essence from the land itself, living a life inherently free and decidedly naturally human, into a guy praying that some distant financial institution determines he has enough fictional wealth to purchase industrially produced and imported necessary food at a glorified warehouse run by the descendants who stole his and his relations access to the land and any sense of independence. Yet Kane's vision of Indigenous folks in the territories now encapsulated by the country of Canada is a surprisingly dominate view of actual contemporary Indigenous existence. And unless we all act like buckskin buffalo killers we aren't Indigenous. It's the sort of thought the leads society and publishers to accept and push fake "Indian" artists like Joseph Boyden and Gwen Benaway. They buy into the colonial stereotypes of what it means to being Indigenous in Canada today. In Boyden's case, it looks at how an ideal colonialized Indian should look, darker skin and all. And pointing out that all of us exist in a familiar world, one where we too struggle with buying our own groceries at a less-than-bougie grocery store, and it's not all Trauma porn and failed buffalo hunts is important. It's important because we are dominated in vision by non-Native imaginings of ourselves. That silencing continues today as it did in Kane's time. Following his take on our experiences is akin to the promotion of work of Preteindians like the aforementioned writers. And maybe writing a poem about it helps. Unlike many other non-stereotypical Indigenous folks I managed to get my voice through and onto the pages of published books or lit mags. My hope is that one day we can deftly illustrate the issue rather than saying, "Boy is that a pretty picture. I wish there were still noble Indians around like that."

LH: *In* Tùkhòne, *you employ variations of the traditional Japanese haiku based on seventeen syllables. How did you adapt this form in developing the subject matter for your book?*

DL: I know I spoke before about how much haiku as form drives my poetic creation process. There is a key connection point between traditional Japanese Buddhist underpinnings of haiku and the teachings of our old ways. Like the slippage between language and metaphors I mentioned earlier, it is not one-for-one, but the connections are engaging and interesting enough. I would argue that western poetic writing, except for maybe Norwegian poetry, tends to not match up well for Indigenous poetry or thought. Or at least Lenape thought, I can't possibly speak for all that First Nations experiences or philosophies. But in concrete aspects, the recasting of the natural world in a way we speak of ourselves and our experiences is so central to haiku and to more traditional Indigenous thought.

I find the thought at the core of haiku that most interested me was the notion of distillation. That the poem itself be stripped down to its most essential elements. As I worked through the haiku as both form and thought action, I approached the individual topic pieces as experience deconstructed into the signifiers that most closely appropriated my reaction as poetic self. Hence you get a lot of these Lenape nouns. Because the essence of those words implies the necessary spirit of the part of creation being discussed. There is also this experiential aspect of bringing the sounds and shapes of those words back into a more sustained usage. Basically, I imported a poetic framework and bent into this quasi-Indigenous thought and word act. And it was relatively achievable because there is a similar natural-world first thought at the core of the haiku form. A spot of shared consciousness if you will.

LH: *In addition to haiku in the second part of this collection, you employ another Japanese form—the haibun—a mixture of essay, journal type notations, and quotations from songs.*
DL: The haibun were a sort of release from the rigidness of the haiku. Limited by season, form, and action the haiku performed in one way. I wish to take broader strokes and perhaps elaborate in way on the process behind those haiku. I wanted a well-rounded book, I suppose, in terms of form. Fellow poet Dorothy Mahoney first introduced me to the form a few years

back. They just seemed to be the perfect mediation act in visible form for tackling the subject of music from Detroit. Perhaps because music is so multifaceted in terms of how one reacts to it. There is a need to leave space to elaborate and really open the work.

LH: *I've observed that you use epigraphs and quotations from rock, jazz, country and other kinds of music, making them an integral part of the poems. Could you elaborate on this?*

DL: I should start with I love music. It's always been a central aspect of my life. My parents brought me to concerts since I was super young, like Charlie Pride, Alabama, Kenny Rogers, Willie Nelson. My world started with country. But my taste has grown over the years. And that music came to form the basis for my memories and engagement with creation. I have a guitar and amp by my desk and use it multiple times every day. A partial act of meditation, I play to break writer's block or dive deeper into what thoughts I throw down on paper.

Popular music is the poetry of the people. It always has been. Artists like Bob Seger, Lightnin' Hopkins, Drake, Merle Haggard, Maestro Fresh Wes, Bob Dylan, Mellencamp—these are collective touchstones for people. If one envisions themselves as a rooted poet, a poet of the people, then one must turn to the touchstones held by those people. Most folks out there have a similar musical connection to the world and their pasts. And if I'm looking at poetry as a shared experience, I believe that including those musical touchstones in the work to be important. It's about building a web of experience with words, connecting what you are doing and making into something familiar. Back in the day, writers would be busy dropping T.S. Eliot, Ben Jonson, Keats' references. And some writers still do that with classic or canonical writers like that. They aren't what I would call voices of the people. People working retail or manual labour very, very rarely stand around listening to or reciting Wordsworth's works. Their memories, their dreams, their experiences are tied to the music of Dylan or Drake or Miley Cyrus. And their dreams and memories are what I am tied to as an artist and a person.

LH: *One of your main targets in poems is capitalism—a protest against the devastating effects of this system on the land and its people. Could you discuss this point with me a little more?*

DL: I should start by saying that Capitalism is a system that has grossly hurt the vast majority of humanity and enriched a scant few. In the totality of the human experience, it has occupied the smallest blip of our collective time. And as far as belief systems go it is among the worst ones around. It's a fundamentalist type of religion that refuses to coexist with any other notions of morality or spirituality. This because it ascribes a value, not a use value but a rather a bizarre concoction of rarity and demand, and strips away any other meaning from everything it touches. There is no room for spirituality nor measures of living beings beyond their ascribed value.

For Indigenous folks, or most folks of even the most remote ecological moral understanding of creation, capitalism is reprehensible. It's an imported and artificial belief system. I think of it, actually, as an on-going global pandemic. Look at all the damage it's done in terms of mass extinctions, genocide, and ecological collapses around the planet. It's a belief system that is choking the life out of our one and only home. Best exemplified by the criminal that was the forty-fifth president of the United States, there is no one person that someone under its belief won't sacrifice to earn more imaginary "money" or promote "growth." A sycamore tree, a redwood tree, a herd of woodland bison, pheasants can't be measured by value in dollars. This is a useless and imagined value, a real weak fetish of temporary human appetite. There is a spirit, a force, an essence behind existing in creation. And destroying those things to create this fetish that is money and growth is as reprehensible an act as murder. It is by most rationale measures purely murder. Capitalism is built on this absurd justification. It's more absurd than extreme religious ceremonies like Christian self-flagellation or genital mutilation because it's actually slowly killing the only thing that is keeping us all alive, the planet. Rather than massive species wide push at something like salvation, the world is following this path so that a couple handfuls of individuals can own more and bigger houses and do things that both scarcity and demand and good common sense holds the majority back from doing.

LH: *Do you feel that it is the responsibility of you as a writer to research and write about Indigenous history in order to map its importance in the Canadian mosaic?*

DL: I believe it is important for me to research and write about Indigenous history if for no other reason than the massive amount of misinformation being presented about it. Returning to Windsor, ON in the early 2010s was a shocking eye-opener in terms of seeing how much of the history of the region predating about 1950 had been constructed on half-truths and outright lies about Indigenous. At the time of this interview there are still local historians proclaiming that the only Indigenous peoples here were brought in by the French, that amazingly this little part of Turtle Island was somehow empty of peoples when these people's ancestors showed up. In the same vein the local government constructs a statue to Chief Tecumseh, who never lived here, actually despised the fact the European descendants were living here, and was not a part of the thirty or more actual chiefs that signed the collection of treaties covering Waawiiyaatanong. I have a responsibility to our ancestors and relations to right the record, to share our experiences, and stop our histories from being co-opted by those that would speak for us and all often in direct opposition to what helps or benefits our various Indigenous communities.

LH: *There have been a number of Indigenous protests over the last thirty years. I remember the Mohawk blockade of the Mercier Bridge in Montreal. More recently, out west, the Wet'suwet'en protested the building of the pipeline over their lands. And then there was the barricade on the Tyendinaga Mohawk Territory, which prevented trains from using the rail lines. Do you support such political actions? Do you think that they will bring necessary change?*
DL: I count Tecumseh and Kisopoko clan of the Shawnee as a substantial part of my ancestry. Perhaps because of that, the fire he kindled for an independent Indigenous homeland has left its embers in me. Oka was a major awakening for me. Witnessing those horrifying images across our family TV screen. And it worsened. I was at a wedding when Dudley George was murdered by the OPP under orders from Mike Harris. I witnessed the hurt and trauma of being Indigenous in contemporary Canada as the wedding reception came to an abrupt end when our chief and elders were called in to diffuse the situation. From all of this, I came to understand the myriad of ways that the state continues to murder and steal from our relations. It's personal. These events are fresh fuel for that ember that my ancestors left with me. Wet'suwet'en, Caledonian, Standing Rock, are simple extensions of Wounded Knee, Gnadenhutten, and Fallen Timbers. Protests are an antiseptic way of framing a war that has not ended since the first puritan murdered our ancestors. These "protestors" are actually our warriors, our protectors, in a war we've all sadly inherited from generations long dead. Will they bring change? They have. In small ways. In big ways, probably not. I am definitely not

as optimistic as I was in my Trent University undergraduate days. But we have to still keep the protests going. They are like embers for justice, for hope, for decolonization. I believe they will ignite a better path forward.

LH: *Recently more and more Indigenous writers have gained a wider readership: Liz Howard, Louise Bernice Halfe, Jordan Abel, and Billy-Ray Belcourt to name a few. Why do you think that Indigenous writers are now being recognized?*

DL: I think first and foremost with the aforementioned writers that they have gained a wider readership because they are supremely talented and are being recognized for that talent and their efforts. I would argue that similar voices have always been there. The problem being that there has concurrently been a system of white supremacy that has continually undermined work by Indigenous creators. I ran into this systemic racism when I first returned to Waawiiyaatanong. I heard from a good number of "respected" poets and writers from the area that I was only getting attention, or grants, or publications because of my Indigenous status. Which sounds like jealousy and to an extent it must have been (and still continues to this day). But also, these words pointed towards a level of disqualification based upon culture and/or "racial" background. And while it was not the dominant reaction to my work and my successes, it was common enough for me to have to learn how to respond professionally to not be perceived as another negative stereotype, the angry aggreged "Indian" artist. I point this out because I don't operate in a vacuum. And highly regarded Indigenous writers have without doubt experienced disturbingly similar instances.

And this is so much to say that racism and white supremacy in the academy and in the more elite levels of writing is most definitely a virus of sorts. And as it's treated and rooted out, cured if you will, we open spaces for Indigenous voices. This is critical because there are fewer reasons to disqualify challenging Indigenous work out of hand. Instead, readers, writers, and editors now have to approach the work of say Louise Bernice Halfe or David Groulx or Richard Van Camp as work of a seasoned and skilled creator. Writers like them have always been here. We've always been here. But the literary scene is finally coming to terms with our existence. What writers like Howard or Abel or Belcourt say or write might not be comfortable for readers. And it might not read like everything else that came before them. But not simply allowing for the disqualification of their work for what have been prejudicial cultural reasons is the primary reason for the recent surge in Indigenous authorship successes. Their successes are reflective of the growing successes of relegating white supremacist thought to the dumpsters that it deserves to inhabit. It is also reflective of a Canadian society that is changing for the better.

LH: *Why did you start the Urban Farmhouse Press? What triggered your interest in publishing others?*

DL: That probably goes back to *READ THIS* and those early days in Montana. But it is the belief that in publishing we form a community for a profession that is fundamentally done in isolation. I also witnessed a real gap in literary publishing in the United States. There were a lot of amazing regional and under-represented voices doing some really phenomenal things. Not every story had to be a dead grandmother story, or trauma porn, or a murder mystery. And not all of them had to come from California or the Atlantic coast. There were places for those, and there still are, but I felt them to be overly prevalent. After spending two semesters teaching Literary Publishing at Indiana University and an absolutely invaluable graduate course on the history of the book for library school,

I felt I had the underpinnings to give a go at filling the gaps. In honesty, I was and have been for a good amount of time, inspired by the work of Lawrence Ferlinghetti as a publisher. He was really a strong literary figure that struck back against unacceptable norms in the literary world. He crafted space for writers that wouldn't normally have been afforded space. Not to mention that full-time paid work was hard to come by in the early years after graduating. I found myself with time and drive and to do something about the inadequacies of literary publishing and a real desire to build a community that espoused similar views on the state of the literary world. So, in 2013, I started the press in our 1876 built farmhouse on the eastside of Indianapolis. Hence the name, Urban Farmhouse Press. We relocated to Waawiiyaatanong later that year, something that we hadn't planned for, but seemed to serve the press in a fantastic way.

LH: *Has this pandemic been difficult for you as a writer?*
DL: Up until the week or so before the pandemic took hold of our world, I was touring. In fact, I would say that the pandemic hit at about the midway point of my touring for *Devil in the Woods*, and that most definitely killed off the social portion of being a poet and writer. I recall being on a GO Bus between Union Station and Hamilton listening to stories about this horrible virus exploding overseas. The abrupt end to the tour made the early isolation of the pandemic perhaps a little harder to deal with. There was an added level of difficulty where I took a position with a Canadian academic press and had to deal, rather privately, with overt racism and harassment from the American director of the press in isolation. If anything in this pandemic, writing became a solace. A way to build a better world than the one I was living in. Because my poetry is so based in experience, the stay-at-home orders

pushed me into more of a fiction first creation mode. A lot of the work that was brewed up during this time was narrator and fiction based. And it's really hard to understand what this pandemic has done to me or society.

LH: *What are you working on now?*

DL: I have become more interested in recent months with longer form works. This is true for both my poetry and my prose. But I've been hard at work on two new book-length epic poems. The first is an epic poem constructed along the lines of Campbell McGrath's extraordinary "Bob Hope poem" from his *Spring Comes to Chicago* collection. It follows a narrator through a trip to a baseball game in contemporary Detroit but uses the original *Magnum PI* series as its method of exploration. It's a lot of commentary on capitalism, war, borders, and colonialism. The second major one is another epic poem about pro-wrestler Rowdy Roddy Piper and his visit to Pelee Island. It's a recasting of myth that explores the spectacle of wrestling with the quiet serenity of a remote community between countries and how one moves between them.

LH: *What was your reaction when you found out that 215 unmarked graves of Indigenous children were found on the grounds of the former Kamloops Indian Residential School and that 751 unmarked graves were found on the site of the Marieval Indian Residential School in Southern Saskatchewan?*

DL: Sad enough, I was far from shocked. Surprised won't even be a word I would use. My grandmother and many of relations were residential school survivors. So knowledge of the horrendous, murderous rampage of government and Christian-based institutions was fairly widespread in our community. I studied under Dr. John Milloy at Trent University. His work was rather central to the Royal Commission of

Indigenous Peoples in the late 1990s. And through him and his work it was clear as day that these mass graves existed. It was also clear that the Catholic Church and the Canadian Government wanted that information and knowledge to be left at the folk level. I don't know how the Canadian people can even consider letting the Catholic Church continue to operate any schools, let alone public ones, and receive tax-free status after unapologetically attempting to commit genocide. Honestly, the Proud Boys and just about every other hate group in this country have done less murdering and damage than the Roman Catholic Church. But here we are. Publicly funded murderers and serial sexual assaulters. It is disgusting and a clear sign that reconciliation is pretty far off from where we are now. Let's face it, most of the Canadian public has already found the next thing in the news cycle to entertain them. And the ground penetrating radar is just getting warmed up at a small number of those institutions of attempted genocide.

May, 2021

Photo credit: Katie Meyer

BRUCE MEYER

Laurence Hutchman: *You were born in Willowdale in the north part of Toronto. What was it like growing up there, and what effect had this place on your early writing? What remains with you of that experience that is a source of inspiration?*

Bruce Meyer: Actually, I was born in Toronto General Hospital at 3:45 p.m. on April 23. Earle Birney had a photograph of himself, E.J. Pratt, Irving Layton, and Leonard Cohen together on Bloor Street at the exact moment I was born. They were celebrating Cohen's first book, *Let Us Compare Mythologies*. I wasn't happy in Willowdale. I wasn't really happy with my education or where I lived until I reached Victoria College and studied with Northrop Frye, Jay Macpherson, Alexandra Johnston, and Ken Bartlett. I wasn't, in retrospect all that happy at university either, although I had a much richer experience there. People have constantly doubted me, questioned what I could do. I would have given anything early on for the sort of mentors who appeared almost like angels and pointed me in the right direction—Gwendolyn MacEwen, Richard Howard, and later David Wevill. The high school, Earl Haig, did not encourage my writing except for two teachers— Gordon Johnson and John Moses—who were mildly encouraging but I know now they didn't know enough themselves to give me the sort of help I needed. Gifted children are cursed with a lack of gifted teachers. I felt like an outsider. The bullies were constantly picking on me. I'd broken my back when I was twelve so I wasn't athletic. But I think the place tempered me for what I wanted to do. It took years for me to sort out the experience, the trauma of it. I learned the history of the area that had once been Oriole. My Uncle ran a local landmark, Dempsey Brothers Hardware Store, that has been started by Joseph Sheppard after whom the east-west street was named. I did have deep connections to the area and tried to write about them but those poems came to naught. Later, when I was at university, life began for me at Victoria College, a place I still love dearly and where I teach one night a week. During my growing years, I'd had to write poetry in secret. At Victoria College, a person was encouraged to write poetry. It was the literary college that had produced Pratt, Atwood, Avison, Lee. I felt like I was part of a tradition there. But the area where I grew up, the Yonge and Sheppard area of north Toronto, was rich in drama and legend. It had been where the 1837 Rebellion was hatched. My uncle, George Dempsey, owned the store at Yonge and Sheppard that had been built by Joseph Sheppard Jr. on his return from transportation to Australia after the Rebellion. My book, *1967: Centennial Year*, about what it was like to be ten years old in 1967 for Canada's hundredth anniversary, is set in that area. I guess it wasn't all bad, but better things happened later.

LH: *You attended Earl Haig Secondary School. I take it you weren't happy there.*

BM: It was a difficult time of life for me. I was captain of the *Reach for the Top* team, and that generated more harm than good. I was a "browner," as they called smart people. I stood third in my graduating year, the highest-ranking arts student in the school. Mr. Johnson taught me grammar and Shakespeare. Mr. Moses encouraged me to write although he didn't know how to help me. I decided I hated the place so much that I'd sneak up on my Grade 13 by going to summer school. My Dad's family, who were miserable to me and all science people, insisted I was doing summer school because I'd failed. I hadn't. I had high grades in subjects I loved. At summer school, I was lucky to get a teacher for Modern Literature. His name was Philip King. He taught me Frost, Eliot, Beckett, Hemingway. I loved that course. I got 98 in it, which is unheard of. He said to me on the last day, "You'll go far."

LH: *Donald Hall in his essay "Four Kinds of Reading" suggests that great readers are born in adolescence. When did you begin to read seriously?*

BM: That's hard to answer. I taught myself to read at the age of three using a tray table that had animals on it and the alphabet around the edge. I write about this in *The Alphabet Table.* I wrote my first poem at five. My first poem was for a friend of my grandmother's. I sold a poem when I was ten. Literature was my salvation as I was growing up, and even now it is the sanity zone in my working life. I read at least two books of poetry per day. I can't get enough literature. The summer I studied with Philip King, my grandmother was dying so I was left pretty much on my own. During my Grade 13 year, there was a strike at the high school so I skipped off and sat in on classes at Victoria College, especially a class taught by one of my mother's former professors, Christopher Love. That is when I decided I wanted to be an English professor. I sat in on Northrop Frye's classes. He eventually became my mentor. I had Jay Macpherson as a professor and fell in love with Romantic Poetry. Alexandra Johnston taught me Medieval Literature and Chaucer and I was addicted to *Troilus and Criseyde.* Ken Bartlett gave me the Renaissance. During my first month at Victoria College, I was asked to take over editing the oldest literary magazine in the country, *Acta Victoriana,* that had been edited by Pratt, Frye, Avison, Atwood, and Lee, and I felt as if I had found a place where people were encouraging me to write. Timothy Findley was Writer-in-Residence one year and he was a tremendous support and teacher. I read everything I could get my hands on. I went to readings. I gave poetry readings at places such as The Axletree Coffee House and the basement of the Main Street Public Library. That's where I met Livesay, Purdy, and Acorn who became a mentor to me along with Gwendolyn MacEwen. MacEwen told me that I was the son she and Milton Acorn would have had if they had stayed married. That's when I was certain I wanted to be a writer. That's where my love of literature became a vow, a vocation, a calling.

LH: *Some of your poems are a tribute to your father. A son's relationship with his father is often complex. What kind of relationship did you have with your father?*

BM: I am still sorting that one out. When I was a child, he used to beat me, badly sometimes, yet he was a part of my life. My first memory is of my father showing me a gas station key ring fob that said "BA" when you turned it one way and "Fill it up" when you turned it the other way. The first book that I loved with a passion and that he read to me was *The Funny Bunny Factor*. I still have a copy of it. He read me history, as well. My mother read me poetry before my afternoon naps—Wordsworth, Coleridge—the greatest hits from John Drinkwater's anthology. But my father, as I grew older, would yell at me if I was lying on my bed reading. He would say I was a good for nothing. I would sneak out in my high school years and go to the Bohemian Embassy and my father would tell me they were going to turn me on to drugs. I said, "No something better—the high of poetry." During university, I met two other poets, Andrew Brooks and Larry Hopperton, and we'd hang out in beery places like the Brunswick House and the Duke of York basement, and read each other poetry. We were joined by Richard Harrison and George Elliott Clarke and James Deahl. Sometimes Pier Giorgio Di Cicco sat in with us. We had the thrill of knowing we were doing something artistically illicit. My father only came around many years later when I was teaching at the U of T. It was my Great Books course for Continuing Literature is a continuum.

LH: *I notice in your work the prevalence of animals. You see them as creatures that we can learn from. This is especially true of your book* Dog Days.

BM: Yes. I have a dog. Her name is Daisy. She is one of the truly great souls I know. Some people have pets. I have a companion. Anatole France said, and I paraphrase, that "One cannot truly know one's own soul until one has looked into the eyes of a dog." That's true with my Daisy. She knows what we say. She is very kind. When Marty Gervais from Black Moss phoned and said he wanted to do a book of new poems, I said: "I had some about dogs but they weren't a book yet." "Send me the dog poems," he said. The next night I received the cover design for *Dog Days*, a yellow tennis ball torn open on a background of grey marble. That book sold like wildfire. It was read by Bob Chelmak on the CKUA radio in Edmonton and it went through four printings. It is now sold out entirely. The book is structured in five acts. The subtitle is *A Comedy of Terriers*.

LH: *Do you see yourself as a spiritual poet?*

BM: I am not a religious poet. I could never toe the party line correctly. I ask too many questions. I am a Protolic. I was raised a Protestant and became a Catholic, and I have lapsed and ended up somewhere in between. That said, I do believe that there's a spirit that inhabits all things. My former officemate, the psychologist Richard Rinaldo, used to argue that we don't have souls and that there's no spirit in things. But I'm a poet. Poets live the life not only of the mind but of the soul. Poets have to recognize that there is a "force that through the green fuse drives the flower," as Dylan Thomas said. I marvel at the passage in Saint Augustine's *Confessions* where he asks, "What is my God?" and everything answers: "We are not your God but He is in us and made us." I don't subscribe to Creationism, but I do subscribe to what I call "the glue and energy theory," that everything is animated and held together by some sort of presiding consciousness. That's poetry. I wouldn't call it religion. I believe in compassion. I believe in the power of the imagination—not prayer but ideas wanting to be something more—to answer our needs and help us solve our problems. Prayer is a form of deep thought or sincere imagination. I've been the recipient of miracles. When my daughter was born, the nurses lost her heartbeat at four a.m. and told us the baby would be stillborn. She was rushed to the neonatal intensive care ward and my wife was worked on by a team of surgeons and nurses. I didn't know where to go. I wandered the halls of St. Michael's Hospital until I found an empty blue room—and there was an old, black rotary phone sitting on the floor. I called my mom and told her to get down to the hospital because the baby wasn't supposed to live past eleven a.m. After I hung up, I had the strange feeling I was being watched. I turned around and there was a life-sized statue of the Virgin Mary staring at me. I said to her, "Please don't take my baby. I want, more than anything in the world to be a father." I got up, went up to the neonatal intensive care ward. The nurses and doctor had given up working on her. She was dying. So, I decided to sing to her. I began to sing "Somewhere Over the Rainbow." The baby opened her eyes and looked at with as if she knew me. Then, suddenly, the heart kicked in. Perfect rhythm. The nurses and the doctor came running. "What have you done?" they asked. "I sang to my baby," I said. The doctor tore up a piece of paper. I asked him what it was. "That was your daughter's death certificate."

LH: *That's a very moving story, Bruce. Thank you for sharing it. Your poems seem to be conceived on an individual stage, but you are aware of a larger whole—the poems and books sometimes seem to have an intertextual relationship.*

BM: My work comes from my life and I believe my life is inextricably bound up with my imagination, the power to think of what can happen in a positive way and to make it happen with a generosity of spirit to others. I don't think a person can wall off portions of life and compartmentalize life from the imagination. The two are constantly conversing. The work comes from a single consciousness. I try to do something new every time I take up my pen. That said, if literature in the greater sense is a conversation, a party, a social network of the printed page so to speak, that same scalability is at work in the lives we live on so many different levels. There's an inner conversation that plays a tremendous role in what a writer or a poet writes. The same pair of eyes, the same senses, the same brain, is at work. I find that I need to be aware of the presence of these epistemological tools because they can lead a writer to repeat himself and I never write the same thing twice. Every work must be new. John Reibetanz once saw a poem of mine in a magazine and before he read who'd written it he said he recognized it as one of mine. That's pleasing and troubling. It is pleasing in that it means I have a distinct voice, yet troubling in that I'm not doing as much with the voice as I could. Should a poet consciously pursue anomalies? Should he rely on the idea of *decoro*, the rules for doing things? *Decoro* is a Renaissance idea from Giorgio Vasari who suggests that every poem has to play by the rules the poet inherits. I suppose that's where I get my interest in form. But within those rules, within those confines of *decoro,* there's a lot of room for play, something James Reaney taught me. Play is the process of reinvigorating reality by inventing a parallel universe that may or may not be real.

LH: *In many of your works, you have chosen to write using traditions such as those of the aubade, villanelle, triolet, and elegy.*

BM: Let's not forget the sestina. I do those, too. They are the Mount Everest of poetic forms. They engage in either ennui or profusion. The first time I wrote one, I sat up all one summer night on the back deck of our first home in Toronto and worked at it until I got it. The high from accomplishing my first sestina is something I'll never forget. I once won a bet—first base, third-row seats at a Phillies game at Veterans Stadium—by writing a sestina with two words per line.

LH: *Why, when there has been such emphasis on experimenting with language, have you chosen more traditional forms? What formalist poets do you read?*

BM: I read all kinds of poems by all kinds of poets. My favourites are Hacker, Larkin, Salter, but there are many others. With Jonathan Barron, my good friend at the University of Southern Mississippi, I co-edited *The Dictionary of Literary Biography* volume on the *American New Formalists,* and at Dana Gioia's insistence, I was included in their ranks with an article on my work. I have had more critical attention from the US, Spain, and even Bangladesh than I've had in Canada. The sad thing about Canadian poetry is that ninety percent of it is monotone blather. It has all the musical power of someone announcing a train is running late, and the trains in Canada are always late. When I was a Ph.D. student, I discovered Larkin. I remember reading *The Whitsun Weddings* on the bus from Toronto to Hamilton, and thinking, "How the hell did he do this?" I was amazed that language could be so fluid, so honest, and yet so sad while doing such wonderful things. Then I thought, why are we so afraid of what language can do in this country, especially with regard to form? We've had some great formal poets—Fred Cogswell, Richard Outram—but we won't go near form, though.

LH: *There is no need to exclude formal poetry from the contemporary canon because the writer employs more traditional elements of style.*

BM: The problem was that, during my three years of Ph.D. work at McMaster (I did my Ph.D. in three years which is unheard of), my first book of poems, *The Open Room*, the one you were at the launch for in 1989, was rejected over 1000 times. Experimentalism, as it was known at the time, was considered to be the voice of poetry. Form was old-fashioned, fascist, right-wing, all sorts of nonsense was attached to received forms. Jeffery Donaldson, himself a very fine poet, sent my manuscript to the American Pulitzer Prize winner, Richard Howard in 1985. Howard wrote back. "What did I want to know?" I asked him, "How should I write?" He responded with a very important message: "There is no right way or wrong way, there is only your way, but consider taking your poems apart and put them back together using meter, rhyme, and form." I tried it. I got another 200 rejections.

Then James Deahl, without telling me, bless him, dropped the manuscript on Gwendolyn MacEwen's desk when she was Writer-in-Residence at the U of T. She told me she loved my poetry, that it shouldn't be rejected, and that she would send it along to Marty Gervais at Black Moss Press with a letter telling him to publish it. She'd spent her last Christmas reading my book. A week after she died the following October,

I got the acceptance letter for *The Open Room*. The book is dedicated to her. *The Open Room* got written up in *MacLean's*. I was interviewed on the CBC along with Sam Gwynn who is a formal poet from Texas and Molly Peacock who was in New York and now lives in Toronto. The US formalist poets had just published an anthology, *Rebel Angels*, edited by Robert McDowell (who ran Story Line Press and who published the US edition of *The Presence* several years later) and Mark Jarman. That anthology made the front pages of *The New York Times* and *The Financial Post*. *Time* magazine did an article on the anthology. It was big news. Who had triggered it? Richard Howard. When he told me to use meter, rhyme, and form, he was telling everyone else to do so as well—Peacock. Salter, Dana Gioia, Marilyn Hacker.

LH: *I'm intrigued by the idea of the effect of other writers on your writing. You appear to have been influenced by Yeats, Neruda, Purdy, and Rilke.*
BM: Thank you. That's a wonderful list. You do me honour. They are my best buddies when it comes to wordsmithing. You are speaking of the voices I love. Don't forget Heaney, Walcott, Lorca, Tranströmer, Young Lee, Larkin, Kooser, Zagajewski, and Billy Collins to name a few. I can't say I have a favourite poet. That would be like the father of a family of twenty kids saying he loves one better than all the others. That would just be wrong. There is a beauty in the written word that inspires awe when the poems move or excite or engage a reader to notice the complexities of the world.

LH: *What poets have inspired you in the past and present time? Are there contemporary poets, many of whom you know personally, that you enjoy reading?*

BM: The aforementioned, of course. I like your work. I always enjoy it when we give a reading together. I adore George Elliott Clarke's work. I heard another poet poo-poo him at a reading and I told her to go to hell. George is gifted because he is expansive. He's someone who isn't afraid of using all the tools and he uses them with grace and power. I love the work of John B. Lee. He's funny, perhaps the best philosophical poet this country has produced, and a poet who has been completely overlooked by the critics because he can entertain a conversation about eternal verities while discussing cows over Sunday dinner with his family. He's truthful. He's genuine. He's memorable. I love the poetry of Marty Gervais because he has a way of reporting on the beautiful actualities of life while being totally honest about what he sees and his reaction to experience. Molly Peacock, Daniel Lockhart, Bruce Hunter, Laurence Hutchman—their work fascinates me because they are looking beyond themselves at what is human and important in our lives. My problem is that I read just about everything. I've had the privilege of knowing and corresponding with Seamus Heaney and Charles Tomlinson. They were mentors to me, not just poets on the page. They answered my questions. They gave me feedback, useful ideas in the engineering of the voice of the heart. I got to know Derek Walcott well when he was in Toronto. I'd go for walks with him. I love the work of Douglas Dunn, for example, and spent a lot of time together when he was here. I don't like poets who chain-smoke, who pretend that poetry is suffering or pose with intense self-awareness and behave in dark, despondent ways or who pretend to be tortured souls. There are many of those in Canada and I won't honour them by listing off their names. They write utter garbage because they refuse to celebrate life and find joy in small things. David Wevill, my mentor, says "the hardest thing to imagine is yourself," and in terms of the poetry that self-imagination engenders is the poetry of celebration. We lose the small but important moments in life when we love others or discover things, and that sense of revelation is what we need to embrace. As for the posing poets, they have always disliked me. Maybe they think I'm not dark enough. I find their poetry hard to take. The photographer, Mark Raynes Roberts, was photographing me and he'd just come for a shoot in downtown Toronto where one of the tortured-soul poets raged against me. Poets I love are the ones who find beautiful ways to make poetry say thank you to life. That's what poetry is: a thank you letter to life.

LH: *Related to the last question is your interest in other writers. During your long writing career, you have met many writers such as Leonard Cohen, Richard Howard, Brian Moore, and Seamus Heaney. You co-authored, with Brian O'Riordan, two books of interviews:* In Their Words *and* Lives and Works. *Why was it important for you to interview these particular writers?*

BM: Alas, I never interviewed Richard Howard or Seamus Heaney, although, as I mentioned, they were wonderful correspondents. I have forty unpublished interviews with British poets, and I hope to do something about those. Yes, I learned about writing, and I interviewed writers because they had something important to say, but the benefit for me was that they taught me things I might not have figured out on my own. Irving Layton taught me how to tell a bad line from a good one, his idea of the "shit detector." Eli Mandel and James Reaney, in particular, taught me that a nation's literature is a family discourse and that poetry is made of the small things in our lives that go missing far too easily. As a young writer, I didn't know where to turn for advice. That's where the interviews had their impact. Brian Moore said that a writer "has to be ruthless." When I asked him what he meant, he said, "steal from your own experience and don't give a damn who questions what you're doing." That's ruthless. Howard told me to find my own way to say what I wanted to say. I found a quote from Thelonius Monk and carried it in my wallet for twenty years. Monk said, "Play your own way. Don't play the way people tell you to play. Play your own way, and eventually people will catch on even if it takes them twenty or thirty years." I had been told by a major Canadian poet to write like this person or that person. That's the worst advice a young writer can receive. The struggle in writing is to find one's own voice, the way of saying things in a way that no one else has said them. To find that, one must read and one must write. The introduction to *Lives and Works* is a pretty good essay on the nature and purpose of literary interviews. But what has stayed with me from all those conversations is that in speaking with people who have turned into bronze statues, such as MacEwen, Purdy, Acorn, and even my beloved Frye, I was giving voice to what it means to be Canadian by asking the writers to take their own vision a step further than what they had put on the page, refine that, and pronounce that. We needed that in Canada. Interviews are a means of breaking what Cohen called "the stony silence on the Seaway." Real criticism asks questions of the source, and we don't practice much of that in Canada. To answer your question, interviewing is a privilege. One learns from asking questions of those who have acquired knowledge and, yes, wisdom, in their own explorations of the connection between life and literature.

LH: *Increasingly, Canadians are interested in the Great War of 1914 to 1918. There has not been much written about this war's poetry by Canadians. You edited* We Wasn't Pals: Canadian Poetry and Prose of the First World War. *What drew you to it and why?*

BM: It was a lost decade of our nation's literature. Barry Callaghan asked me if I could find any information about Frank Prewett and that began a fifteen-year quest once I recognized Prewett was only one of many Canadian writers who were in the trenches. I showed the original books to Barry Callaghan while we were playing the ponies one day in Bigliardi's Bar with Austin Clarke. "My God," said Barry. "Does anyone know about this stuff? This is amazing!" Barry Callaghan put the work in the order it is in now, but the search, the digging, the hunt that lasted fifteen years and took me through barn shops, junk bins in second-hand bookstores, and library discard piles, was my work. I felt I had to give voice to the poets and fiction writers of the war, the trench poets, the nurses who had treated the wounded in France or England, the airmen who had been shot down, the soldiers who did not survive the war but foresaw their inevitable deaths. They needed to have their say. They needed to be heard. We had lost ten years of our nation's literature about the moment we became a nation. We bled ourselves into existence on Vimy Ridge and at Passchendaele. The problem was that the uber-critic of the age, E.K. Brown, wrote a book that everyone thought was gospel, *On Canadian Poetry*. In one sentence, he trashed some of our most important writing: "Nothing of note or worth was written during the war." Just like that. Poof. Ten years of our literature gone. My good friend and continual mentor, Barry Callaghan, set my quest for our trench literature in motion. Robert Graves had told Callaghan about Prewett. I became a literary bloodhound. I hunted for manuscripts, literally hauling myself up ropes into the attics of abandoned houses to find a missing generation of authors. When I was doing my CBC broadcasts with Michael Enright, we were having coffee one day. Enright is a great listener. I told him about the lost ten years of Can Lit. We decided to do a Remembrance Day broadcast in 2000. When Enright put the idea to his production team and said we had a lost literature, they responded it was probably lost for a reason and should stay that way. He insisted and overruled them. We did the broadcast and we got an enormous response. More work came out of the void. What the World War One experience tells me is that as a nation we are resistant to anything that is not announced at a cocktail party. We want the pizzazz of the moment. We want the press release, not the revelation. We desire the splash, not the depth of the still pond. We embrace the popular but forsake the unpopular truth. It is going to bite us someday. What we ignore will be a wound upon our nation. There are probably secrets waiting out there that will shatter the illusions of who and what we are as a civilized people. We will pay the price for believing marketing and simpering showmen over true but lost voices. We need to find the bravery to seek ourselves. *We Wasn't Pals* was a bestseller in 2000. It changed people's perceptions but only after the book rattled them.

LH: *In your work, you are not only concerned with smaller individual elements but a larger vision. The poems are precise transformations of history, encyclopaedic in scope, reminding me of Hugh Hood's presentation of historical Toronto. Why are you so fascinated with local history?*

BM: I live here. History is in my face. That said, I consider history to be multifold. Yes, there are the larger events that have taken place here. I'm fascinated by what we lose and how easily we lose it. I found the first baseball stadium in Toronto, Sunlight Park. My friend, the Don Valley historian Charles Sauriol, told me I'd have a hard time proving Sunlight Park ever existed. I went through all 15,000 images in the James Collection in the basement of City Hall. I went through 40,000 images in the Baldwin Room Collection of Toronto

Public Library. In every image that came close to showing the park, the park was hiding, just out of frame. I found newspaper articles about games played there—the first Canadian professional sports championship game, won by Toronto, on September 13, 1885. And on Christmas Eve I found two huge triptychs. There it was, Sunlight Park, in both items, as seen from a balloon anchored over Toronto Harbour. I called my friends, the baseball historians Bill Humber and Russell Field, and told them I had found the grail. We stared at the images. I had proven the place existed. I had found the unknown.

LH: *In some of your poems you act like an archaeologist. They are like palimpsests evoking different layers of history. For example, in the poem "Victoria Square" you speak to your daughter about the people buried beneath you in a small public park:*

> *I wanted to show my daughter the place*
> *where pioneers were once remembered—*
> *four hundred or more bodies—not a trace*

> *among them left on stone; the peasants,*
> *the founders, the defenders, the cursed,*
> *lie beneath us like sleeping tenants.*

BM: I'm glad you said that. Purdy was an archaeologist of our collective experience. In the case of Victoria Square, there is this enormous, buried history that we refuse to acknowledge. Heaney, one of my favourite poets, does the same thing in terms of digging through the layers of Ireland's past. Why we don't embrace the same process is beyond me. Heaney and I exchanged letters after he released *Field Work*. I pointed out that he'd been going down through the layers of Irish bogs progressively in his books and that he'd finally hit rock bottom.

I asked him where he'd go from there, and he responded, in his playful manner, that there was something beneath even the bedrock and he was working on it. His next book was *Station Island*, which is about Purgatory, the underworld, the nether region that is not beyond redemption, his Ireland. I think poets are looking for the afterlife. They are eschatological by nature. All the great epics contain a *nekusis* scene, a harrowing of Hell. *The Odyssey, The Aeneid, The Commedia Divina, Paradise Lost, Station Island, Omeros.* They are all about the search for the blessings of the eternal. That timelessness, that eternity, is where poetry lives. Shakespeare's "Sonnet 18" ends with the line: "So long lives this and this gives life to thee." Poets seek the eternal, though to say so today is highly unfashionable. There's a line from Horace that keeps entering my life: *litera scripta manet.* The written word survives. We want to know several things: Who are we? What is our purpose here? What will become of us? I weep for poets who say we have no souls and that we have no possibility of living forever. In our words, we live. Knowing our history is extremely helpful because it tells us where we can begin to look if we want to be part of the broader human memory.

LH: *Your poetry is about the possibility of the imagination and how to formulate important questions in modern times. Despite the present condition of the world, your poems have a tone of optimism: "You can make a song out of anything you put your mind to."*

BM: Poetry is song, and song, a lyric, whether it laments or celebrates, remembers something important. A poem is a container for the exponential wonder of a moment. I don't think the world is a bad place, as I've said. As someone who is fascinated by history, I think there have been far worse times when I could have lived. Freud says at the end of *Civilization and Its Discontents* that the early part of the last century left us with one overwhelming question: Will we blow ourselves up? He predicted the bomb. I take Faulkner's route. I don't think we'll destroy ourselves. There are moments when we seem to be expressing a will to self-destruction because at the root of that will is a failure to recognize that other people are human beings, too, and without others, we would not exist. I write on behalf of love. It is the only thing I can do. To ignore that, to ignore the need to recognize the absolute, indisputable necessity of human kindness and compassion is to fail the language. Language is what brings us together. It is not for pushing us apart. We are all different but we are also all the same, a paradox that resides at the complicated core of human relationships. I love learning about the other, perhaps because I love learning about who I am and who others are. The Tower of Babel story is not about the origin of national languages but of our consistent failure to learn from each other, to understand what another person is saying. Each of us has our own language, not just a mother tongue, but an inner tongue, a voice that is personal. Being human means we have to learn a plethora of languages, and even then, it is hard to completely know another person. But that's a test we're all given. My greatest fear is that we will be lazy with our minds and lazy with our poetry. Our salvation resides in critical thinking because critical thinking, selecting, asking questions, seeking connections, desiring to know how love can teach us more than what we think we know is what poetry is all about. I am not sure poetry can save the world, but it is as good a place as any to start.

LH: *George Elliott Clarke comments on* The Obsession Book of Timbuktu *that "Bruce Meyer knows that the secret of good poetry is obsession … To read Meyer is to share his passion for beauty whether it is 'obsession and February'." Can you speak about this book in terms of desire, obsession, and beauty?*

BM: Poetry is obsession. It is obsession if someone makes a life's work of it. Unfortunately, as I point out In the introduction to *The Obsession Book of Timbuktu*, the lyric is dying—that vehicle which sings in celebration and laments at what we have lost. It is an obsession when it acts as a millstone around one's neck. I become physically ill if I can't write. Sometimes I can't write as well as I want. I throw huge amounts of material aside. Sometimes, I go back to it years later. In the back of my mind, I have a goal I want to reach, and in that respect, it is like the historical Timbuktu was to Europe, an obsession, an unattainable desire or destination that will never be satisfied or reached and the farther point one can travel both physically and imaginatively.

LH: Testing the Elements *is one of my favourites among your books. On its back cover, a critic wrote: "To record experience with passion and crafted detail transforms the transitory into the attainable." Could you comment on this quotation?*

BM: He was being generous. I'm never sure I reach that point. I'm glad he or she is satisfied. The front cover is one of my favourites. Michael Callaghan came up with the image and he knows me well. He knows I beat up on myself a great deal. I keep writing because there is something new that I discover every day. That's a nice quote on the back of the book, but I can't take it seriously. If I did, I wouldn't have anything more to write for.

LH: *The poem, "The Movie Being Filmed Across the Street from My Hotel Window" is an ekphrastic poem in which you use key strategies to express your experiences. What was the genesis of the poem?*

BM: That's one of my "concert pieces." I was on an Ontario Arts Council Jury one year and they put me up in the Intercontinental Hotel on Bloor Street. On check-in, the clerk offered me a quiet room at the back. "No," I said, "I want a room overlooking Bloor Street, one of the ones with a bay window so I can sit in a chair and watch to see if anyone I know is going by." I saw people I hadn't seen in years. In the middle of the night, I was asleep in the buff, and I was awakened by someone on a megaphone and flashing blue police car lights. The voice hollered, "Everyone come out slowly with your hands up! We have the place surrounded! I ran to the bathroom and grabbed the fluffy robe they offer guests, and because of my equatorial expanse, it wouldn't meet across my girth. So there I was with a robe that wouldn't close and my underwear and shoes somewhere in the dark. I went to the window and looked out with a drape wrapped around my middle, and I realized the police cruisers said NYPD and that they were filming a movie in front of the Royal Conservatory. That's where the poem comes from. The line that the poem repeats is "We are always somewhere else in our dreams." Dreams fascinate me, not for their content or narrative matter—everyone has dreams—but in the way they are creative structures of the unconscious mind. I realize it is the one poem that comes closest to an *ars poetica* for me. I am also fascinated by Medieval and early Renaissance painting. In every major city I visit—New York, London, Ottawa—I always go to the main art gallery and the first thing I want to see are paintings from that strange period in the Western imagination when we believed what we saw or invested belief in a moment or a perception. That's the ultimate in audience participation—not the holler back stuff that poets try to evoke or that bad local theatre engages in where the audience has to get up on stage. I loathe that sort of thing. For me, art is ritual. A Catholic mass is the purest form of theatre I've witnessed, and I was a Catholic for a long time before I lapsed. What I found in Catholicism was the conversation between idea and action, the demonstration of thought as a form of performance. They even fed me. But what they fed me was an idea, the living enactment of the insubstantial, the pageant that fades as Shakespeare called it; and that, for me is what poetry should strive for. It should be theatre of the mind in a very private way. The poets I love and admire do that. Take a look at Heaney's "Postscript," or "Tuesday, June 9, 1991" by Billy Collins. Those poems do that. What passes as experimental poetry, or even intellectual poetry, lets me down because it won't engage the theatrical at the core of our brains.

LH: *In "Musée de Bonne Chance," you find connections between the personal and the objective events of the RMS Titanic sinking on the night your grandparents were wed.*

BM: Yes. My father's parents. As they said their vows—they were married late at night in my great grandmother's front parlour on Dunn Avenue in Toronto—the Titanic struck the iceberg. I think that became a metaphor for all their family relationships. My father's mother, who wrote a book I can't locate, had given up going to university on a full scholarship (she was the top student in Ontario when she graduated from Parkdale Collegiate) to marry my paternal grandfather and inherit a large estate. My father's father was a very strange man. Angry, temperamental, full of himself with delusions of grandeur, he was ten feet from McKinley when that president was assassinated in Buffalo. He burned through my grandmother's fortune. We discovered he may have had another family in New York City. He crossed the border and would stay away for three months at a time. In the later years of their marriage, my very literary grandmother who I would have loved to have known referred to my grandfather as "that man," and would never speak to him directly. That portion of the family's past is a miasma to me. I've looked into it, but the more I found the less I liked what I saw. It was the antithesis of my mother's parents who were saints and heroes to me.

LH: *Your book* The Seasons *was rewarded with a literary prize in the United States.*

BM: Yes. That book went entirely unnoticed here in Canada. It was given the IP Medal as the best book of poems in North America for 2014.

LH: *It is partially modelled on Pablo Neruda's* Cien Sonetas de Amor. *The poems are dedicated to your wife.*

BM: Yes, I was drawn to Neruda. Neruda's *sonetas* are the most beautiful poems written in the twentieth century. Mine are more about reality than about images and dreams. I started penning them while I was riding the bus four hours a day back and forth to Orillia and Barrie during the years I was working all over the place as a part-timer. I would look out the window at the same landscape I saw every day and think about the things my wife and I had done together, the memories I wanted to record of the little things in our lives that might otherwise go missing. The details of life that escape us are the grains of sand that contain our love. Structurally, the sonnets in *The Seasons* are meant to sound as if they have been translated. The secret in them is their titles. The titles are in square brackets after the poems, as afterthoughts. What I was striving for was a bridge between Eastern and Western poetry. Western poetry loves sound, sounds of all kinds. Eastern poetry is about the eye, the little vision. A haiku is a "word picture." I wanted to fuse the two traditions, the little sound and the intersected moment made of other moments. To me, that fusion is a record of living, the material that life and living leave behind for just an instant, the ripples in the pond of experience and reality. The one image that will never leave me because it is the most beautiful image of all is that of looking in my wife's green eyes as she said her marriage vows to me. I wasn't thinking of jewels in the earth as Neruda does, although he probably found that was a suitable objective correlative for what he wanted to express to Mathilde.

LH: *In* The Seasons *you present a philosophy of love. You are giving various definitions of love and different portraits of it. Can you comment on this?*

BM: The last line of the book is going to appear on my gravestone. I'll be buried, I hope, in a plot (next to Kerry), in Mount Pleasant Cemetery in Toronto. The plot is contiguous to the one that contains the fifteen bodies from the *Empress of Ireland* disaster. It has a nice view of Yonge Street. In any case, the final line is "To be is to live and to live is to love." You're right. *The Seasons* is an *ars amoria*, though I refrained from any Ovidian bawdy stuff which is kind of insincere to me. Love is the hardest thing to write about. Heaney wouldn't put the word to paper. It is not one thing. It exists in everything we do. The problem is that we're busy doing what we need to do or what takes us out of ourselves—what Joseph Campbell called 'finding our bliss' or just the daily junk we have to do to survive—that we don't perceive or even suspect its presence when it is right there among us. I don't think the world is an evil place. I think people who refuse to act out of love are evil. They, not the world, are to blame. People who cannot find the humanity in others or who deny it for themselves do the world tremendous harm. I admire Emmanuel Levinas, the great philosopher. He lost his entire family in the Holocaust, yet he professed to see the face of God in every human being. That's a triumph of what love does for us. We can't define love precisely; we can only notice it, and it is hard to see most of the time but it is there. The most unacknowledged human desire, the most overlooked form of love is the desire not to harm others but to welcome them into our experience as they welcome us into theirs. Bravo. Amen. That's what poetry

235

does. It invites everyone into the conversation, be it the great conversation of the ideas of literature or the small, whispered conversations of personal moments. And it isn't about what we talk about, but why we talk. I said in *The Golden Thread* that literature is the process in which we write ourselves into existence. We need to listen to each other. Why? Because silence is death. Poetry lasts longer than life, and because of that we can talk not over death in a scream or a shout but through and beyond it and remind each other of what we have lived for and what we have loved.

January 7, 2019

Photo credit: Steven Payne

AL MORITZ

Laurence Hutchman: *Some poets at certain times in their lives will turn attention to their ancestry, as for instance Robert Lowell in* Life Studies *or Brian Bartlett in his book* The Watchmaker's Table. *Your father's and mother's family are from different nationalities. I'm curious if any one of your forebears was involved in writing?*

Al Moritz: Not that I know of, and I'm pretty certain that I can say "no". They were from poor peasant classes, in both Hungary and Italy. Both my parents were well-educated and were teachers. My father was a professor of biology and of science education, and my mother was a teacher with a Master of Education degree and who served sometimes as an assistant principal. Both could write well. My mother eventually helped write—was the major author of—a history of our town, Niles, Ohio.

LH: *In various interviews, you have talked about the key literary influences in your early life. Were there books other than poetry that influenced your formative years—ones from the world of philosophy, psychology, or science?*

AM: What are one's formative years? Early childhood? Up through late adolescence? If the former, then the answer is "no"; if the latter, then "yes." In childhood everything that influenced me you could call poetry. Firstly, when I was an illiterate young child, I loved the poetry I heard at Mass: the Psalms, Isaiah and Jeremiah, parts of the mass liturgy, sequences, litanies … Then, I loved the poems and stories that were read or told to me, including ones that my father made up, and ones that a child learned, at least in those days, from other children. Because that was still the era when children played using children's rhymes and learned them from each other, in a tradition belonging wholly to children and not provided by adults. And this included the traditional songs: every child knew "Jimmy Crack Corn", "Buffalo Gals Won't You Come Out Tonight", "I've Been Workin' on the Railroad", "The Erie Canal", "Red River Valley", "The Streets of Laredo", "Sixteen Men on a Dead Man's Chest", "Get Along Little Dogies"—dozens of them, truly. There were of course skipping rhymes, "Ring Around the Rosie", "London Bridges Falling Down", many things like that.

Then, when I could read, I got immersed in long versions of the great legends and myths: the stories of Arthur, for instance, and the whole story of Troy, right from the gods raising Troy's walls, and the apple of discord, to the homecoming of Ulysses. I remember the great version, along with all the other principal myths, by Gustav Schwab; I remember the book, with its introduction by Werner Jaeger. This reading was my main activity in late grade 1 through grade 3. Of course, it has always continued. Then, I got interested in what you could call the "tale"—that form of short story. Stevenson, Chesterton and the like. Poe. Toward the end of third grade, looking for some more Poe stories in the Niles library, I found a big "complete works" with his poetry. I was mesmerized—a very Poe-appropriate word!—and from that moment I've wanted to be a poet.

I read a lot of nonfiction in boyhood but it was, more or less, adventure. The stories of the great bush pilots, the World War I aces, polar exploration, Stanley and Livingston, the discovery of the Mayan cities in the Guatemala jungles, pirates of the Spanish main, mysterious ship disasters. Also history. Ancient Greek history, the Dorians, Crete, all that. My childhood friend Paul Shaker has just reminded me that in mid-grade school we read the histories of James Breasted, some of which were in that library. I remember reading a lot of biographies too: Pasteur, for instance. Wiley Post. Glenn Curtiss. And *The Microbe Hunters*. *The Voyage of the Beagle* was a book I read at that time. And the history of the Mayan and other American civilizations as far as it was known then. I could multiply subject areas but that gives an idea. Also in mid-primary-school through middle school I got "obsessed" successively with humour, science fiction, and murder mysteries: I read an awful lot of those. I read Alfred Hitchcock's paperback anthologies of classic and recent horror stories.

That was about coeval with the coming of the sort of nonfiction you mentioned. Around grade 9, my father had me read a book entitled *Ecology*, which was an introduction to the science of living systems, and at the same time he had me read *Silent Spring* by Rachel Carson. These were influential. Then the next year he had me read Dewey. My first Deweys were *Reconstruction in Philosophy* and *Education and Experience*. I still have my father's copy of the latter book. In mid-high school, while reading Dante in John Ciardi's then new translation, and trying to do it thoroughly, to learn everything in all the notes and introductions, I was led—by what connection I can't remember—to read a book called *The Essential Newman*. Both made profound impressions.

From inside school, though, nothing of this sort came to me. There wasn't, in our school, any presence of philosophy. By the end of high school I'd begun to read a little more widely in it on my own, and I knew a bit of Nietzsche, I had read Will Durant's *The History of Philosophy*, with brief sketches of the "great philosophers". I had read *A Primer of Freudian Psychology*, *The ABC of Relativity*, *The Universe and Dr. Einstein*, and a book I still possess that gives brief biographies and outlines of the thought of the chief modern philosophical psychologists: Freud, Adler, Jung and quite a few others. Rank. Bettelheim. The other thing I can remember along these lines was *The Feminine Mystique*. I didn't read it then, but I heard a long radio interview with Betty Friedan discussing it and that impressed me and stayed with me. From school I did learn the U.S. Constitution: in grade 11, I got so many detentions that I had to copy the whole thing out by hand four times: it was one of the punishments. Not four times in a row, I mean. Once at a time was the punishment. But I got it four times. You had to copy it every time you collected seven detentions.

In terms of nonfiction, the most influential books on me in adolescence were books about poetry, which were usually filled with poetry as examples of what the authors were saying. When I was 14 and 15, I read *Understanding Poetry* by Brooks and Warren, *In Pursuit of Poetry* by Robert Hillyer, various biographies of poets, *Poetry Handbook* by Babette Deutsch, *Discovering Poetry* by Elizabeth Drew. It was in the latter book that I learned that, in addition to Sir Walter Raleigh the poet and pirate I had long known all about, there was another Sir Walter Raleigh who was a modern literary critic, and who loved Christina Rossetti's work. And that's how I first learned of Christina Rossetti! Elizabeth Drew, I remember, quoted Raleigh to the effect that he was going to lecture on Christina's poems but you couldn't lecture on pure poetry, and that Christina's poems made him not want to lecture but just cry. These books were a wonderland of one thing leading on to another like that.

As soon as you get to university, of course there's a lot of nonfiction! To discuss it would be endless. That's still one's formative period, right? Eighteen, nineteen, twenty? I remember reading, in a psychology text in my first undergraduate year, that one's impressionable age is over by 20. I was almost 19! What that made me do was to sit down immediately and read *Hamlet* seven times in a row without stopping. I took more than a day over it. Didn't sleep. Drank a certain amount of bourbon. I knew what I wanted to be impressed by, while there was still time!

However, to stay with nonfiction and not say too much, I'll mention just a couple of things. Right at the beginning of my undergraduate years I had a profound encounter with the thought of Bergson, and that is still and always continuing. I recognized the kinship between elements of his vision and that of Leibniz in the *Monadology*, which I also read and loved then: I was studying the "rationalists" at that time. Then, I've always stayed with Dewey. Dewey is a sort of greater Aristotle. If by "philosopher" we mean a person who devotes a supreme intelligence passionately, tirelessly to the understanding and betterment of human life, then Dewey is the greatest philosopher who ever lived . And a far greater twentieth-century figure than, say, Einstein. Far smarter. Smarter right down to the foundation of his thought: the choice of the right, the important, things to think about. That choice, of course, is the main component of intelligence. I read a lot of Freud—*The Interpretation of Dreams, The Psychoanalysis of Everyday Life, Lectures on Psychoanalysis, The Future of an Illusion, Moses and Monotheism*. I read a lot of Nietzsche. I was impressed and influenced especially by Nietzsche. But these thinkers are not the equals of Dewey and Bergson and Leibniz and Spinoza etc.

LH: *I remember how turbulent the times were in the late 1960s in modern American history: the war in Vietnam, the TET offensive, racial riots, the assassinations of Martin Luther King and Robert Kennedy. As an American citizen, how was your life affected by these events? What was your reaction as a young poet to the war and the rise of violence?*

243

AM: This has been a major factor in my life. I have just got done publishing a book about it, *The Garden: a poem and an essay,* from the young publishing company Gordon Hill Press. As to racial justice, my parents sensitized me to this: they took the part of African American students and teachers in the Niles schools, where African Americans were very few and isolated and faced great prejudice. My mother did this back to the 1930s. Then I was fascinated—astonished, I might say—by the 1957 struggle over the integration of Little Rock Central High: I watched it persistently on television and read about it in the newspapers. I was 11. The next year, I noticed tiny newspaper stories about battles in Laos, and began keeping a scrapbook of these and began realizing there was a war in Laos involving the United States: at first a very low-level one, and very much kept quiet, but a real one, which seemed to be growing. So I'd already discovered this myself before it became clear the U.S.A. had "taken over" from France in Vietnam. Taken over the guardianship of colonialism. Or, I should say, of *that* colonialism too.

I naturally become very aware of the growing protest movements: the initial anti-war movement of the early 60s, while I was in high school, 1961-65, and things like the growing clarity by Martin Luther King and others about including anti-colonialism in social justice thought and activism. All of this grew to its peak exactly when I was in university, 1965-69, and I participated. I've written about it in the "Author's Afterword" to *The Garden*. That book was a revival and publication, at long last, of a book I wrote but never entirely finished in 1992, sparked by the 1991 beating of Rodney King and the related uprising in South Central Los Angeles a year later.

LH: *We are now living through the devastating time of the coronavirus pandemic, which has had an impact on the world's economy, causing massive social disruptions, family isolation and deaths* *of millions of people. As Poet Laureate of Toronto, you reacted to this grave situation by writing the poem "Thoughts in the Time of Plague," which was published in the* Toronto Star *last year: March 2020, near the pandemic's start. Then again, you responded in March 2020 with your poem "Exactly Here the Marvel Spoke", which was also published in the* Star, *as well as in other venues. How has this pandemic affected your writing?*

AM: It took over much of my work during the laureateship, and yet it has seemed congruent with other laureate work. When offered the position, I liked the idea, as I never would have done earlier, of bending my hermetic approach toward the public dimensions of poetry. As soon as I accepted, I found myself called on for a poem to be part of the one-year commemoration ceremony of the Yonge Street van attack that killed 10 and injured 16 in Toronto. Then, only a few months later, there was a poem to write and deliver for the one-year commemoration ceremony of the mass shooting on Danforth Avenue. Well, the City does not require the laureate to write anything. But I'd taken the post with my own full intention of addressing such things as these, although I did not suspect perhaps how many there would be and how severe.

The responsibility left me feeling that I must write a poem that puts a "happy ending" or a "silver lining" on disturbing and destructive events: the spiritual superiority and survival of the victims, for instance. But isn't this a valid requirement? Ought we not to think of the *work* of hope, the enormous, intense *effort* hope requires? And the way in which we owe this difficult work to others, we all owe it to all of us, more almost than any other thing, more than anything but justice: justice which is synonymous with poetry. So the effort I've felt in writing these laureate poems, including the pandemic ones, has caused me to ponder whether I've done the work of hope enough in my private poetry, and what it really takes to arrive at an honest, sufficient, grounded hope. I have always been obsessed with this, but I can say that the laureateship experience has further intensified the effort, has further shown me how central and serious it is.

LH: *I would like to return to your early years now, specifically when you attended Marquette University in the late sixties and early seventies. Were there programs or particular professors that drew you to this university?*

AM: I had paid zero attention to university during high school. In February of my senior year, my father said to me, "Well, aren't you going to university?" I had no desire to be anything but a poet, and I'd recently been reading biographies of great writers who had worked in journalism—Mark Twain was one, Don Marquis was another. Hemingway was current: he had died only four years before, and I was reading him. So I made a snap decision for journalism and chose Marquette because it had, at least in those days, I don't know about now, one of the top journalism programs. Also it was a Catholic university, which would satisfy my parents, and it was quite far away, which satisfied me. While there, I was a terrible student. Until the middle of third year, I almost never went to classes or handed in assignments. I remember having begun to read Dostoevsky in late second year and just staying in my room and reading and reading his novels instead of going to any of my final exams. Also, you could still hitchhike in those days and for years I spent a lot of time hitchhiking all around the United States, some of it with a friend or two, some of it alone.

As for teachers ... No. Like all university students, I was still a teenager when I started and I retained fully my childhood suspicion of adults, amounting almost to contempt, sometimes to hatred. So I never drew close to any professor, just as I'd always given almost all adults as wide a berth as I could. And that persisted through graduate school. So I never had any mentor or any association with a teacher. There were professors who, I think, were well disposed toward me, but I kept my distance, a total distance. When I met Theresa, we decided that I should graduate on time. That was the middle of third year. So in the final three semesters, I took as many courses as they'd let me and got very high grades and managed to squeeze in just barely enough credits to graduate and get my average up to a middling B from D or nearly.

The exception I must make about teachers is a beloved one, Professor Lou Belden of the College of Journalism—a member of the Belden Brick family, Ohio industrial royalty. He and his wife Jean more or less rescued Theresa, who had an impoverished and difficult childhood, by taking her into their house throughout her undergraduate years. This elimination of room and board costs was what allowed her to attend, and the Beldens were wonderful second parents to her and became beloved to me too. We were intimate with them until their deaths.

LH: *At Marquette University you met your future wife, Theresa. She was also studying journalism and would later specialize in Medieval literature. Could you share some details about the time and circumstances of your meeting?*

AM: We knew each other and noticed each other from the beginning of undergrad, since we were both in the College of Journalism and the required first-year courses. We drew close in third year. I became less anti-social and started working on the Marquette *Tribune*, the student newspaper, as a cultural writer and sometime news reporter—covering the student protests from inside, for instance. Theresa was one of the chief editors, and in fourth year she was the editorial page editor. That was one way we came close: we were often at the office after hours. Ordering in pizza from Angelo's. After that, what else would you expect? I got a lot of free tickets to things in my role, so we had our courtship partly in going to performances of the *Marat/Sade* and *Waiting for Godot* and the visiting Berlin Symphony Orchestra, and attending the Milwaukee Art Museum's programs of German Expressionist films and Scandinavian silent films and the like. *Ordet*! *El Topo*! *The Trial of Joan of Arc*! *A nous la liberté*!

Theresa was majoring in Spanish as well as journalism and that was another of her gifts to me: through her I began reading Spanish-language poetry, which became an abiding axis of my thought and experience. Another gift was medieval studies, which gave me Toronto. While I was doing my doctorate, Theresa marked time by doing two master's degrees, in Spanish and in Medieval Studies, at Marquette. She was an absolutely outstanding student, got interested in an aspect of medieval studies I won't bother to go into, wrote a book on it based on her master's thesis that got published by Ohio State University Press, and wanted to proceed to the doctorate. The U of T had the best medieval studies in North America and so we came to Toronto. That's why I'm here. We just loved it and we became citizens and have stayed ever since. I was happy to think of myself as going into voluntary political exile from the United States, although that was not the prompt and chief motive of our move.

LH: *Your Ph.D. dissertation was on eighteenth and nineteenth century British poetry and was influenced by such writers as Wordsworth, Keats, and Shelley. I see in your work parallels with Woodsworth's idea of the mind watching itself, Keats's "negative capability"—his idea of the poet as a chameleon, and Shelley's shifting narrative perspectives. Your ideas seem to have been strongly influenced by the aesthetics of these English Romantic Poets.*

AM: I regard English and German Romanticism as my Ur-poetry and I regard myself as a Romantic. You mention interesting factors but they're rather peripheral ones to me. From Wordsworth I derive many things, but the chief one is the vision, short-lived in him but of the essence of the first Romanticism, that the world in its truth is marvellous and it only seems miserable because we insist on seeing that way, following a deadening human-created tradition to which we limit or enslave ourselves. Well, "seems" is the wrong word. It *is* miserable, but because we make it so by the way we decide to see it. We do not think that we decide on purpose to see things as ugliness and hopelessness, and refuse and fail to see beauty, but so we do, with a "purpose" beneath and beyond what is usually thought of by that term. And our seeing determines existence. "If they lack the vision, the people die," says the book of *Wisdom*. "God did not create death and does not rejoice in the death of his creatures," it says elsewhere. Exactly. Great poetry in that book! If we could "open our eyes", we would find ourselves in paradise. But we don't want to. The cell door is unlocked and we prefer not to open it. Blake was still clearer and more unremitting than Wordsworth about this vision. He says, "How do you know but ev'ry bird that cuts the airy way / Is an immense world of delight, closed by your senses five?" It's partly a rhetorical question—"you" *do* know that each bird is infinite if you're William Blake!—and partly a straight question: Why don't you know, since you ought to, since you possess the inherent but inactive nature that would show you if you really looked.

I recognized this vision as mine.

I derive further from the Romantics the recognition that this vision is threatened by the possibility or temptation of a tragic materialism: perhaps it is threated primordially, but it is certainly threatened in our times. Poetry is unlike music in that its materials are words, which are sensuous existents, are sounds, yes, but which also are concepts. A poem cannot help but have all the concepts that belong to all its words within its substance. The poem is not argument or reasoning, but it always carries, in its very body, argument and reasoning, truth and error, prejudice and openness, exclusions and the thirst for justice and openness, all the determinations of history and culture, all the firmness of them, the sloppiness, the arrogance, the humility. It is these things that the poem is made out of, just as the pot is made out of clay and the symphony is made out of sounds and the painting out of colours and shapes. So it contains the truth of the vision and, on the other hand, it contains all of humanity's weaknesses and barriers and tentative approaches and wrong turns. It contains this divergence, this struggle.

Imagine an object of surpassing, mysterious beauty and when you bend close, in its transparent impenetrable surface you see this whole struggle swimming, transforming itself, playing out its entire history, past and to come. That is poetry.

That is not *all* that poetry is: It is much more besides, infinitely much. But it is, magnificently and heroically, among all the other things, *that*.

This struggle to continue the vision in the face of constant doubt and contradiction occurs necessarily. So the poem tends to be the mixture of vision and the barriers and objections to vision. This is another thing I derive from Romanticism: for instance, the famous interplay between "Intimations of Immortality" and "Dejection: an Ode", and the fact that the intimations ode actually contains the same interplay within itself. It would be too lengthy to go into the details of this, the various aspects and transmutations of it that I read in Shelley, Keats, Tennyson, Browning, Dickinson, Whitman, Hölderlin, Goethe, Emily Brontë, Mörike, Novalis, Hopkins, Blake, Clare, Wordsworth, etc.

LH: *I've observed that your work is not in the vein of the Beat poets or Black Mountain poets such as William Carlos Williams, who write more in "the American grain." Your interest is rather more internationally oriented. I'm thinking of such writers as Robert Bly, Juan Ramón Jiménez, Czesław Miłosz, Octavio Paz and Pablo Neruda. What drew you to reading the works of these writers?*

AM: Well, to put it very simply, they are great. In fact, just to speak of the period of my youth and maturity, the second half of the twentieth century, Miłosz and Paz, along with Yves Bonnefoy of France, were in that period the three greatest and most important creators active in any human field, by a long distance. You could maybe put Beckett with them. It was a great period for poetry. Someone who doesn't know the work of these poets fails to be our contemporary, no matter how up-to-date he/she may be in technology, politics, pop, the sciences, the arts, etc.

I have to affirm, though, that I also love the other poets that you mention. I can remember the great summer when I was 23 and just moving back to Milwaukee to begin graduate school. I was working as a columnist and reporter for the Milwaukee *Sentinel*, and I was simultaneously reading, obsessively, repeatedly, Byron's *Don Juan* and William Carlos Williams's *Early Poems*, the first volume of the old two-volume Williams from New Directions: this was 1971. And I kept thinking to myself, Byron is teaching me to mock and satirize everything—almost everything—and Williams is teaching me to love everything—almost everything.

LH: *It seems that Ludwig Zeller, the Chilean poet and artist, was an important literary figure in your life. You became friends with him and his wife, the artist Susana Wald. You also translated one of his novels. Was it the striking surreal imagery in his painting* *and writing that provoked your own imagination, or was it a different aesthetic that influenced you to find new approaches for refining your techniques in writing?*

AM: I was interested in Surrealism. Breton was and is a favourite poet: a figure as important for the first half of the twentieth century as Paz or Milosz or Bonnefoy is for the second. He retrieved the romantic vision: "Everything leads us to believe that there exists a spot in the mind from which life and death, the real and the imaginary, the past and the future, the high and the low, the communicable and the incommunicable will cease to appear contradictory."

And he attacked what he called human "miserablism": the tradition I mentioned of believing everything is tragic, painful, ugly, small, and impossible. So when I learned that a truly wonderful third-generation Surrealist was in Toronto, I had to meet him. Ludwig did not disappoint: a never-ending fund of beauty, fearlessness, exploration, and also of community, love, geniality. A genius of poetry and of friendship. Truly, he was a center. A center of a different world that was yet within this one and was the truth of this one. Spiritually, creatively, and socially a magnet, a bringer-together in both art and life.

LH: *John Ashbery is one of the most important and influential poets of the latter half of the 20th century. You have said in an interview with James Lindsay that you discovered him at the age of 19. Did you know him personally? What did you find in him that was so important to you? Like Ashbery's work, your poems require time from the reader to decipher them, line after line.*

AM: I discovered Ashbery when one of the things that I was doing instead of attending classes was going through the Marquette library trying to read all the poetry. Arriving at the modern and contemporary American shelves, I found Ashbery. At the time, he had published *Some Trees, Rivers and*

Mountains, The Tennis Court Oath, and a superbly chosen, very short "selected poems" with the British publisher Jonathan Cape. Not long afterwards *The Double Dream of Spring* came out. How I loved these books!

A lot's been written about Ashbery, and I don't want to add more in a speedy, little-considered way. Ashbery was an example of openness—in many ways the chief example, along with some other poets and some people in the social justice struggle, King and John Lewis and the like. Ashbery was a unique part of a great, similar movement in poetry at that time. It showed itself in many brilliant ways. For all the supposed instability of his poetry, it maintained a clear tension between the remaking of vision as a way of seeing the hidden beauty of fact, the essential glory, and on the other hand, all the drifts of melancholy, ennui, theoretical confusion, temptations to anomie and despair. One only has to look at the way that the early, beautiful, profound poem "The Instruction Manual" can be read as an inversion and transfiguration of *Nausea.* Or the way in which "The Skaters" ends in an "ideal" reconfiguration of the year, stating it blandly as if this new order of the months and seasons is just exactly the one we all know. That is to say, the one we impose.

LH: *Sue Sinclair in an interview "Al Moritz on Beauty," wrote that your "intellectual engagement is animated by a sense of moral urgency." Why is it so important for the poet to speak about moral issues concerning our humanity? I've noticed that sometimes you criticize the injustice of political figures as in the poems "Kissinger at the Funeral of Nixon" and "The Death of Francisco Franco."*

AM: I more or less hate the word "moral". Well, I don't hate any words, but I do come close to hating some of the ways they're used. What does "moral" mean? The background meaning, which I can accept as applied to my work, is simply the totality of the human context and operation of our decision-making and willing. But people usually use the word to mean an evaluative or "judgmental" approach to conduct, and this usually carries with it the selection of and adherence to some scheme of behaviour. In that common meaning of "moral", my poetry is distinctly anti-moral. Its morality is freedom from all that. The human being in love, true love, is superior to all schemas. All schemas are simply other "things" of the world in which we are. They're human things, and they're like and yet unlike the "things" that Jiménez and Rilke emphasized: rose, pitcher, thorn tree. But the point is, they are in us, we are not in them, dominated by them, unless we let ourselves be, choose to be. This is my morality and I guess I'm urgent about it.

LH: *Many of your poems express empathy. In "The Ruined Cottage," one observes the fascinating juxtaposing of Wordsworth's poem, the desolation of 19th century England and the brutality exhibited by the two drunken men who upset the breakfast of the two women and their children.*

AM: Poor people. A deep distress hath humanized my soul, Wordsworth says. Forgotten, disregarded, or forever unseen misery and disaster and death is precious to me. Profound poetry of the poor and of the dead, Wallace Stevens says, and I've taken that as a motto since I first read it when 18. We are fully responsible to give the life of common happiness that they deserved to people who were deprived, tortured, killed long ago. Yet we never sweat blood over this, we never even think about it, we never do anything to discharge the responsibility, unless you count the pallid "to make sure it will never happen again" culture, the "giving a better life to our children" culture. For example, we listen placidly when great economists with Nobel Prizes and professorships at Yale and Oxford explain to us that it's a natural social "evolution" that first immigrants receive slave treatment, their children manage to struggle up to better circumstances, and finally maybe their grandchildren are normal members of society. How does that help the grandfather, the grandmother? And how did they deserve less than the grandchildren? Weren't they, too, someone's grand-children? And since we know about this unjust constantly repeated social "evolution", which Professor Complacency or CEO Self-satisfaction has just unnecessarily explained to us, isn't the only truly intelligent thing that can come from the knowledge to change it utterly, to never let it happen again?

I simply *hate* all this way of figuring on the normal his-torical operations of society as a sort of fact of nature. It's common, omnipresent, and totally, totally false and wrong, But it's such a background belief, or acceptance, of the "lead-ers"—read, ruiners—of our society that it's a thing that rarely even gets said.

You could say, simply, that the vision of society held by power, finance, technology, science and the like is expressed in the common-sense saying, "It's a jungle out there." A cor-ollary to this is the culture of "child-proofing", the idea that education and experience are for convincing us of this and hardening us. On the other hand and in complete contrast, the vision of society inherent to poetry is expressed in Blake's line, "Creating the beautiful house for the piteous sufferer."

I suppose that people don't even realize that they think this cruel defeatism—they perhaps don't actually "think" it, they simply live it, as if it belongs to the order given by God or na-ture. In fact, the truth is just the opposite. The communion of saints: the communion of the suffering and destroyed. Those who died in deprivation and injustice, since they were just as alive as we are, are alive still, are just as alive as we are right now. There is no difference of degree of "now-ness" between one now and another. I don't know how often I've said this explicitly. But it's just poetry, so no one notices. But they have to start noticing poetry, in fact they have to start putting it at the head and center of all human endeavours, or our world will die. Maybe this is what was meant by moral urgency?

LH: *I think that as poets we favour some of our works out of sentiment or just because they more accurately represent our aesthetics. In* The Sparrow: Selected Poems, *one poem "We Decided This Was All" stands out and marks the introduction of this book. This particular poem seems to represent your philosophy of life, what you do and what you intend to do?*

AM: Well, yes and no! I pulled out two poems from my work to serve as an introduction and a conclusion to *The Sparrow*. "We Decided This Was All" is from *The Tradition*, 1986, which to me begins a middle phase of my poetry. The poem was written about 1983. That was the "introduction". The "conclusion", a poem entitled "The Last Thing", is from *Black Orchid*, my second book. The poem was written in 1973 or 1974, about a decade earlier. So the poem I saw as my conclusion came before the one I saw as my introduction, but then in *The Sparrow* it had to come after.

"We Decided This Was All" expresses the human decision to create and believe in misery, limitation, cruelty, exclusion. It expresses the resulting horrors, the engulfment of hopeful human beings in man-made misery and self-thwarting and belittlement: what we generally term greatness and success. Things such as the creation of empires, like that of the Nazis, alluded to at the beginning of the poem, and the creation of the industrial totalized environment and dictatorship of technology, referred to later. The poem dramatizes the creative person, the "I" speaking the poem, as growing up knowing the splendour of the world and then learning the human-made part of its truth: what we have decided was all there is, the cruel, squalid order that keeps repeating, what we decided to profit by, submit others to if they should try to avoid it, make them learn it, obey it, bow down to it, acknowledge our superior eminence within the ash-heap that it is.

The poem represents the way that this "knowledge" penetrates inside the creative person and is hard to shake. It produces an internal contention between original innocence and so-called realism. Or it can wholly tilt the person toward a habitual, dampened despair. At the end of "We Decided This Was All", the poet, looking back over his life and searching for the "glory and the freshness of a dream" that he once possessed, finds in himself only the pan-human decision that life is a grim, banal contention that will end six feet under. He concludes that, for a human being, it is impossible to achieve anything substantial, or even something small and one's own: a tiny sculpture of pebbles. Even retaining that much aspiration, to build so small but to build, would be an ember of innocence and true perception. But does this poet now even possess that much?

"The Last Thing" was earlier but is later, more the goal and the unseen reality. It's very Ashberian, in my transformation of Ashbery. The "last things"—death, judgment, hell, and heaven—are exceeded by the true last thing, human glory and grandeur in a simple playing out of freedom in which all possibilities will come round, even though there will never be an end to new possibilities. Being, the poem says, brings "me here to you, or you to me" as "this fable plays at playing out / all its proliferating hopes". I think that someone who understands these two poems will see that *The Sparrow* moves between them.

LH: *At first it arrives purely as an interest, then it becomes an important part of life. Some see writing as a mission. As a poet you are very conscious of what poetry represents. In your opinion what "tools" does a writer require to use in order to explore his subconscious and bring out what is even unknown to himself in poems?*

AM: The tools of poetry are first of all discovery and release. Architecture and versification are also and absolutely necessary, but the true discipline is to allow yourself to hear and to speak beyond the misconceptions and trivia that surround you, to be able to separate reception and inspiration from a frenzy of regurgitation of cultural errors. To be able to separate creativity from speed. To be able to discover and to make yourself in the interplay of discovery and making. Jiménez says, "I don't know how to say it, to say myself, / because my own word / is not yet made." That's the whole poem and it's a bigger one than Joyce's *Ulysses*.

Another tool of poetry is to recognize that you are a craftsman, a maker and worker, and that when we human beings say that truth or motivation is a beam of light or a torrent, strikes from heaven or rises as a fountain from within and beneath, we mean that our tools and our craft do this too, not just our enlightenment and our energy. It's not as if over here there is "inspiration" and over there we have "prosody." Both of them arise out of the dark; both of them are crafted with skill in the light. Together they move toward being a building or a ship and turn into—reveal themselves as—a tree. Our craft is our enlightenment, our tools are our energy, our painstaking architecture is our vision. If we were angels, then construction would be simultaneous with thought and would be easy in the sense of there being no separation from conceiving and bringing forth. As human beings, we have to labour to join the two and we have to labour even to recognize that they're aspects of the same thing. But we do have to achieve the recognition.

But poetry is precisely the art, the human endeavour, that is closest to the thought that originates it, as Hannah Arendt points out in *The Human Condition*.

LH: *We as poets travel intensively to the places that we know by heart backward and forward in time. Place plays an important role in a writer's life. One thinks of Joyce, Faulkner and Williams. Mahoning was your place. In the poem "Visit Home" you speak of returning to Mahoning in a rather negative tone; there is a sadness in your voice: "Burnt, dried out, crumbled, / it would not let me remember how to love it." What made you see it with such clarity? Was it the passage of time or because you are accustomed to a different Canadian landscape?*

AM: That's a great question. The final part of it, your final sentence, strikes me. I had never thought of such a possibility. Yes, *Mahoning* was in part enabled by distances of time, but also of place: I kept going home, and thinking I should go home "more", whatever that means—but I wasn't there, as the title "Visit Home" indicates, where "visit" is a both a noun and a hortative. I think what happened is this. I'd always thought of my relationship to "home" as best expressed "essentially", in my poems that see that home is childhood, innocent and glorious perception, and leaving home is experience: bitter opposition and the schooling and training in the counsels of bitterness. So I didn't think of writing about my place. I felt uninterested in the American poetic tradition of place and roots. But was I uninterested? I loved Williams, as I've said, and I've loved and reread *Paterson* since my early twenties: *Mahoning* has various quotations from and a lot of allusions to *Paterson*. In the middle 1980s, I began thinking I should write about my own specific original place. One spur to this was reading an essay on American poetry of origins by M.L. Rosenthal, which made me think back to my reading of Williams and Olson and others, a lot of others. But this wouldn't have been a sufficient spur without another and sharper one, a renewed and deep reading of Yves Bonnefoy. His is a poetry also of rootedness in many ways. And his manner, his angle of approach, his *literary* "rootedness" in Romanticism and Symbolism and Surrealism, helped me feel that I could approach this subject, and my particular roots, in my own way. A way that in texture and architecture would be completely different from Williams or Olson, though spiritually it might be quite close to them.

You've mentioned my selected poems, *The Sparrow*. When I was first contending with my publisher's urgent wish that I produce a selected poems—an idea I hadn't entertained on my own—I came up with many idiosyncratic possibilities that were, I could see, never to be tolerated by actual publishing! Nevertheless, they had true meaning to me. And one of them was that a good "selected poems" for me would be simply to reprint *Mahoning* (which is both a single book-length poem in sequential form and a collection of poems) along with a very few early poems that clearly lead up to it and a very few later poems that clearly lead out from it.

LH: *In the poem "Artisan and Clerk" you are returning again to the American Northeast to the subject hard for you to ignore— the lost industry of the land you know well. Using an ironic tone the speaker talks about empty factories: "Like ghosts leaving their bodies those factories / were leaving us." The deterioration of the towns has had a great effect upon you. You are critical of business and its shareholders, who are looking for cheaper labour in order to have more profit. What is your position on this subject now when we hear politicians talking about returning jobs to America? Do you see it as another card for them to play with potential voters or a real solution?*

AM: It depends on the politician, the degree to which the mission is sincere or false, an opportunistic slogan. The real trouble is that the United States is so rich and powerful that it is better equipped at all times to "return jobs" to itself than are other countries. The fact that even the United States is so full of unemployment and underemployment and poverty and near poverty and helplessness before debt and disease, etc.—this fact ought to lead us to think about the entire world economic system. Does it, and can it, provide enough for the huge populations that it remorselessly produces, both for reasons that are "automatic" and for reasons that are intended—to use an anthropomorphism? The system needs huge numbers of people massed together to be workers and consumers. It needs the underemployed and unemployed whose existence keeps wages low. And it needs the unemployable, who are as they are because the system avoids paying for them, since it would cost money and require work aiming at no profit—and besides, the truly miserable provide a salutary, educational image to you and me of what could happen to us if we don't behave and perform well. Does it, and can it, provide enough for the huge populations it requires and produces? No, probably not. Not even in the richest countries—only in the few most privileged pockets within them. It's a failed system, in this regard as in so many others.

LH: *The provocative poem "The Sentinel," in the book with the same title, shows that the assigned guard has been told to be vigilant and to look for the presence of a possible enemy, but he only reports the mundane things that happen within the camp. His superiors accuse him of being a traitor. Perhaps it is an analogy to the poet, much like the poet in A.M. Klein's "The Portrait of Poet as Landscape." One critic has suggested that the sentinel is a symbol of the poet—one who is a witness of his time, but his vision is not accepted by society. Would you agree with this interpretation?*

AM: I would agree with the interpretation. However, to express that meaning was not my goal in writing the poem. What's important about that interpretation, I think, is to be sure you don't take "the poet" as meaning just people who write verse. For me, "the poet" is the sensitive person, the person who retains, and struggles to maintain and extend, openness and responsiveness. The poets of life. Within that group, the poets of life, the poets of the art of verse are a vital sub-category. "The Sentinel" is about the whole category, everyone who is "a sensitive and a creative soul," as Wordsworth says. Which is, probably, all of us, at least in certain moments. I think that everyone, reading "The Sentinel", would recognize that he or she experiences such moments of being placed out on the edge, with a responsibility to *save* which seems impossible to discharge without help, and which is unhelped and little thanked, and which is a loneliness and seems a threat of death. But if a reader hears that the poem is about "the poet", this reader is liable to think, "That's not me," and that would be wrong and unhelpful. The poet is the representative person, as Emerson said.

LH: *Let's go back to the sequence poem. In your notes on it, you spoke about possible models taken from Shakespeare, Tennyson, Whitman, Seferis, and Lagerkvist. Bp nichol once said: "In a long poem I have the time to tell you that in all its faces or, at least, in as many faces as I've seen so far." What compelled you to write this book as a sequence poem?*

AM: I wanted to sing the going on from day to day and I wanted to bring out that just going on is not different from having an idea and a goal, even though to rational figuring, the two are mutually exclusive. I also wanted to express that it's nonsense to say that a journey is more important than its goal. I wanted to express that this piece of conventional modern wisdom is premised on a complete misunderstanding of "goal". It doesn't mean a stoppage in some sort of jail cell that's supposed to be, on the other hand, wonderful, or sufficient—Beulah-land! It means arriving through adventure at a place of a truer, more fulfilled adventuring. One truly arrives, but the travelling and changing and new delight and surprise doesn't end, in fact it only begins again more deeply. It "ends" in a new territory to explore. The goal is an end to our sometimes invigorating, sometimes terrifying wandering that is truly an end to it but is at the same time a new place, a new world, a new enterprise. That's the goal.

I wanted to express that in *this* wandering of ours here and now, we have a foretaste of the transfiguring arrival and the transfigured journeying in the new place. This is because each day arrives at the next day, and if days arrive at new days, then also moments at new moments, and steps at further steps: each one arrives at another one, where everything is different, if we could grasp it. Our lives, our days, our steps, are not the whole journey and the whole vast new country of the goal … but also, they are—they are the whole thing, already, prophetically and really.

I wanted the book to express this in its form. So it's written to make each page, which is usually just a short text, complete and separate and independent, and yet completely immersed in the flow that moves from the previous page to the next one. Each page is independent of those around it and dependent on them, separate from them and a part of them. Each page is a day or night or moment seen as it is, as a complete and defined vast era of time which is yet only a wavelet in the course of a life. Each page was a step, which is a complete and separate event and only a momentary aspect of a progress. "The longest journey begins and ends and continues and remains in its every single step," you might say.

The book thus contradicts, in its form, the common idea today that forces, eras, "underlying" formations, are real, whereas specific things—such as we human beings ourselves—are only temporary embodiments of them. That is a sort of recrudescent Platonism: the ideas are truer than things, but we think today that because we have a "scientific" concept of our ideas, somehow these ideas are concrete existents. No. They have no existence except in and as the individual things that exist. The whole vector of modern and contemporary intellectuality is pointed in the wrong direction. *Sequence* expresses that. The book does not, I hope, make a totalizing claim on behalf of the individual thing as against the underlying anatomy or flow. The true vision is to rebalance the two, balance them properly. It is the individual that is most real and for which the rest exists, the structures and forces that are, only, in things.

To talk some poetic shop, then, another aspect of *Sequence's* formal expressiveness is to show the flaws of "open field" theory and the related theories of poetry and the falsity of the idea that "the lyric" is characterized by "closure" and that closure is wrong. None of this is so. *Sequence* shows that the traditional book with separate pages which yet are all part and parcel of each other, is the most advanced possible form, and is well and permanently beyond all "experimental" innovations. There is closure in the lyric, but it is not a closing off; it is ending and definition as they really exist, as vital aspects of continuing and remaining. There is the "open", but it does not exalt "field" above the little girl or the horse or the stone in the field, or the moment of loss sung with a beautiful "final line".

LH: *One of the salient features of your sequence poem is that time is fluid; you roam back and forth between ancient and present time, often dissolving the periods of time by moving from*

contemporary Ontario with its "Huge tractors—Freightliner, Pe-
terbilt" to the French writer, Anaïs Nin, then to Juan Ramón in
late 19th century Spain and finally to the boy in ancient Babylon,
and conclude with the phrase, "I am him." What was the pur-
pose of these unexpected shifts? To extend our perception of seeing
things behind the things?

AM: Yes, time is fluid. You'll notice for example—besides the example you gave—that section III of the book is a biographical narrative of (presumably) the speaker and that section IX is an entirely different biographical narrative of the same person (presumably), in an entirely different mode, with different incidents, and in different landscape. You'll notice that in the first of these stories, section III, if you think about the time-line, the speaker presents himself as—he is—a young boy around 1960 and also around 1930 and also in the mid to late nineteenth century. That's how I'd put it. The reader might not be able to come up with such precise dates, but would see the same "slippages" of time I'm talking about. Well, time is fluid. So it's like a wave. A breaking wave. The combing over of the wave as it breaks is part of the internal creation of the wave—is the wave—and so the wave is always being produced by the flowing back into it of its forward-breaking. Its future comes into and makes its past-present, its main bulk up till now. That's one of the directions of time's flow. Another of its directions—as it says in *Sequence* p. 49—is that time, from everywhere it is, from everywhere it begins, flows into *you*. That is the direction of time: from around you, into you. All of time rays into you, like a star that receives rays from all corners rather than sends them. Or better, the way a star's light not only leaves the star but stays attached to the star and returns to it. Otherwise you wouldn't be able to climb back along the way of the light and see the star. A certain portion of water may depart from the source, but the river doesn't.

LH: *In our contemporary life, we continually encounter violence in many forms. The newspapers and television are full of violence. Your poetry often deals with this subject in a hard and direct manner. In a later section of* Sequence, *you react to the murder of a child. Was it difficult to write this part of the poem?*

AM: Yes. But the murdered girl is a bare, brief allusion there. And that final section, part X, similarly presents and suggests many kinds of death in engaging death itself, death which is always the same thing and is different in every case, since it's always the death of a certain one. In the early cantos of *The Heights of Machu Picchu*, Neruda deals mightily with the idea of "my" death, and with the human being's deprivation of his/her "own" death in the massification of modern society and the demeaning of workers.

In section III of *Sequence* there are particular deaths fully engaged. The wasting away and death of the narrator's mother after five years of forcible separation from her husband by her birth family: her kidnapping and imprisonment, in other words. Then, later, the death of the narrator's father himself: shot but he survives and later commits suicide, hanging himself from a tree. I can point to many, many deaths in the book. There's the cavalcade of all the dead, p. 128, where the narrator himself says he has no wishes because "I'm dead. I've always been dead / and a dead man can't wish." There are forecasts of death, sightings of those soon to be dead, like the chained prisoners along the roadside on p. 94 and the dying lepers at the disease-poisoned oases, for instance on p. 99. On. p. 56, there's the hopeful/hopeless attempt at prophecy, premised on the destruction of the speaker's family, perhaps of his entire people: "The whole valley of the dead bodies and the ashes / will be sacred. The city / will be built again on its mound. / The children will come back, will be / as they were of old …" There are the deaths of the geological eons: "bone ends of utterly forgotten beasts / poking through the sand," in the poem on p. 58.

Violence in the sense you name—that the world is brutish and seems to be getting more so—is actually dealt with more directly in poems from other books. For instance, "Stabbing" in *Black Orchid*. A particular murder. Or the slaughter of war in "Beirut 1983". There are a lot of others.

LH: *Poetry is often criticized for being too elitist, where a lot of it resides in an ivory tower and is addressed to a small audience. Do you see it this way? Is it possible to make poetry more accessible to the general public? Poets now, especially younger ones, use liberty to write and to perform spoken word poems expressing the complex realities of our time.*

AM: I read an interview in which Stephen Sondheim vigorously rejected the suggestion that he was a poet. Of course, he is a poet. Obviously and undeniably. Then what did he mean? Probably that he'd been taught poetry in school, and what he was taught is not the sort of thing he writes and which he identifies with the term "poetry". If we forget about such distinctions, then it immediately becomes evident that poetry is everywhere. For instance, the works of Stephen Sondheim. Poetry's the greatest art, true, but it's also the most common, which is part of its greatness.

When we say that poetry isn't popular and that it's ivory tower and that it plays to a small cadre audience, things like that, we're talking about a certain kind of poetry. This kind, or zone, of poetry has certain characteristics. I'll name a few. One: it has the Symbolist and Modernist and Surrealist heritage of attacking a rapacious and vulgar society by creating a poetry so other, so complete in itself, that you cannot enter it except by totally preferring it to the general state of society, because this art takes a total effort to enter, a total commitment. Two: it has the history of protest poetry and counter-culture poetry—for instance, the Beats—who created to a great extent a popular poetry that yet remained isolated in a relatively small sector of society because of its own, differently expressed, total opposition to the general behaviour.

Three: Today, this poetry continues to express, more severely and persistently than any other cultural work, a devastating critique of the dominant society and, most importantly, a vision and example of a completely different way of regarding life. As a result of the two historical factors, and some other factors, but especially of this factor of shattering critique and transcendent example, poetry is repugnant both to the large structures and forces of society and, unfortunately, to the individual persons who must fill out the structures and obey the forces. Such persons do not want—or rarely want—to see what they're constrained to, and to see it is hopeless and wrong. They've largely absorbed the dominant culture's propaganda that it is a total world and there is nothing outside it but a withering vacuum. So people don't want to know that it's suicidal and inhuman. "Where else is there to go?" they think. "How difficult it would be to be different—I could never do it, and if I did, no one else would be doing it and I'd be an outcast," they think. So the messenger, the angel, is not welcome. The angel poetry is instinctively disregarded, held at a distance. In its place is put the alternative view, the "thank-God-it's-Friday-living-for-the-weekend" form of taking comfort in the perquisites of slavery that civilization has recently developed, as a means to defuse revolutionary dissatisfaction. There's also the termite morality: I might as well eat the trunk and the roots and the branches because it probably won't die till after I'm gone. To which the powerful add their own variation: might as well eat everything because even if it dies and falls down, there might still be life in the ruins and I'll still survive and be top-ant in the world of sawdust. Mad Max. Zombie apocalypse.

Poetry's unpopularity is primarily due to its magnificence in a world of self-belittlement and denial and milquetoast but real despair. It's also due to poetry's questioning in a world that likes to pride itself on realistic and reasoned inquiry but which in fact is the most dogma-bound and empty-faith-based example of rigid dimness that humanity has ever created.

LH: *The book* Rest on the Flight into Egypt, *which almost seems to be a study of artworks, reminds me of Picasso's studies of Velasquez. You achieve this with words by sketching portraits of subjects from different angles and perspectives to create a multifaceted view of reality. Is this a fair assessment?*

AM: I think so. With a proviso. The book engages a lot of artworks, but it also contains a lot that hasn't got anything to do with artworks but is immediate experience. And its dialogues with artworks always enact one of my basic principles: the poem (or painting or whatever) is not separate from life, is not some sort of enclave against life—an ivory tower. It's not separate from life except as each "part" of life is separate from the whole. And like every other "part" of life, but more intensely and completely, the artwork encapsulates the whole and sends us back to the whole, always, with increased vigour and thrust. Life turns into art; then art magnifies life and the thirst to dive into it; then that dive results in a further art— and so forth unendingly, in ceaseless creative interchange of ever greater vividness and wholeness of experience. Life and art: they're "communicating vessels," in Breton's great metaphor. If art has an aspect of being a "retreat" from life, a withdrawal, a shelter, it's mainly in the sense of a monk's retreat: to absorb and pray and rest and gather strength and come back wiser and stronger. And in a similar way, life has an aspect of being a retreat from art, and to the same end. To come back to the human heart again to create further poems.

July, 2021

Photo credit: Peter Sinclair

SUE SINCLAIR

Laurence Hutchman: *You are a keen observer of nature, often finding ingenious connections between things. How did the landscape of Newfoundland, where you grew up, affect you?*

Sue Sinclair: Thoroughly. My parents are Scottish, and I felt dislocated culturally in Newfoundland when we moved there from Ontario, where I was born. I didn't talk like a Newfoundlander or eat like a Newfoundlander or have the generations-deep social connections of a Newfoundlander. I did have the privilege of a white body and a cultural background that wasn't looked down upon, and I hadn't yet entirely connected my presence there to the genocide of the Beothuk people, so I wasn't yet aware of being out of place in that sense. My relatively minor sense of cultural dislocation, however, did turn me toward the non-human, as did a tendency toward shyness. In short, when I arrived in Newfoundland as a seven-year-old and began figuring out how to live there, the non-human dimensions of that place seemed easier to get to know that the people, were easier for me to build relationship with. This was an unconscious orientation at the time.

I'm also full of gratitude to my parents, who taught my brother and I to take the time to observe and marvel at the non-human world—we did heaps of hiking and had field guides as bibles. My mother would send my brother and me out on scavenger hunts to find, for example, five white flowers, then we'd identify them all. So I learned to look and to look closely. My dad is never without a camera and when I was growing up mostly made pictures of rock, water and plants, and although photography can be reduced to a mere click of a button and/or a power-grab, in his hands it's a form of careful looking. I'd help him out in the darkroom and look at multiple almost identical versions of the same picture to notice the differences. So literal and metaphorical regard for the non-human was built into my family of origin.

LH: *In the 1990s you came to the University of New Brunswick to work on an M.A. in Creative Writing. What was it like working with Don McKay and Jan Zwicky?*

SS: Oh, just life-altering. They helped me to understand what it means to live a life in poetry, which for them went beyond putting words on a page—the words were the least of it. I learned from them to see poetry as part of a more general orientation toward the world beyond the self. Poetry for them is part of cultivating a caring and attentive regard for and response to the worlds of which we are a part. Caring attention has been a principle I've tried to live by and write toward ever since. I'm drawn to a morality based in attention: how can a person know what an apt response to anyone or anything is without first paying close attention to that person, thing, ecosystem etc.? How can you know what's called for? That connection of poetry, attention and ethics is the primary legacy I feel I'm carrying from Don and Jan.

LH: *I know that you completed your Ph.D in philosophy at the University of Toronto on the topic of beauty. I'm fascinated by the fact that you chose philosophy as your path to poetry. How is it that you came to be interested in philosophy and related this interest to poetry?*

SS: I've always been drawn to poetry; I didn't discover philosophy till I went to university. My mother had a hunch I would enjoy studying philosophy, so I tried it out, and I was lucky to have two phenomenal teachers for that first-year survey course: Cyril Welch—perhaps not incidentally married to a poet—and Paul Bogaard. They both had a gift for showing how the abstract world of thought can have a bearing on how a person might live, how it might connect to material life. Which made philosophy feel like a meaningful endeavour rather than a conceptual game, which it can be at its worst.

At its best, philosophy can be world-changing; it can change how you see things and hence how you relate to other beings. So can poetry. And I love the way in which poetry can enact the relationship between the conceptual and the material that was given space in my introduction to philosophy. As an artefact made of language, the poem can deploy all of language's flexibility in terms of being able to signify concepts but also being able to call to a person's body, their somatic self. A poem can speak to me in many ways at once, which is powerful and allows me to respond as a fully integrated self. "There is nothing here that does not see you" but also there is no part of you that is not seen. ("Archaic Torso of Apollo," Rainer Maria Rilke, translation by Stephen Mitchell)

Going back to Don McKay as a mentor, one of the most valuable things he did for me was not to insist on the common poetry rule that the concrete is always preferable to the abstract. When abstractions weren't working for me, he didn't tell me to steer away from them; he made it clear that they could work, even if they weren't working in the particular poem I'd given him. So there was room for philosophy if we're thinking about philosophy as operating on an abstract plane. But then there was Jan Zwicky's teaching through *Lyric Philosophy* that poetry can be a way of thinking. She defines philosophy as "thinking in love with clarity," which creates room for poetry to count as philosophy. Her work made me think deeply about what thinking is. For me, it's ultimately

273

about tuning into relationships, seeing connections. And that can happen for me in the realms of both poetry and philosophy, insofar as they're distinct, although this understanding of thought also handily blurs the line between the two. Both can be means of sighting relationships.

LH: *Although you have an interest in analytical philosophy, I see that your philosophical approach has more affinity to contemporary philosophy such as phenomenology, the study of consciousness from the first-person point of view. In your poetry you are concerned with the personal perception of the world in many forms. Were you influenced by the phenomenologists Nietzsche, Heidegger, Husserl, and Maurice Merleau-Ponty?*

SS: I am very interested in the phenomenologists, it's true, less so Nietzsche (despite the fact that I've written a poem about him) than Merleau-Ponty's studies of the body as capable of pre-linguistic, pre-conceptual thought and Emmanuel Levinas' phenomenological ethics. I'd specify that I'm ultimately less concerned with consciousness as an object of attention than as a means of attention: I'm invested in consciousness as consciousness-of and the relationship-with that it enables. And I'm interested in consciousness as offering possibilities for relationship. So I'm drawn to Merleau-Ponty's study of the body as engaged in pre-linguistic orientation toward and relationship with the world in which I participate. And I'm interested in Levinas' vision of this relationship-with as the foundation on which my very existence is built. I suppose we could look at poetry as the trace of consciousness-of if we see consciousness in this very broad sense, i.e. 1) as including body and 2) as part of an absolutely foundational ethical response to an other.

I'm interested in poetry as an invitation to be attuned to the world around us in both conceptual and pre-conceptual ways. But in that sense, my poetry may not be phenomenological in that it isn't necessarily thinking *about* consciousness; it's more inviting particular forms of consciousness. I suppose for me, phenomenology sheds light on what poetry does, but it isn't what poetry does—my poetry mostly isn't about consciousness but is an enactment of consciousness-of; it's an opening into relationship-with.

LH: *Your work is often epistemological or concerned with gaining knowledge of the world that often has an almost "mysterious ineffability." Yeats said, "that we could not know the world, but we could embody a truth." Would you agree with this?*

SS: Hmm, I wonder if I'm concerned with gaining knowledge-of … something about the idea of gaining knowledge puts me off, perhaps because I'm immersed in a capitalist context where it's hard not to hear "gaining knowledge" as synonymous with "gaining ownership," trying to pin the world down so as to exert control over it. And "gaining knowledge" seems focused on knowledge as an inert thing rather than on an enacted effort of attention that is part of a relational unfolding. Maybe this distinction is my version of Yeats' difference between knowing the word and embodying a truth? Maybe. Truth as a noun makes me squeamish though, even as something embodied.

To be clear: I'm not saying I'm free of an impulse to reify the world I'm immersed in—maybe some of that impulse is in me. But I try to lean in other directions. I do want to know everything I can about the world—I'm currently on a fungus kick and am deep into field guides (thanks, Mum!), soaking up information, but the information is ultimately directing me back to the fungi themselves, is part of learning to better perceive the fungi I encounter.

I think I'm ultimately thirsting for intimacy-with. Yes, that's the more primary impulse: insofar as I want to gain knowledge of the world, it's in an effort to become more intimate with the strange place I'm immersed in. It's a form of approach, of attempting to be present to the world. But you're right, Laurence, that I've lived with a profound sense of the world's strangeness, of the ultimate otherness of others. And the effort to be mindful and appropriately awed by the strangeness of the other-than-human world definitely shows up in my poems. Further: if this is how it is with the other-than-human, other-than-Sue world, if there's a fundamental mystery there, a distance that bears respecting, there may be something presumptive and potentially intrusive about striving even for intimacy—does the world reciprocates that desire for intimacy, want me that close?

This is how I've thought of things for a long time—I've been hyper-aware of the need to respect the otherness of others. But lately I've been turning a corner, have been thinking that I may have exaggerated the otherness of others and am not mindful enough of the forms and moments of intimacy and closeness that coexist with forms and moments of otherness. I'm thinking, for example, of Robin Wall Kimmerer in *Braiding Sweetgrass*, writing about her deep understanding of the land as loving her back. I don't know if I can meet her there, though I see what she means about the land sustaining me and that being a kind of love. I'm feeling this out as a possible way of relating to land, trying it on.

LH: *I'm intrigued with how you explore the different concepts of beauty. For example, in the poem "Reply to Rilke" you see pain and sorrow as part of the beauty of life.*

SS: Elsewhere in *Heaven's Thieves* I quote Francis Bacon's famous line, "no beauty without a measure of strangeness." I see pain or sorrow as part of this strangeness. Maybe as a result of this strangeness? I.e. the world is a little strange, a little withheld, even in its beauty, so the fulfilment of beauty's "promise of happiness" is always at least somewhat deferred? If we think of this happiness as an utter harmony of self and beautiful other?

I say "promise of happiness" in reference to Alexander Nehamas and Theodor Adorno's picking up of this characterization of beauty from Stendhal, and when I say "even in its beauty," I'm thinking of Immanuel Kant arguing, more or less, that beauty helps us to feel at home in the world—to see it as a place that isn't as strange as we might think it. Now he had particular Kantian reasons for believing that we might think the world strange and a particular Kantian way in which he thought beauty made us feel at home, but the idea of beauty helping us to feel at home in a sometimes strange-feeling world is resonant regardless of what I may think of his Kantian apparatus. And yet …

I do think beauty can have the effect of making a person feel at home in the world, feel that their bodies and their aesthetic tendencies are well-matched to the world. As though beauty is a call I'm well-built to hear and respond to: there's a fit there (if not quite the mind-centric fit Kant had in mind). But beauty can also be profoundly alienating—when, for instance, a person doesn't feel up to beauty. I'm thinking about when we're in no fit state to be interested in a promise of happiness (a promise that has no place in the Kantian beautiverse, to be clear). When in the depths of grief, perhaps. That said, I don't think we're *ever* entirely up to beauty—can we ever even receive it as fully as we might like, for example? So even when beauty is at its most hospitable and inviting, there's perhaps a sliver of sadness, of mourning. Hence the poem.

But I find myself wondering what Kimmerer would make of this idea that we're not up to the beauty of the world—she who loves and feels herself loved by the land. I imagine this love as involving forgiveness for and acceptance of inevitable

277

(and even maybe also evitable?) human inadequacy. Would that allow a person to feel satisfied with receiving beauty to the best of their abilities and not to mourn a counterfactual infinitude of reception such that this person wouldn't feel the sliver of sadness? I wonder …

LH: *Your poems are often about hard-to-reach places, or places that are not easily accessible to normal discourse. I.e., they go beyond the limits of ordinary language to express as T.S. Eliot wrote "the inexpressible."*

SS: I love poetry for its willingness to bring on its own failure, for its willingness to work language in such a way that it falls vividly short of the world beyond it. The material world, with its ungeneralizable haecceities or "thisnesses," outstrips language every time. And there's the (moral and epistemological) problem of foreground and background, which we're stuck with: to say "this" is always to fail to say "that," when this and that (and that and that and that…) are co-existent.

The poetry I love best has no illusions about its limits, brings us to the furthest threshold of what's possible in language, then lets us go. This kind of poetry is maybe not exactly expressing the inexpressible, but it does bring us to awareness of the inexpressible. It skirts the mystery of what-is, and in its patent inability to name that mystery, we feel the power of what lies beyond the poem.

I like poems that hold space for silence, that sound a note so you can hear how far it travels through the silence. Maybe that's what it means to "go beyond the limits of ordinary language."

LH: *You frequently write about light. Why do you find it so interesting? Can you please elaborate on this?*

SS: Hmm, the more I think about it, the more I see that light functions a bit like a god for me. I think light and I think utter clarity. Which is something I crave, though I know it's out of reach. I work hard to embrace the inevitable partiality of my understanding, to accept my limitations and the ways in which I will always be troubled by doubt and misgivings, which are apt to the world I live in. Even so, there's a part of me that goes on craving utter clarity. The ease of utter clarity. A god's ease.

Relatedly, I imagine light as flawless. There's a kind of perfection about light that is seductive to me as a mere human mired in imperfections.

So light is beyond me, is always more than I can be. And it's distant from me in that way, in the way that a god exceeds the human, can't really ever be in touch with or hope to inhabit the messy human situation. That's the god's flaw: flawlessness. I imagine being messily human as the one thing that lies beyond a god's powers, the light's power.

But light touches me. Despite this ontological distance, despite the fact that I will always be light's other, it touches me, illuminates my world. It doesn't leave me alone in my insufficiencies. It's very different from me, but it's with me. Light beaming down from the sky feels like a little bit of love, a little bit of grace.

LH: *I've observed that you use personification often to animate things in nature, but you also use the opposite of personification or chremamorphism, where the human is treated as an object. Why do you like to use these devices in the representation of certain realities in your poetry?*

SS: This is a question I've been turning over for years. I'm drawn to personification--I think because as I experience it, it requires of me an intense effort of empathy. So there's always an element of chremamorphism at work in that personification. But I'm very aware of the moral danger of making the non-human over in our own image—especially the worst-case scenario of turning the non-human into goofily cartoonish versions of ourselves, creating an invitation to condescend to the non-human as falling hopelessly, even laughably short of the human—as though we're really all that.

But there are different ways of personifying. Don McKay, for instance, in *Vis à Vis*, proposes a respectful form of personification that offers the non-human a "face" as a kind of ambassadorial gift from one culture to another. Yet I understand that even more apparently benign forms of personification run the risk of effecting an intrusive imposition of the human image upon the non-human. Gift or imposition? Who decides?

Another question worth considering, however: is what gets called personification always personification or is it recognition of animacy in what gets called inanimate?

Even in cases that seem like clear personification, where the animacy in question looks a lot like a human style of animacy, might these yet offer a valuable invitation to readers to see those non-human beings as active subjects rather than inert objects (as the dominant culture of my contemporary world encourages me to see them)? Personification might offer some resistance to this mode of engagement, invite me to consider other-than-human beings as having a perspective, as being protagonists of their own stories rather than props in mine.

Finally, there's personification's inevitable failure at transforming the non-human world into humans. As a form of metaphor, it always contains an "is not" alongside its "is." Yes, that failure to transform can result in the hierarchically-driven condescension mentioned above, but empathic, attentive personification can reveal differences that may make a human sigh with envy. John Berger writes about this in "Animal

World": in anthropomorphizing, he says, a person "measures [themself], as [they are], against the animal. Occasionally with undiluted pride. Often with surreptitious envy."

Now chremamorphism—that feels far less controversial to me. It involves some of the same valuable empathic effort with far less risk of disrespecting the non-human: I allow myself to be transformed rather than imposing transformation on the other. I imaginatively invite the non-human into my being rather than risk imposing my being on the non-human. Yet I also hold to the idea that sensitive personification and chremamorphism are both elements of one and the same gesture: in imagining the other as me, I also imagine me as the other, and vice versa. So I think the necessary self-openness and self-vulnerability of chremamorphism is also part of other-aware, other-respectful personification.

Personification is a site of tension for me, but I return to it over and over again because of what I said at the outset: the effort of empathy it demands feels valuable. And perhaps any attempted empathy risks unwarranted projection … perhaps … hence the tension …

LH: *You are very visual in your poems, expressing unusual and striking metaphors. I see that you are sometimes drawn to ekphrastic poems, such as in* Heaven's Thieves *as in the natures mortes of Dutch painter Pieter Claesz, the Sagrada Familia by Gaudi, and the photographs of the French photographer, Eugène Atget. What is it that attracts you to writing ekphrastic poems?*

SS: The workaday world requires of me, of most of us, modes of engagement that are more linear and ends-directed than they are attentive and resonance-sensitive. I can easily fall into these sometimes necessary but ultimately unsatisfying modes of being. Works of visual art are like poems in that they're invitations into presence; they ask me to pause with them. They alert my sensitivities, draw me into being hyper-attentive, open me up to resonances. So of course I write poems in response! Visual art puts me in a poem-y frame of mind. It helps me to inhabit the world in resonance-sensitive, fully present way that reading and writing poetry also helps me to do. It's a state of grace, this way of being in the world, and I'm hungry for it.

Dance, by the way, also invites me into this open and sensitive mode of being, but I've found it challenging to respond to dance with poems. I think that the kinaesthetic dimension of this art form has made it more recalcitrant to language for me—I must be responding in a more deeply somatic way than I do to either poetry or visual art. I kind of like that about dance, much as I would also love to be able to respond to dance in writing. I enjoy that it engages me at a level that appears to be a-linguistic.

LH: *In my interview with Louis Dudek when referring to a bouquet of chrysanthemums he said, "They cry out to be praised." Rilke in "The Second Elegy" of the* Duino *Elegies wrote: "Begin again, always anew, your ever-inadequate praising." In your work, there is this sense of the need to praise. For example, in "Bach's Harpsichord in F Minor," you evoke the different elements that you praise.*

SS: I think poetry can be importantly critical and politically challenging, and directly so, but I do also cherish praise poems. And I think they have a role to play in the political landscape.

For me, offering or enacting praise is tied into the effort of being attentive to what's here—being alive to what does "call out to be praised" and staying in touch with what's precious about the worlds I belong to. Of course, there's the worry that in praising a chrysanthemum I may be overlooking or turning my back on the troubles and injustices at work in those worlds. A person might wonder how I can spend time praising a chrysanthemum when, for instance, the climate on which all beings, chrysanthemum included, rely is in peril. But need it be either/or? I have trouble imagining fighting for a world if stripped of the ability to praise it.

We could also be worried that sociopolitical injustice may be rendered invisible by the praise poem—I'm thinking here about an untitled Lucille Clifton poem that opens Camille Dunghy's *Black Nature*. The poem asks why, when the poet begins a poem in praise of nature, "is there under that poem, always / an other poem." It's not hard to guess what other poem upsets the writing of the praise-filled nature poem.

I don't dispute that a writer may experience some of the unease with the nature ode described by Clifton's poem. How could I? Why would I want to? That friction seems important. But rather than do away with praise poems, I'd prefer to work on building a world in which everyone has the privilege of writing praise poems (or singing praise songs or offering praise in whatever way a person might choose). The point for me is to create room for more people from a wider variety of backgrounds to write praise poetry if they feel moved to. Praise poems remind me of the world I want to stand up for and help to grow. I think they're an important part of a poetic ecology that also includes rants and protest poems and call-out poems and whatever other kind of politically inflected poem a person may write; I think they all need each other. And of course praise and protest can co-exist within a single poem, an approach to which I'm increasingly drawn. C.A. Conrad's poetry comes to mind as an example—often working as both celebration and protest.

As I think back on this reply to your question, it's interesting to me that Dudek didn't feel the need that I do to hold some space for the praise poem, to argue for it as a valuable part of a larger poetic ecology. Perhaps I'm wrong to perceive it as needing support, but I'm obviously feeling some pressure.

LH: *In your poems, you often develop your ideas as permutations of an argument. For example, in the poem "Sympathy" from* Mortal Arguments, *you speak of the difficulty of escaping from the "self." Can you please comment on this idea?*

SS: I'm interested in the question of what counts as an argument. What counts as a reason? Can an image be a reason? "Argument With Rilke," for instance, tries this out, offering a pretty clear rational argument but also arguing via images.

I'm also interested in the extent to which a poem can include traditional argument—in the sense of offering a logically coherent position and rationale—and still retain its poemness. I suppose I mean by this that I don't want the argument to overwhelm the other elements that come together to make the poem. I don't want the resonances among those elements to get flattened. Argument does tend to take up a lot of oxygen in whatever room it enters, so I'm curious about how to balance argument with image, sound, breath etc. How to include it as one element among others.

Mortal Arguments is grounded in the idea that every mortal being is an argument for the care of that being. It's not complicated: to be mortal is to be open to harm and is hence to deserve care. It gets complicated when we consider that different beings expose this vulnerability to different degrees, in different moments, and with differing degrees of agency, but it remains that any time I encounter mortality, I encounter my responsibility to care. The book wants to show how deep-rooted the call for care is and that it's everywhere around us. It's also struggling with the reality that we can't possible care enough, that we simply don't have that power to respond to everything around us with the depth of care that it deserves.

I don't know that I'd say "Sympathy" argues, but it's definitely premised on a certain understanding of ethical life. The poem worries about not being able to decentre the self, to use

Iris Murdoch's term. It worries about the speaker's inability to get past their own concerns, needs and desires in order to care properly for others. But this is a worry that I've outgrown, to some extent. It seems to me now that the call for self-erasure, to become "the self, selfless," is a rather extreme form of ethics, an uncompromising ethics that isn't caring enough toward the self—and it generates friction when I put on my feminist hat and think about sociopolitical invitations or demands that women be selfless carers when that selfless care isn't or isn't consistently reciprocated. Still, there's something to the idea that the self can't be at the centre of an ethical life. But maybe it can share that centre. Or maybe sometimes it's right for the self to be centred and sometimes it's right for it to be de-centred … What's interesting to me about "Sympathy" is its preoccupation with self—it's self-centred, enacting the very problem it wants out of. What a conundrum!

LH: *In the introduction to Jan Zwicky's* Wittgenstein Elegies, *you wrote: "The reflective listener makes no claim beyond that of listening seriously—attending to tone, mood, gestures both linguistic and physical—then reflecting these back to the speaker." Could you elaborate on this concept?*

SS: I'm not quite sure where I learned about reflective listening—from my therapist maybe? At its core it's empathy, is a matter of tuning in and then responding in a way that shows you're tuned in. It's a modest form of engagement: it doesn't propose solutions; it just says, "I'm here with you." If that really is a modest claim! By which I just mean that it's hard to be fully present to others. As a teacher I try to be a reflective listener, to dial into what students are saying and reflect it back to them so they know that they're worth listening to and that we're bound together in the effort of whatever exploration is underway in the classroom. In the case of Zwicky's

Wittgenstein Elegies ... well, knowing that Wittgenstein felt desperately misunderstood most of his life, I often felt that in the *Elegies*, the fundamental gesture was one of *I hear you. You are not alone.*

I wonder, is that what I'm saying in the fungi poems I'm writing just now? I do think I'm trying to write in a way that says to the fungus, *I hear you*. And that's a bit different from reflective listening in a classroom setting—the fungus obviously can't literally hear me. The poem, the reflective response, falls on deaf ears in the case of the fungus. The responsive *I hear you* is in some sense just as distant from the mushrooms who will never hear or understand my poems as Zwicky's reflective-listener response is from a long-dead Wittgenstein who will never hear her *Elegies*. So why make these fruitless gestures? Said elsewise: how might these gestures be fruitful?

I think here of a small passage from Kate Cayley's poem "Lent," in which a minister, breaking bread, "wears a small smile that suggests he knows the futility of what he does, and does it anyway, from love, from habit, from the way the two become, over time, indistinguishable from one another." Poems for me are a habit of leaning out with love. And even if the chanterelles, for instance, can't feel me leaning out toward them, the poems bring me to presence regardless. Writing a poem about chanterelles with the drive of wanting to say, truly, *I hear you*, makes me feel my way as far as I can into what it might be to be a chanterelle. And to feel the relation between us. So maybe the poem isn't really about what I can reflect back to the chanterelle but about the preparatory attention that reflective listening requires. Or the poem is a kind of benign diagnostic: how fully can I say *I hear you*?

October, 2021

Photo credit: Unknown

COLLEEN THIBAUDEAU

Laurence Hutchman: *Your mother was born in Ireland and your father was Canadian, Acadian by descent. Can you comment on this?*
Colleen Thibaudeau: I think those who come from other countries to Canada have to be a little more scrappy. You have to really scrap or you're not going to find your place. But mother was of course Northern Irish. It was First World War time when my mom and dad met. They were both in a rather emotional state. Like Dad is going back to what he knows is going to be worse. He had gone out of university, remember, the university battalion that was formed in Canada at U. of T. He was a U.C. person in political science mainly and hoping to be a bilingual journalist, even though the Thibaudeaus all spoke English because they had always married people like these Stuarts. So Mom having been the only girl and youngest in a family of boys was by her nature extremely belligerent or you might say if you were using the negative "contrary?"

Dad had just told us things, like that we are French, but we're not from Quebec. Then he told us about his ancestors, the two brothers getting away from the deportation. They went somewhere like New York State or Pennsylvania. Before the Battle of the Thames in 1812, they offered to go as guides with the Americans into Canada. They said they knew a route via Windsor, and they would take them to where the British were. In the night they took off and went to find Tecumseh. They didn't tell where they were, but the Americans realized their guides were gone. They went on a big march, but these ones met up with Tecumseh and the York volunteers and the British, the Redcoats up there at Moravia town. They were in that battle, and then out of that they had a chance to marry with the widows of the Butler's Rangers. That way you would get a double land grant: one for helping as soldiers and one through that widow. So I think this is the Acadian part, although dad never used that word.

LH: *There are Thibodeaus in Northern New Brunswick, a moving company.*

CT: That sounds like us. Yes, well you see you have to remember also these particular guys. They were freethinkers. They were not Catholic by this time, they married Methodists. That was a nice, kindly middle of the way religion, that could include people of any kind that were not like the establishment, Anglican Church of England. You see many people have two religions within their family. My mom had Church of Ireland through her dad, that's just established from the Anglican Church and Presbyterian through her mom. But the Methodism which then went into the United Church etc. as did some Presbyterian and some Baptist.

LH: *I want to turn to your poetry now. Your poems are quite different from most English Canadian poetry. David Helwig commenting on your subject matter said, "It is penetrated by dream, nightmare, and a sense of history."*

CT: Well, I don't know. Are they really poems? Then you get those awful reviews. David Helwig is kind, but other people say things like, "A three-year-old child could do better." You know, because you're trying to be simple, like I come from a primitive surrealism type of thing.

LH: *Do you meet Margaret Avison at this time?*

CT: Margaret Avison would tell me what she's reading, which is Cavafy, Carson McCullers. I mean the world was highly intellectual, *The New Yorker*. I had never heard of any of these things. I was amazed. Then I owe a debt also to people like Miriam Waddington, whom I would have seen. In her *First Statement* stuff I identified with Miriam. You see she's coming a bit from Dylan Thomas; I think so, more than from Auden. You see I love also Vernon Watkins.

LH: *It's imagination connected to myth and history.*

CT: Well, we worked hard in our studies. I think I might get the mythy stuff from my mom. You see the Thibaudeaus, the Acadian side, that's just all hard work, slogging away. When my parents met in Belfast, the one topic of conversation they had in common that was not sad like about war and death was *The Celtic Twilight.*

Dad was away doing this tight security work; we all thought he worked in the munitions. The Northern Irish underplay everything. You might be sitting on a like a bushel of rubies or something, but they're not going to say that. Mom through Dad knew about *The Celtic Twilight* from a British officer that he had met with a lot who was from Dublin, and he knew all about Yeats's plays and that Mom knew all Yeats's poetry. You see Mom wanted Yeats read at her funeral and we had a hard time getting the right things. I finally did a bit of "Among School Children" and MacNeice of course; she had read about MacNeice and liked him.

That's later, you see Mom was born actually at Greencastle out there. I wanted to tell you about Mom and the fairy tree and all that. She was always telling us, up the mountain, up the rushy glen, about the big statue or a big tombstone of the crusader, and something about the way the foot or boot is that shows whether or not he died over there or came home. Well, you see I must have just absorbed all this countryside, Irish funny stuff. Mom's born 1901. She had a privileged kind of upbringing. Her dad paid for her to go to school. He sent her to the model school. The boys went to the church school, you see which would not be good. She had this wonderful, experimental education.

LH: *Your poems have something in common with Quebec poetry; in fact, you translated some Quebecois poets.*
CT: Well just little bits and pieces I had to do. This was an offshoot of the university women's club book group. We decide on the number of books we will read that year. Well, at one point for some reason, I had a chance to do something on Quebec literature. Probably we all scrambled for something, and I tried to translate little bits and pieces. Later I did a paper on Roch Carrier, and I had met him because Jamie, my husband by that time, was teaching French Canadian in his Canadian lit translation course. They liberated a lot of material, and they worked with bringing in guests such as Paul Chamberland. I had to go with a friend to translate when we met Paul Chamberland at the airport. When we went to Manitoba, I lost complete contact with everything that had gone on before, except I kept the thread of the French by once a month going to the St. Boniface Library, that was so far on so many buses and cold etc. and then you had a seven-mile hike from the University bus stop over to where we lived.

LH: *You had a connection with French through your French-Canadian studies at the University of Toronto.*
CT: The connection with U of T with France was through Robert Finch mainly and through all those other courses that you had to take. And of course I lived in Angers for a year in 1951. I taught English conversation as an assistant in the lycée but lived out which was good.

LH: *There are other influences in your work. One thinks of Virginia Woolf and the empathy you have with people and situations in many poems—Rilke in "The Elastic Moment," Wallace Stevens in "The Blue of the Swimming Pool," and e.e. cummings with your word-play. Richard Stingle has traced some of these in his essay on you. Have you been conscious of any literary influences on your work?*

CT: Yeah, I think I made a big leap around the time of meeting those people like Margaret Avison, Alice Boissonneault, the librarians, the help of the Jackman family—like not having to cook your meals, you know when you're a student. They had a big library too on entirely different types of stuff, the world of the *New Yorker*, Mary McCarthy and the Southern writers. It seemed at that time nearly everybody was big on the southern writers—McLuhan was certainly and John Crowe Ransom. And Avison still relates back to certain things. If we're talking on the phone or something like that she'll say "as so and so says or as John Frederick Nims says," which would not be a name I would have followed. Margaret had that big West Coast connection as well later. At the same time running parallel to that Jamie had always very much been interested in the Sitwells—that was the stylistic influence and that type of aristocratic country life. Virginia Woolf also was a big influence on him.

So I not only have the dreamy, idealistic qualities of nature. Well at the same time though, I've done a lot of gritty jobs, and I always had like Jamie loved to explore back alleys. Our daughter and son are both the same. We relate to people who are cooking out of an ashcan and so on for some reason. One thing that Weaver liked. He always said to me: "You've got an interesting style, Colleen," you know what people will do when they're a student and have been to war etc. "But you don't have anything to write about." I said: "What about all my tobacco material?" "Well, maybe, maybe."

You know then McLuhan opened up so many different avenues. That was one of the main things that he was talking about; he hadn't yet gone into the big time with the American money. So he's doing like the Southerns, *The Kenyon Review*, *The Sewanee Review* and all that sort of stuff; he was doing F.R. Leavis and Q.D. Leavis. You see he put me onto Q.D. Leavis to use her stuff and Empson's *Some Versions of Pastoral*. In my thesis, Roper and Bissell didn't so much know about this, but they weren't anti-McLuhan. They were interested in all of this interweaving; now what I wrote was not down the Roper line.

LH: *Your poetry is inclusive—that is in it you try to bring together many apparently disparate elements. I'm thinking of "Poem" (from 1949) with its references to the shy girl, Brueghel, the socialist boy, Rita Hayworth, the Mayfair Washing Machine Company.*
CT: That would have been written after I came back from that '47 summer in Montreal. It was just accidental that the *First Statement, Northern Review* people befriended me. They'd come into the store where I was working. Like John and Irving would come into the store to say "hi." You know as they're passing through the town in summer. They were very kind.

LH: *Do you remember writing "The Elastic Moment"?*
CT: The Elastic Moment" too came out of that summer in Montreal period where I was living on Jeanne Mance, but I was walking all the time. I got to the mountain or wherever I could. So anyway like in that particular poem … I'm trying to think of what the aesthetic was. We had had a very wonderful whole year with Reid MacCallum in aesthetics, and then the following year was in a philosophy course. The third year we had Leibnitz. Within Leibnitz you have a concept that I find very interesting, and this is what he stressed what

he had formulated during those wars of religion. It's almost understandable as a concept—except if you come from a very divided race or religion or you see it all around. You will remember this all of your life and that is that doctrine of the reconciliation of opposites. Now we didn't do the monads and the other stuff so much, but the doctrine of the reconciliation of opposites we were on that all year because dear Reid MacCallum. Margaret Avison also knew Reid MacCallum.

LH: *There is something in your personal makeup, which lends itself to an incorporation of different elements. It seems to me very much the way you react to people.*

CT: Well, I don't know. We don't know ourselves very well, do we? I was very fortunate I think as a child; I was the eldest. Also, neither my mother nor father believed boys and girls should be brought up according to any particular what they now call "gender identification or gender roles." We were just thrown out in the world like MacCallum always said, "head-first into a bowl of fruit salad." That's your perceptions when you're a little child like when you sit there on your tree and the world is all whirling around. It's not particularly religious, and it's not psychological, and it's not physical, it's just what happens. You see everything through a kaleidoscope. Now, you gradually begin to sort it out. You, in fact, get pushed and indoctrinated and stuff is presented to you. You don't know how to reject it at first. My mother was very tied in with the Welsh miners and all of that. You see she identified with the working class, but her politics, strangely enough, were not with the working class. So I grew up with all of these opposites. My dad also had a conflict. He came from very simple really farming people whose mothers were very religious. He himself was one of these Thibaudeau men who was a freethinker. What that means is that they cannot go along with the idea that you indoctrinate other people. That's why it's so weird that I got into that *Christian Poetry in Canada*, except when you see that they can include doubt and all manner of different denominational etc. But there's other people, like Margaret Avison's work.

LH: *There's also the visionary quality in your work. You empha-size the unity of experience in "We're all aswim in one big sea" in the poem "King's Park, Manitoba." It reminds me of a George Johnston poem.*

CT: Well maybe that was what people were like more in those days. You have to remember that up until 1950, like what they call the post-war, we didn't have any technology, as we know it now. We had radio. And we had cars, but they weren't causing much of a problem in wartime especially because the gas was rationed. People did everything themselves. And on Saturday night you went to Hambles and lined up for fish and chips like that was the greatest thing and brought them home. You see my mom was from the sea. Maybe that's a strand here. I was brought up on all sorts of sea lore because of this Belfast harbour connection. She wasn't like conventionally religious because she had as I say on one side of the family Church of Ireland and on the other side was Presbyterian, and they had to go to both churches. Like every Sunday they went to both. But, she went to the model school, which didn't stress that but probably stressed more humanist values.

She could still remember how we went around the Gaspé Bay, and we saw all. We saw all of the Champlain country be-cause we had to go all around the Finger Lakes, and we went over on Ferries like into New Brunswick it must have been— that kind that you pull on ropes. And they knew there was going to be a war; it started just as we went into high school … But in August we went to all those places like Walden, and dad said, "Oh what would Thoreau have said 'Empty package of Lucky Strikes'." People were very careful in those days. There not only weren't all the goods around, but they were more protective of the environment, I think. That's the sea. Now, I'm just trying to think, my poem. Of course, the sea also is vast because in the sea many people are drowned or are burned up on ships or that and go into the sea. I have quite a bit about that now. Now in that particular poem that you're talking about that's the one were the dolphin baby says it, that's little John out in his carriage and he's born July 16th. So, the little baby, so it's not too long since it's left the womb.

LH: *Women were beginning to be more active in the development of modern Canadian literature.*
CT: Doris Anderson, then the editor of *Chatelaine*, was associated with the Status of Women. See people talk about the feminist movement as if it had just started unexpectedly in the States somewhere whereas it has been going on forever. Doris was also interested in writing obviously. She's done novels. She was doing an M.A. at the time that I'm doing mine. Then my friend Phyllis Gotlieb. You see she came over to UC. We had taken in our fourth-year creative writing together, we were always good friends. Phyllis obviously with the Jewish aspects was helping me with a lot of good descriptions of various things, give me an example of like how she remembered as a little child seeing such and such a ceremony.

LH: *You met A.M. Klein. Could you talk about this meeting?*
CT: I met him in December of '49, just before Christmas. I went directly to his law office. He granted a ten minute meeting, but during the course of that the poor man, he had I don't know how many phone calls because he was also running *The Jewish Chronicle*. He would have also been with many

committees that were trying to deal with the aftermath of the concentration camps, the resettlement of people, here, there. I had read his "Oxen of the Sun," and obviously I did read all his works and loved them very much somehow without being from that world at all. Now his skin was beautiful like parchment, very dark, sparkling eyes. And very slick blacky hair at that time and he was into all that Joyce, all that very tough stuff, working. He worked on his own. He worked with others and it was always Smith, Klein. He was like totally into all of the world's activities type of Jewish person. That's what they're committed to doing that, that's all. Yes, extending themselves infinitely, but I felt that he was getting older. He should not have had to deal with that alone.

LH: *Later you and James published in Alan Crawley's* Contemporary Verse

CT: I was trying to think about how that connection would have come about. I am trying to pinpoint where P.K. Page would have been, etc. I don't know. You see P.K. Page worked in Montreal. She also worked at the film board. I connect Alan and P.K. because much later on the West Coast I met him for the first time—that would be the Easter of '69 when we were judging together. He included me graciously. She read everything to him from a high school contest. Bushel, they came in bushel baskets, like that's a farming community there, the Squamish Peninsula. So I met Alan Crawley and his wife. But at the time that the first run through of *Contemporary Verse* it could have been Birney who was helping us then. He was for a brief time the editor of The Canadian Authors Association publication and he asked us for material. I wonder whether Weaver was the contact. Crawley and Birney had seen those little things in *Northern Review*. Now the poem in *Northern Review*, one of them I remember is "Can Maude come out and play with me."

LH: *What kind of a relationship did you and Jamie have with Alan Crawley?*

CT: It would be more through Jamie. He was wonderful. I hoped I might have some of his letters. I sold subscriptions to all of these things. My poor parents subscribed to *Northern Review,* they subscribed to *Contemporary Verse.* So I had come a little bit through Weaver, and those people were all very socialist cause people. Then I had come from like what you'd call very young childhood feeling that I wasn't prejudiced against people like Agnes Macphail and also the role of history at that time, that instinctive awful thing that is in people where they tear apart anybody who they can classify as establishment. But it did seem that when you talk about imagination and that Crawley and his magazine and Birney seemed to be coming from a different interpretation of things. Now with Earl Birney, always you have to remember his childhood setting out in Banff and that wonderful feeling of being in the mountains you know, and it makes you proportionate to your surroundings. It's different from an urban upbringing. Jamie on the farm is coming from an outdoor environment where you're king.

LH: *You were friends as well as worked with Margaret Avison during your years at University of Toronto.*

CT: Margaret Avison, we were back in that summer of '46. Did I recall where I met Margaret? She wanted to meet Jamie, but they did it in a very roundabout way. How was that done? I think I met Margaret before finding her in the library. Frye had invited both of us to Eaton's College Street to meet and she had her favourite—I think Boston Cream pie. The idea was that then Jamie and then Margaret would get together which is what happened and they all liked each other you see. Now how Frye happened to do this. He knew Avison. He didn't know me. Like I was the only go-between.

LH: *Did you exchange poems at that time?*

CT: I don't think so, except in books? But that would be the time of *Contemporary Verse* and the *Northern Review*, and *The Undergrad* was getting going. You see Frye and Margaret would have seen our stuff in those publications, which to me didn't mean anything.

LH: *You wrote your thesis "Recent Canadian Poetry in the 1940s" under the direction of Marshall McLuhan.*

CT: He was my third person as it were, because I had done it in that grad year. I graduated with a B.A. from University College in Eng Lang Lit, a very funny put-together subject in '48-'49, I'm doing my M.A. I had never done any modern, so I hit McLuhan without any modern's background other than what I had sort of picked up myself because I put together such a funny B.A. I had however done an awful lot of French with Robert Finch. We went for our French to University College. Jamie, of course, was doing classics. You could put together quite a different kind of packet in Eng Lang Lit. I had kept on with philosophy. I kept on with French right to the fourth year; most of the teaching was in English. I had Robillard for Marquis de Sade, and all of that, and then you go into Finch, and he used more French in his teaching and we did Baudelaire and Verlaine and all those people. And then he was going on to what McLuhan was then teaching which was Laforgue and Corbière just as a sideline. I had always run over to St. Mike's and I had taken Aquinas. Some of our '47 grads would be like people like Don Heron. They were at Vic see, and Trinity also had a full contingent of very interesting people and all the little university magazines were of a pretty high calibre. Paul Arthur and Kathy Harmon had gotten tired of being on *The Undergrad*, the university college literary magazine. Something happened there. They founded their own thing called *Here and*

Now. They did that I think when we were in our third year. So these people are operating on what they now say a global scale.

LH: *A.M. Klein's was one of the most important works in your thesis.*
CT: Oh it was excellent. You see that's where I would first encounter like they had excerpts from Klein's "Oxen of the Sun," work that he was doing. They tied in with Montreal in quite an interesting way. They had also probably had Birney; he'd be on the West Coast by then. He was from U of T, but he had gone overseas and then returned. About *Here and Now* they brought Stephen Spender, who was on a lecture tour and they tapped into from whatever that was from the States. It was Paul Arthur whose dad was Eric Arthur, the architect, who had come out of the navy and studied a bit or knew about the Swiss magazine *Graphus* which was quite a beautiful typography set up. So *Here and Now* was very visually beautiful. Have you ever seen it, Laurence? Now a person like me, you see, we're in this very small setting of classes and people who knew each other. Here I am getting a poem in an international journal. But this is only one of those accidents of wartime. I'm right at hand, I can put it right in their hands.

LH: *What got you interested in writing on modern Canadian poetry? It was very new at the time, and yours was one of the first theses on the subject.*
CT: Well, as I was saying, we went into this M.A. year. Claude Bissell was coming back from the Italian campaign and Le Pan. Now all of this ferment of the returning men. It was his ambition to set up an M.A. level Canadian course. It combined history and literature. He taught the literature and Creighton taught the history, so it was a very heavy reading and out of that he also wanted to get one student at least

working on Canadian poetry on their M.A., so I would be sort of a natural one to do this. Before I had stuff printed in *Contemporary Verse* and also by '47, *Northern Review* took something. And then in the summer of '47, I went to work in Montreal in Eaton's, so I actually met John Sutherland and Irving Layton, and Audrey and those people.

LH: *You had a close connection with* Northern Review.
CT: I was only in Montreal for two months. Now originally I got an idea that maybe I would switch gears. A lot of people switch in their third year. If you were in moderns, you would have a chance to go to Smith. So why wouldn't I switch and try to finish in Montreal, the old Saint Thomas More Institute it was, that then became Sir George Williams and now Concordia. However, I was only there for such a short time because it was too expensive. My original thing was to work to find out about Quebec poetry. Now I went there to try to learn French, which was always an ambition and because we spoke English, of course, at home.

LH: *You met Irving Layton and John Sutherland at this time.*
CT: They were hand setting their magazine *Northern Review* by this time, and they did it all. There was no Canada Council or anything like we're just talking about selling ads. And their friend, Ernesto Cuevas, he was also very good at selling ads.

LH: *What kind of man was John Sutherland?*
CT: John was very nice and they had a bit of recreation. They played tennis and they looked really well and he was very clean, like your idea of a Maritime sailor. This was my idea of John, and they had me over several times. I wonder whether John was on some kind of disability pension. He did also work at many other things, and Irving taught a course out at Macdonald Institute.

LH: *What was your impression of Irving Layton?*

CT: I liked Irving too. I went there too one Saturday night. They gave lovely instructions on how you're going to get there on the buses and that. Betty Sutherland, the sister of Donald Sutherland, an artist was Irving's wife, and I met little Maxie. Little Maxie was allowed to smoke cigars like while he was still in diapers just for a minute to keep him quiet—how you do with children. And Betty and Audrey Aikman who was John Sutherland's wife. They were night proofreaders on *The Gazette.* I think people more in those days were casual in one sense, that everybody was quite poor. These people were living I would think would be kind of a bohemian, Washington Square type of thing, but it didn't seem like a New York thing. I had been to New York with my mum. When I left, I said listen this is nothing to do with writing. I want to help you guys. I'm going to run three different areas and trying to get your magazines in, so I helped them out in a business way.

LH: *Your thesis had a political perspective.*

CT: I never had a copy of it for years; we moved so much.

LH: *In your thesis you were critical of the poets of* Preview *suggesting they could have had more of a sense of humour and "the naive delight in the strange productions of the imagination." Do you remember what you meant by this?*

CT: No, for goodness sake, I don't remember. Isn't that awful. That's a young person speaking of the people who are older. Obviously if you were doing this in order of rank, it would have to be either P.K. Page or Miriam Waddington or Dorothy Livesay—there were others. Those were some of the major people at that time. Miriam and Patrick Waddington also were connected with *First Statement.*

LH: *Do you feel closer in your aesthetics to the poets of* First Statement?

CT: These are funny questions, you know because I never thought of that. Isn't that weird? I never thought of relating all this through the little magazines. Why? The reason *Preview*. They were trying to do this deliberate type through Patrick Anderson whom I later did interview for the thesis. He was in his bathtub there in Montreal. You just talked to his feet— very clean, very wet. It's one of those little Montreal situations, you know were there's two rooms, parts of two rooms, a one and a halfer, so you take away the bathtub. So he was in his bathtub and I interviewed him, and somebody else was there and Jamie. I did those interviews for the thesis—all in a bundle during the Christmas vacation of 1948.

You see to remember all the time I didn't have any moderns to guide me. I was only beginning to put the moderns together at the time that I was doing the thesis. Therefore I approached *The Preview* way of writing; their techniques were just fresh. That's a much more a gentle version of that kind of diction, I think. So that there's two things that's unusual in those *Preview* people is their diction or their technique and that possibly is coming like through Auden and those people. Also, the other unusual, wonderful thing, of course is that they formed a group. They were anti-fascist, that they kept going.

LH: *Did you have any clear idea what the people in* First Statement *were doing? Layton and Dudek were deriving their influence from American rather than an English influence.*

CT: No, I don't think I did. I had a very clear idea of what they were doing except they seemed simpler in their diction, but where they came from. I still don't know to this day. You see if you remember John Sutherland was a Maritimer. He's a

New Brunswicker. Well you should be getting to know them now, Laurence. Now, they think differently. Did you notice that already? So we're dealing with a New Brunswick person. You just recognize the people right away.

July, 1991
London, Ontario

BIOGRAPHICAL NOTES

Brian Bartlett

Brian Bartlett was born in 1953 in St. Stephen, New Brunswick, and after the age of four he grew up in Fredericton. He has published 14 collections and chapbooks of poetry, and four books of prose (one of his writings about poetry, the others of nature writing); he has also edited several volumes of other poets' works. Bartlett received a B.A. in English from the University of New Brunswick, an M.A. from Concordia University, and a Ph.D from the Université de Montréal. Since 1990 he has lived in K'jipuktuk/Halifax, where he taught Creative Writing and various fields of literature at Saint Mary's University for nearly 30 years. His poetry has been honoured with *The Malahat Review* Long Poem Prize twice, the Petra Kenney International Poetry Prize , the Atlantic Poetry Prize, and the Acorn-Plantos Award for People's Poetry. Bartlett's wife, Karen Dahl, is a Senior Manager in the Halifax Regional Library system, and they have two children, Josh and Laura.

Roo Borson

Roo Borson is a poet and occasional essayist. Her books include the collaborative works *Introduction to the Introduction to Wang Wei* by Pain Not Bread (Roo Borson, Kim Maltman, and Andy Patton) published by Brick Books, and *Box Kite: Prose Poems by Baziju* (Roo Borson and Kim Maltman) published by House of Anansi Press. Her most recent solo work is a triptych of poetry books linked through imagery and formal variation: *Short Journey Upriver Toward* Ōishida, followed by *Rain; road; an open boat*, followed by *Cardinal in the Eastern White Cedar*, published by McClelland & Stewart/Penguin Random House. She has served as Writer in Residence at Western University, Concordia University, Massey College at the University of Toronto, Green College at the University of British Columbia, and at the University of Guelph.

She won the CBC Literary Competition in 1982 and 1989. *Short Journey Upriver Toward Oishida* was awarded the Griffin Poetry Prize, the Governor General's Award, and the Pat Lowther Award. Born in Berkeley, California in 1952, she currently lives in Toronto with poet and theoretical physicist Kim Maltman. Their combined literary archives are held, alongside the archives of Pain Not Bread, at Library and Archives Canada.

George Elliott Clarke

George Elliott Clarke was born in 1960 in Windsor, Nova Scotia, but grew up in North End Halifax, the province's capital. Holding an Honours English B.A. from the University of Waterloo (1984), a Dalhousie University M.A. in English (1989), and a Ph.D in English from Queen's University (1993), he is a prized professor, poet, playwright, novelist, and literary critic. Currently a professor of English at the University of Toronto (1999-), "GEC" has taught English and Canadian Studies at Duke University (1994-99), served as the Seagram's Visiting Chair at McGill University (1998-99), was a Noted Scholar at the University of British Columbia (2002), and later the 27th William Lyon Mackenzie King Visiting Professor in Canadian Studies at Harvard University (2013-14). He has published some 23 poetry "projects," five verse-plays, four opera libretti, two novels, and two books of criticism. Clarke has won the Archibald Lampman Award, the Portia White Prize for Artistic Achievement, the Governor General's Literary Award for Poetry, the Dr. Martin Luther King Jr. Achievement Award, the Pierre Elliott Trudeau Fellowship Prize, the Poesia Premiul (Romania), the Dartmouth Book Award for Fiction, and the Eric Hoffer Book Award for Poetry (US). He also served as Toronto's fourth Poet Laureate (2012-15) and Canada's seventh Parliamentary Poet Laureate (2016-17). Appointed to the Order of Nova Scotia (2006), and the Order of Canada (2008), he is also a Fellow of the Royal Canadian Geographical Society (2017).

M. Travis Lane

M. Travis Lane was born on September 23, 1934 in San Antonio, Texas. In 1956 she graduated from Vassar College with a Bachelor of Arts degree and earned an M.A. and her Ph.D from Cornell University. She moved from the United States to Fredericton, New Brunswick with her husband, Lauriat Lane Jr. Travis Lane has published 18 books of poetry and *Heart on Fist: Essays and Reviews: 1970-2016*. Lane won the Pat Lowther Award in 1980, and the Atlantic Poetry Prize in 2001 and 2002, Alden Nowlan Award for Excellence in English Literature in 2003, and Lieutenant-Governor's Award for High Achievement in English Literary Arts in 2016. Travis Lane also worked as an honorary research associate in the English Department at the University of New Brunswick, and has taught a number of courses in the English Department. She is well known for her literary reviews in *The Fiddlehead*. She was a founding member of the Writers' Federation of New Brunswick. She lives in Fredericton, New Brunswick. She has a daughter, Hannah Marguerite Lane, and a son, Lauriat Lane III.

John B. Lee

John B. Lee grew up on the farm near the village of Highgate, Ontario. He graduated with a B.A. in Honours English, a B.Ed. and M.A. from the University of Western Ontario. He has published more than fifty books, ten chapbooks, seven non-fiction titles, and edited eleven anthologies. He was named Poet Laureate of the city of Brantford in perpetuity, Poet Laureate of Norfolk County for life and Poet Laureate of Canada Cuba Literary Alliance (2020-2022). He is the recipient of nearly one hundred international literary awards. His work has been translated into several languages. He and wife Cathy live in a lake house overlook Mackenzie King Long Point Bay on the south coast of Lake Erie in the town of Port Dover, Ontario. They have two married sons and four grandsons.

Daniel Lockhart

D.A. Lockhart is the author of eight poetry collections, including *Go Down Odawa Way* (Kegedonce, 2021) and *Bearmen Descend Upon Gimli* (Frontenac House, 2021). His work has appeared in *Best Canadian Poetry in English 2019, New Poetry from the Midwest, TriQuarterly, ARC Poetry Magazine, Grain, Belt,* and *The Malahat Review* among many others. He is a Turtle Clan member of Eelünaapéewi Lahkéewiit (Lenape), a registered member of the Moravian of the Thames First Nation, and currently resides at the south shore of Waawiiyaatanong (Windsor, ON-Detroit, MI) and Pelee Island. He is the publisher at Urban Farmhouse Press and the poetry editor at the *Windsor Review.*

Bruce Meyer

Bruce Meyer was born and grew up in Toronto, and received his B.A. and M.A. at the University of Toronto and his Ph.D at McMaster University. Bruce Meyer is a professor, broadcaster, poet and short story writer. At present, he is a professor of Writing and Communications at Georgian College in Barrie where he teaches Poetry, Comparative Literature, and Non-Fiction, and a visiting associate at Victoria College at the University of Toronto. He has published more than 68 books of poetry, sixty books of fiction, poetry, flash fiction, and non-fiction. Meyer has been active on the Canadian literary scene serving as director of the Writing Program at the University of Toronto School of Continuing Studies, and has won numerous awards including the E.J. Pratt Gold Medal and Prize for Poetry, 1980, 1981, and the Gwendolyn MacEwen Prize for Poetry, 2015, 2016. He lives with his wife, Kerry, and daughter, Katie, in Barrie. His most recent books are *Down in the Ground* (fiction, Guernica Editions, 2020), *Grace of Falling Stars* (poetry, Black Moss Press, 2021), *The Hours: Stories from a Pandemic* (short fiction, *Ace of Swords*, 2021) and *Toast Soldiers* (short stories, Crowsnest Books, 2021).

Al Moritz

A.F. Moritz's most recent books of poems are *The Garden: a poem and an essay* (Gordon Hill, 2021), *As Far As You Know* (Anansi, 2020) and *The Sparrow: Selected Poems* (Anansi, 2018), as well as a new edition of poems in Greek translation selected from *The Sparrow* (Vakxikon, 2021). He has published twenty-three volumes of poetry. His work has received the Guggenheim Fellowship, the Griffin Poetry Prize, the Award in Literature of the American Academy of Arts and Letters, the Bess Hokin Award of *Poetry* magazine, the Elizabeth Matchett Stover Award of the *Southwest Review*, the ReLit Award, selection to the Princeton Series of Contemporary Poets, and three of his books have been named finalists for the Governor General's Award. He is presently the Poet Laureate of the City of Toronto (2019-2023), the sixth poet to hold that office.

Sue Sinclair

Sue Sinclair was born in Guelph, Ontario, and grew up in St. John's, Newfoundland. She received her B.A. from Mount Alison University. She received an M.A. in English & Creative Writing from the University of New Brunswick then completed her M.A. and Ph.D in Philosophy at the University of Toronto where her dissertation was on the subject of beauty. At present, she is a professor in the English Department of the University of New Brunswick. She is the editor of *The Fiddlehead* and a poetry editor at Brick Books. She has published five books of poetry. Sinclair has won the International Independent Publisher's Award for Poetry and the Pat Lowther Award and has twice been nominated for the Atlantic Poetry Prize. She lives with the poet Nick Thran and their daughter Abigail in Fredericton.

Colleen Thibaudeau

Colleen Thibaudeau was born in 1925 in Toronto and grew up in St. Thomas, Ontario. Her father was of Acadian descent and her mother from Belfast, Northern Ireland. She completed her B.A. and M.A. in English with a specialization in contemporary Canadian poetry at the University of Toronto.

She married the Canadian poet and playwright, James Reaney, and they had four children. Thibaudeau published six books of poems. She died in London, Ontario in 2012. The League of Canadian Poets established the Colleen Thibaudeau Award for Outstanding Contribution in her memory.

ACKNOWLEDGMENTS

I would like to thank Patrycja Williams, Brian Bartlett, and especially Eva Kolacz for careful readings of the manuscript and making essential suggestions. I would like to thank Michael Mirolla for publishing *In the Writers' Words Volume II* and for his continued support of Canadian literature. And finally, I would like to express my thanks to the poets who contributed to this book. It was such a pleasure to work with you.

*

"An Interview with Roo Borson." *The River review / La Revue rivière*. Number 2, 1993

Lee, John B. "These Were the Stories That Needed to be Told." *Carousel* 10, 1994.

ABOUT THE EDITOR

Laurence Hutchman was born in Belfast, Northern Ireland, and grew up in Toronto. He received a Ph.D from the Université de Montreal and has taught at several universities. For twenty-three years he was a professor of English literature at the Université de Moncton at the Edmundston Campus. Hutchman has published twelve books of poetry, co-edited the anthology *Coastlines: the Poetry of Atlantic Canada* and edited *In the Writers' Words*. His poetry has received many grants and awards, including the Alden Nowlan Award for Excellence and has been translated into numerous languages. In 2017 he was named poet laureate of Emery, north Toronto. He lives with his wife, the artist and poet Eva Kolacz, in Victoria, BC.

Printed in February 2022
by Gauvin Press,
Gatineau, Québec